To Dad —
with our love,

Philip & Jill X

Christmas 1988.

CONFESSIONS
of a
CONSERVATIVE
LIBERAL

John Habgood
Archbishop of York

First published in Great Britain 1988
SPCK
Holy Trinity Church
Marylebone Road
London NW1 4DU

British Library Cataloguing in Publication Data

Habgood, John, *1927–*
    Confessions of a conservative liberal.
    I. Title
    252′.03

    ISBN 0-281-04384-1

Photoset & printed in Great Britain by
WBC Ltd., Bristol

Contents

Acknowledgements

THANKS ARE DUE to the following for permission to reprint copyright material:

G. J. Palmer & Sons Ltd, for an article which first appeared in *The Church Times* on 2 January 1987 (chapter 35).

Times Newspapers Ltd, for articles which appeared in *The Times Higher Education Supplement* on 2 January 1987 (chapter 30), and in *The Times* on 22 September and 6 October 1984 (chapter 15), 3 October 1987 (chapter 19) and 13 February 1987 (chapter 26).

Introduction

IN CASE THE word 'confessions' excites the wrong expectations I had better admit from the start that I am using it in its broadest sense. To confess is to speak out about what one is and what one believes. The essence of confession is the desire to be true to oneself, to face reality, and to set out the ground on which one stands.

I am not concerned in this book with the more usual and narrower meaning of confession. One's sins are for the most part only too obvious, whereas faith can easily be hidden, or misrepresented, or glimpsed only in unrelated bits. The book is a confession of faith, not of a formal kind, but faith as expressed in the daily business of trying to communicate the Christian gospel. It contains the sort of things I say or write when I am asked for a lecture or essay or sermon, usually on some special occasion. Unfortunately there are no examples of sermons and talks in ordinary parishes. I seldom write these down, and such addresses are usually too heavily dependent on time and place to be worth reproducing elsewhere, even if there were scripts available. As a confession of faith, therefore, this book lacks an important dimension. It is strongly slanted in the direction of public issues rather than personal religion; if it were a book of parish sermons the bias would be the other way.

This latter point needs underlining because bishops and archbishops are frequently accused of meddling in politics when they should be saving souls, and I am conscious that my selection of topics may reinforce that impression. But the criticism fails to distinguish between what is reported in the media and what is actually said and done. It also ignores the fact that public issues are usually more news-worthy and book-worthy than personal ones. Furthermore reportage in the press or through broadcasting almost invariably destroys the balance of statements and, through a process of highlighting only what fits a previously determined image, can lead in the long run to extraordinary distortions. Sometimes when I read in the press what I am supposed to have said I am amazed.

All of which leads me to see a value in setting out some statements at length, if only to illustrate the rather complex meaning of the second half of my title.

The phrase 'Conservative Liberal' is not meant to be confusing but to help dispel confusion. I am genuinely perplexed by labels, and the word 'liberal' in particular has become positively chameleon-like. The General Synod has heard liberalism described as 'a cancer in the Church of England', and there are those who seem to imagine that any faith short of fundamentalism is really a form of apostasy. There are others for whom liberalism seems to be synonymous with 'nice and undemanding', and there are yet others for whom it represents the broad mainstream of Christian tradition.

I am unwilling to let the word go because for me it represents an openness in the search for truth which I believe is profoundly necessary for the health of religion. We grow in knowledge only insofar as we are prepared to criticize what we think we know already. True knowledge is tested knowledge, just as true faith has to be sifted by doubt. That is why an illiberal faith must in the end be untrue to a gospel which promises abundant life and growth.

Openness in the search for truth also entails a positive, but again critical, approach to secular knowledge. I confess that I have no patience with those who indulge in facile dismissals of the whole scientific enterprise, or who do not seem to have grasped the huge change which occurred in human consciousness through the development of historical perspective. I do not see how it is possible to hold that Christ was truly incarnate in a universe created by God without treating the actual form of that universe, its historical development and our human capacity to understand it, with utter seriousness.

If this is liberalism, then I am a liberal; but I see it as in no way entailing a subjection of faith to secularism or the travesty of liberalism described in the term, 'anything goes'. It is essentially about honesty, but an honesty rooted in what God has given us, both in revelation and in the created world.

Hence 'conservative'. This too is a word with many meanings, and polemical attempts to depict conservatism, whether in church or state, as the great enemy, are as neurotic and absurd as the resistance to change which such attacks can sometimes provoke. The essence of conservatism, as I see it, is to treasure what is given by tradition, what is best from the past, and what has proved itself by its durability. It is to display a certain humility towards the things we have received and may not fully understand, and so to conserve them as potentially fruitful for the future. It is to respect continuity. 'If democracy means that I give a man a vote despite the fact that he is my chauffeur', wrote G. K. Chesterton, 'tradition means that I give a man a vote despite the fact that he is my great-great-grandfather.' Or to put it another way: 'Tradition is the living faith of the dead; traditionalism is the dead faith of the living.'

I am unwilling to lose either conservatism or liberalism in the sense in which I have defined them. In fact I regard it as essential for the Church of England (and not the Church of England only) to contain both. But it is not enough for a Church to have members who just hold to one or the other perspective unless there is a real meeting of minds, and preferably a combination of both perspectives in the same people. Such tensions as exist ought ideally to be within people rather than between them, and I believe that Christian experience is deeply impoverished unless this is happening. I hope some of the pieces in this book will help to illustrate why.

The book falls into five main sections. The first follows up the theme of my enthronement sermon on 'Public Faith'. This is part of a continuing attempt to spell out the public role of religion in a pluralist society. I began to explore the theme in my earlier book, *Church and Nation in a Secular Age* (Darton, Longman and Todd, 1983), but my perception of the need to do so has increased considerably since I became archbishop. Whatever else an archbishop may or may not be or do he cannot avoid being even more of a public figure than a bishop, and viewed as in some sense representing public Christian values.

The second section gathers together some of the things I have written on controversies concerning faith. These are mostly short pieces written for the York Diocesan Leaflet and intended to help ordinary parishioners find their way through the often complex arguments without being seduced by over-simplifications. I have felt it right to include a specially written article on the 1987 Crockford Preface in this section. Since I was myself at one stage in the affair heavily criticized by the press I am conscious of the danger of being defensive. On the other hand, there are aspects of the story which have not yet been told, and I believe they should be, if only to deter the growth of an unhelpful mythology.

The third section is more concerned with strictly intellectual and theoretical matters. It centres on the question, What basis can there be for making Christian moral judgements which are seen to have some validity outside the Christian community? This is an important question for Christians to answer if we are to do more than just talk to each other. It is also a potentially illuminating question in the face of internal ethical disputes within the Christian community. These usually need a critical examination of methods and assumptions if there is to be any hope of resolving them. The lecture on Making Moral Decisions is a highly compressed summary of a very large subject, some details of which are spelt out in the lectures which follow. It was originally delivered to a conference of church leaders who I was confident would be able to fill in the details for themselves.

Section four consists mostly of sermons on particular aspects of morality, and the final section deals with specifically ecclesiastical topics. In terms of my total writing and speaking this section is grossly under-represented but, for reasons already mentioned, I have chosen to put the emphasis elsewhere.

The biggest challenges facing the churches today concern the credibility of the gospel. This is not just an intellectual matter: credibility has to be demonstrated as much by what the churches do as by what they say. But it has an intellectual dimension to it, and if I concentrate on that it is because that is where most of the recent argument has been, and where some of the toughest work still remains to be done.

I hope this book will be helpful in showing how one twentieth-century Christian tries to hold together liberalism's concern for truth and conservatism's respect for what is given us in historical revelation. The tension is not a new one, and has never been better expressed than in a superb description of Christ in the (probably) second-century Epistle to Diognetus: 'This is he who was from the beginning, who appeared new and was found to be old, and is ever born young in the hearts of the saints.'

I am grateful to my Lay Assistant, Raymond Barker, for suggesting this book and helping to gather the materials for it, and to my secretaries, Daphne Wood, Jane Wegelius and Anne Broadbent, for all the extra work they had to do in typing it.

Above all I am grateful to those companions in the faith who have been willing to listen to a stumbling disciple trying to express something of its rich diversity.

PART I
PUBLIC FAITH

1
Public Faith

Enthronement sermon preached in York Minster
18 November 1983

THERE ARE MOMENTS, and this is surely one of them, when public life in its broadest aspects has to be reminded of its religious roots. The pomp and splendour of today's worship may seem, for much of the time, to focus uncomfortably on a single individual. But an Archbishop is important, not for what he is in himself, but for what he represents. And what he represents, among many other things, is the public face of the Christian Church. If he can reach out beyond his own Church, if he can be seen as a friend and colleague and representative figure within a still wider religious fellowship, so much the better. But whether it is seen narrowly or broadly, his job is a public one, and that is why his enthronement is rightly regarded as a major public event.

Part of the meaning of this service, therefore, is that it is a reassertion of public faith. Like all great acts of worship it tries to express in words and ritual and music something of the glory of God. And it sets this vision of God's glory in the widest possible public frame.

But can this really be done honestly and credibly in Britain in the twentieth century? It was all very well for some of my medieval forebears to make great claims for themselves, to wield great powers, and even to provide great feasts for all and sundry after their enthronements. One newspaper has described the guests at such a feast as eating their way through the equivalent of a miniature zoo.

Today's world is different; we live in a country at least partially divided into different religions and cultures; a country conscious of deep social divisions, divisions made even more apparent by our present economic strains; a country with many uncertainties about its aims and values. We have seen the public dimensions of faith steadily eroded. There are many whose religion only surfaces on those odd occasions when it still seems natural to celebrate some vaguely religious aspect of national life. Others go to the opposite extreme and are so filled with the joy and peace of a simple personal relationship with Christ, that they wonder whether the public dimensions of faith are worth preserving. Others doubt whether it even makes sense to speak of public faith in an age with so uncertain a grip on religious realities.

Yet I cannot escape a verse from Psalm 11, itself written in an age of uncertainty and division:

If the foundations are destroyed, what can the just man do?

Public faith is about the foundations; it is about the things which bind us together, and the values we share, and the goals we pursue. The psalmist refuses to separate this concern with foundations from individual, personal, goodness and faith. 'What shall the just man do?'

Of course, sometimes there has to be a separation. Sometimes the most shining examples of personal faith are found just where the going is hardest and the public opposition to religion most intense. But most of us for most of the time depend far more than we care to admit on some kind of public validation of the things which matter to us. We don't want just to be individuals. We want to belong to a society which helps us to be what, at our deepest and best, we know we ought to be.

And this includes belief in God. We are told, I believe rightly, that the most urgent question facing Christians today concerns the depth and reality of our belief in God. Surely one of the major obstacles to such belief is precisely this erosion of the public religious frame of reference. It is not for nothing that it is hard to talk about God these days in ordinary conversation without creating embarrassment.

There is no shortage of highly individualized beliefs. In fact I am constantly amazed at what people *do* believe; half-remembered bible stories, odd bits of science fiction, snippets of proverbial wisdom passed on through grandmothers or glossy magazines. There is evidence, too, of a huge and largely unrecognized reservoir of religious experience in all sorts of people who would be horrified to class themselves as religious. There seems to be a widespread diffuse awareness of some sort of religious reality, which can attach itself to whatever materials happen to be around.

What is lacking is a focused awareness, a public frame, a shared faith, which can sharpen vague feelings into prayer and commitment and action. But how is it possible to begin to refocus in a society so fragmented, so critical, so suspicious of authority? And how dare an Archbishop, how dare a ceremony like this, witness to the need for a public framework of faith without seeming impertinent or blind?

Here lies a lifetime's work. But it is a work which I am convinced, under God, is possible, and I want to offer just one hint about where to start. I see no ultimate contradiction between relying on a coherent public framework of faith, and being critically aware of its limitations. In fact it is only by alternating between belief and doubt that we come to know anything at all.

It is the coherence of faith which makes it powerful and effective. A jackdaw kind of religion, a nugget of gold here, a strip of tinsel there, this belief or that belief picked out of context while the unattractive bits are ignored, such a hotch-potch faith provides no defence against mere self-indulgence. To believe only what you like, is to believe only in yourself.

This is the real importance of conservatism in religion and why faith needs to be public. A shared framework gives us criteria by which to judge ourselves. It is a sign that true faith is not a mere matter of choice, but a response to the loving, demanding, disturbing reality of God. 'Repent and believe the gospel' . . . believe it as something given, not something merely chosen or made up.

But when the response is made, that is not the whole story. Even the most coherent faith only touches the hem of the robe of the infinite and everlasting God. And its very coherence can be a temptation to complacency and self-sufficiency and intolerance. That is why there has to be radical criticism as well. That is why a public faith can never be a settled static order. That is why the Church must be forever building and forever pulling down; forever thankful for what it has received, and forever conscious of its inability to receive it in all its fulness.

It is in the combination of these two, in the match between the believing heart and the critical mind, that true faith grows strong.

So what is the meaning of our worship today, this assertion of public faith? Not, I hope, a mere puffing up of Christian self-importance. I see it as a sign and promise of God's grace. A sign of the God who gives himself to us, and in so doing reveals his infinite depths. A promise that beyond our separations as Christians, as people, as one nation in a divided world, there is an ultimate unity. And a reminder of how fragile and how vulnerable our life is together, and yet how securely we can be held in the loving hands of God.

2
The Naked Public Square

Lecture to a Conference of School Chaplains at Queen Ethelburga's School, Harrogate
3 April 1985

I TAKE MY title from a recently published American book, *The Naked Public Square* by Richard Neuhaus (Eerdmans 1984), subtitled *Religion and Democracy in America*, an analysis of why the Moral Majority has entered so deeply into public life in the United States. Its thesis is that the movement has tried to fill the vacuum left by the traditional liberal religious establishment in the latter's overreaction to pluralism and consequent withdrawal from any definite moral stance. Liberal democracy in America needs a religious basis, and without it could rapidly become totalitarian. It follows that if the liberal establishment leaves its position at the centre of public life, then those who in their bones feel that America is basically a Christian nation inevitably move in to provide the necessary moral framework. In the background, of course, is the somewhat absurd situation created by the First Amendment to the US Constitution, which disallows any overt expression of religion in public institutions. There is also, as in Britain, an attempt to go to great lengths in deference to minority rights. Given this scenario, we find the liberal establishment sawing off the branch on which it is sitting, though failing to realize that if a nation loses its central Christian commitment, then it is likely to lose those very attitudes and beliefs which encourage respect and tolerance for social deviants and minorities.

However, in the American scene the Moral Majority can be no real substitute for traditional liberal protestantism because, despite the fact that it has moved into the public sphere, the faith it represents is still essentially private in not being open to public criticism. Fundamentalist thinking forms a closed circle which is impregnable to external influence. This gives it great strength, but its weakness is that, by not moving in a public world where truth claims can readily be tested, it remains essentially a private faith, no matter how far its adherents become politicized.

I was intrigued by this book because in many ways it echoes some of the themes which have been in my own mind, and a recent meeting with the author in New York confirmed this impression. In my Enthronement Sermon I attempted to articulate a concept which I call 'Public Faith'. I see this as a necessary counterbalance to the tendency for religion to be treated more and more as a purely private matter, marginalized into a hobby, an interest for people who happen to like that kind of thing. The Editor of *The Times* devoted an entire leading article to an attack on my sermon which he interpreted idiosyncratically as an attempt to reduce Christianity to some lowest common denominator defined by counting heads, in contrast with the noble individualism which *The Times* itself has espoused under its new management.

Clearly the notion of public faith needs to be spelt out more fully. In my reply to the leading article I defined it thus: 'I am not talking about some nationally or internationally imposed creed, nor is it the lowest common denominator of popular piety. It is the framework of assumptions, mostly drawn from the great historic expressions of religious faith, which makes the public articulation of personal faith both possible and fruitful.' In other words, we can only justify what we believe, and can only articulate it effectively, if there is a public framework within which this can be done.

Let me give some examples. I start with one outside the sphere of religion. Some months ago I had the pleasure of meeting a former Governor of the Bank of England and was able to ask a question which I had always longed to ask someone in his position. I reminded him of the promise on the face of a bank note where it says, 'I Promise to Pay the Bearer on Demand the Sum of One Pound', and then asked, 'If in your capacity as Governor of the Bank of England I had given you a pound note and said, please honour that promise, what would you have given me?' He replied, 'I would have given you another pound note.'

In other words, money is money is money. The currency is a faith system. Indeed the language of faith is quite explicitly used, as when dealers describe, say, the degree of confidence in sterling. It is only because people believe that these particular pieces of paper can be exchanged for goods and services that money has any value. It is true that the pieces of paper have to be backed in some way by real goods and real services, so that although the system depends on faith, it is not a blind and empty faith. But confidence can be lost, and because nowadays money markets in one part of the world or another are open every hour out of the twenty-four, jittery reactions in Japan can easily escalate to crashes in Wall Street. It is not unlike what happens when exaggerated stories of ecclesiastical rumpuses are flashed round the world to those who have no means of evaluating the truth of them.

Money, then, is closely bound up with public faith of a kind. So is language. It is a system of shared meaning without which human development is impossible. Wittgenstein's 'The limits of my language are the limits of my world' sums it up. The other day I was reading a version of the New Testament in pidgin English from Papua New Guinea and it was remarkable to see how the range of religious meaning was narrowed by the limitations of the language. I would find it hard, for instance, to go on thinking of God as Big Fella.

Profound communication on any subject requires not only an adequate language, but also a nuanced understanding of it. Think for example of the difference between the sentences, 'I live in York', and 'I am living in York'. English allows a subtle distinction here which cannot be conveyed in languages like French with only one form of the present tense. To speak a language well entails being able to pick up these subtle differences, as well as being able to hear the resonances in language from the literary past. I remember once having dinner with one of the mechanics' unions in the coal industry concerned with the separation of coal. The members were all wearing badges with the Latin version of the motto, 'Nothing shall separate us'. There were two obvious levels on which this could be read, as a statement about their technology, and as a statement about their union. Those I spoke to were unaware of a third set of resonances from St Paul's 'Nothing shall separate us from the love of God'. It added a new dimension to coal separation.

In the World Council of Churches, where there is the constant problem of having to work in six languages, the limitations of not being able to use nuanced language are all too obvious. This is one reason why documents from international bodies are usually written in such appalling jargon. It is also the reason why it is almost impossible to tell jokes in such circumstances, a factor which I am sure contributes to the general feeling of heavy-handedness conveyed by world ecumenism.

All this is obvious and familiar. In spelling it out I am simply trying to make the point that if human beings are to relate to one another in matters which are at all deep or sophisticated, there has to be some public framework in which the relationship can be expressed.

Coming closer to the heart of what I have to say, think for a moment about the meaning of the world 'nation'. What is it that makes people feel they belong to a particular nation, apart from formal indicators such as the possession of an appropriate passport? One approach to that kind of question is to ask what nationhood means to a group of people who claim it, but are denied it. I remember a conversation some years ago with an Israeli international lawyer on the subject of Palestinian nationhood. His criteria were common language, common geography, shared history and, most interesting of all, shared suffering. It is a fact that most nations have been born out of wars, and there seems a good case for saying that Palestinian national identity has derived at least in part from the struggles and frustrations of the years since 1948. In a more settled situation I believe it is important to go beyond the lawyer's criteria and see nationhood as including some ability to recognize signals within a shared culture and at least some measure of shared values.

In pursuing this line of thought I now turn to questions nearer to our own country. How much pluralism can be tolerated within a nation without threatening its cohesion and stability? What are likely to be the long-term consequences of the creation in many parts of the world of secular states within which different religions are simply regarded as minority interests? I have already referred to the attempt to fill the religious vacuum in the United States. India is another example, and I suspect that, like the United States, it can exist nominally as a secular society precisely because its secularism is so deeply religious. In some other parts of the world it is the reactions against secularism which provide a striking example of what happens when a sense of identity and culture are in danger of being eroded. Fundamentalism as a worldwide phenomenon must surely owe a great deal to this sense of erosion.

In suggesting that religion, or some substitute for religion, has an inescapable public role in the maintenance of culture and national stability I am not trying to make a bid for a return to belief in a unitary state bonded together by an official faith. Those days are obviously past. A mature democracy can cope with a good deal of fragmentation into subcultures, provided there is seen to be some family relationship between them. In other words, for a society to cohere its members do not all have to believe or do the same thing, but there need to be bridges between them, links between the different subcultures so that they are seen to belong within the same set of family relationships. Thus, the questions to be asked about, say, Muslim minorities in

Britain are not how their culture can be integrated into British society, nor how they can be tolerated as some totally separate subculture. The fruitful questions, surely, are about the kind of bridges which can be built between Muslims and other groups, while allowing each to be itself within a more general culture which still, in Britain, remains centred on our Christian inheritance.

I accept the view that historically religion has been the main provider of the framework for social life. It has been the carrier, or one of the main carriers, of culture, the upholder of values, and a source of identity. British culture still stands basically within the Christian tradition and most British people, however little they actually do about the Christian faith, would be unwilling to drop the label Christian. Will Herberg's classic social analysis of the United States in his book *Catholic, Protestant, Jew* (New York, Doubleday, 1955), put forward the thesis that in the great melting pot which the United States prides itself on being, one of the main means by which people define their identity is in terms of their religious grouping. Indeed the strong link between ethnic and religious groupings in the United States is obvious to anyone who drives down a Main Street and looks at the names of the churches.

The reverse side of this link between religion and culture is the dependence of religion itself on some form of common culture. Many of our difficulties as clergy spring from the loss of a common nuanced vocabulary which enables widespread communication on religious matters. Words like 'sin' or 'salvation', or even 'God', lack the necessary resonances or, worse, have picked up unhelpful ones, with the result that in society at large it is difficult to communicate using a technical Christian vocabulary without risking gross misunderstanding. It is also unwise to rely on people's ability to pick up the meaning of symbols or to hear the echoes of familiar Christian stories. There are thus huge restrictions on modern preaching and it is all too rare to find a congregation where biblical allusions can be used with confidence.

Thus, while I would want to claim that our nation still feels, and wants to go on feeling, a continuity with Christian tradition, the actual relationship between our present culture and the churches is under severe strain. Many churches are no longer willing to play a role as guardians of culture and carriers of identity. There are strong pressures to raise the barriers between Christians and non-Christians and to build little enclaves where Christians can be themselves, can speak their own language and build their own culture. Hence the attraction of house churches, and groups, and Christian Unions, and holy huddles. A major disadvantage of that policy is that when Christians simply talk to each other they cease to be credible. Truth claims have to be made in the public world, and in a form which relates to the common culture. If that culture is simply rejected on the grounds that it can no longer convey any adequate Christian understanding then the situation is serious indeed, and there are signs that even the Church of England in some of its manifestations is beginning to go down that road. One result will be the even more rapid secularization of the general culture.

If my analysis has any validity, then clearly strains in the system must not be ignored. Rude things which politicians sometimes say about bishops, and bishops say about politicians, are symptoms of the strains, which is why I have felt it worth trying to spell out how they arise. It is probably not too much of a caricature to say that typical English public religion combines rigidity and consistency of practice with a wide variety of private opinion. Provided people do and say the right things in a reassuring manner, the content of belief does not seem to matter too much, as long as it is kept private. It is the repeating of familiar words, whether from the Prayer Book or the Creeds, or well-loved hymns, which provides feelings of reassurance. It is the familiar occasions, as when the British Legion gathers in the Albert Hall, or the midnight mass, or carols at Christmas time, which become the public religious expressions of a residual Christian culture which may in practice be linked with private beliefs having little to do with the Christian faith as normally understood. Robert Towler, the sociologist, has produced an analysis of letters sent to John Robinson after the publication of *Honest to God*. The letters are significant because they are an expression of the raw, uninhibited kind of religion which people will often expose when they are writing to somebody they do not know personally, and particularly when they are responding to a threat to their assurance. The common religion of the ordinary Englishman on this analysis appears as something very different from what centuries of Christian teaching might have been thought to have conveyed. It relies heavily on concepts of fate, destiny, something to hold onto against the arbitrariness and uncertainties of life, the belief that one's number is somehow written in heaven. My own part in the events surrounding the consecration of David Jenkins as Bishop of Durham led to a very similar correspondence, and I can confirm the strange mixture of beliefs which this revealed, closely linked with a strong adherence to particular forms of words.

Robert Towler has more recently moved to become Research Officer for the Independent Broadcasting Authority. When I asked him about the switch from being a sociologist of religion to becoming a media researcher his reply was, 'There is no difference at all really, because I am still dealing with mythology. Television is the generator of the new mythology, the new stories in terms of which large numbers of people understand their own lives.' This is surely the significance of soap operas. They are our twentieth-century parables and the nearer they are to the kind of reality with which people can identify, the more influence they are likely to have in helping to generate a common framework of meaning, but one very different from what most people overtly profess.

In this situation and in the light of the developments I have been describing, it seems to me that the role of the public guardians of faith becomes a crucial one. The present Bishop of Peterborough, in talking about the relationship between the Church and the media, referred tellingly to 'the handful of people who hold the bridge between the past and the future. Woe betide a society if these people fail.' This handful of people is nowadays a somewhat beleaguered group who need great support and who rightly feel alarm when some of those to whom they look for support seem to express only their own opinions. The need, as I see it, is for public expressions of faith which are broad enough to be inclusive, the ability to live and move within our great Christian heritage and not be narrowed by it, but also faith which is firm and definite enough to give some reassurance that what is being carried through into the future is genuinely rooted in what we have received from the past. If there are to be prophetic voices they have to speak within this tradition and out of these shared convictions. It is exceedingly difficult to prophesy within a community where there are no shared convictions to which to recall those to whom one is prophesying. All the great Hebrew prophets were essentially recalling people to a faith they already professed, albeit very inadequately. This is a further reason, therefore, why churches should remain within the public square and seek to clothe it. Not only are their truth claims likely to be suspect if they do not, but their prophetic voice is likely to be speaking in a vacuum, where no resonances are heard and no response evoked.

Let me end by drawing attention to some practical implications of what I have been saying. Without the attempt to nurture shared convictions within a society, public ethics themselves become problematic. Those who believe themselves to be living in an ethical jungle are likely to feel that they cannot afford to be high-minded. Business ethics are a case in point. The pressures are enormous on some people to behave in ways they may personally regard as unethical, but which from a business point of view they cannot resist for fear of losing their competitiveness. Professional codes of ethics can be a way of building some limited protection against this kind of pressure in situations where the general moral framework of society is not strong enough to provide the assurance that fair dealing is the best policy. Unfortunately, though, many professional codes suffer from the same defect as inward-looking churches. They become slanted primarily towards the protection of the profession rather than towards the well-being of the general public.

The absence of a common culture makes itself felt also in international affairs, notably in terms of defence policy. Attitudes towards defence depend on where one begins. Those who begin from within the Christian tradition, and decide on moral grounds that nuclear weapons are appalling and must be abolished, may see a first practical step towards realizing this aim in the building up of trust between nations. It is a policy which depends on the assumption that potential enemies analyse the issues in more or less similar terms. But supposing the potential enemies are operating on radically different assumptions; supposing they do not respond to the same signals; and supposing they regard moves towards disarmament as evidence of weakness rather than of the desire to build up trust; in such cases a very different defence policy may be appropriate. Divergent policies arise, not from disagreements about the morality of nuclear weapons, nor from technical disagreements about their effectiveness or lack of it, but from different shared perceptions of how nations behave and how they respond to one another. Putting it bluntly, the hard-liners say, 'You can't trust the Russians to behave as we do.'

Many political strains arise from the fact that there is no real agreement about the premises from which arguments start. The cry for social justice may take very different shapes depending on what concepts of justice are being used. There are those who see justice primarily in terms of just deserts. 'What I have is mine because I have deserved it.' There are others who see justice primarily in terms of just distribution. 'Justice is to give to everybody in accordance with their

needs.' Unless these differences are recognized and some effort made
to transcend them, there is no possibility of having a sensible political
discussion about the pursuit of just policies. As I see it, the public role
of the churches in the political sphere, in the field of business ethics, in
the face of international issues and in many other aspects of public life,
is to try to provide a public language, a means of exploring public
values, aims and assumptions, against a transcendent background
which puts them all in question.

This is a much more difficult role, but in the long run a much more
rewarding one, than becoming embroiled in party political battles on
the mistaken assumption that there can be clear Christian answers in
the confused and complex world of public policy. The General Synod
Board for Social Responsibility is shortly going to set up a working
party for just this kind of exercise under the title *Goals for our Future
Society* [This report was published by Church House Publishing in
1987 under the title *Changing Britain: Social Diversity and Moral
Unity*]. I have the unenviable task of chairing it, but I believe it is a
worthwhile task which may help the churches to define more clearly
their public role in a way which is consistent with belief in the God
in whom all true values are ultimately rooted, and by whom all merely
human values are ultimately judged.

3

Church and State

Lecture broadcast by Radio Newcastle during the miners' strike
10 September 1984

I SUPPOSE MOST of us have had anxious thoughts this summer as day after day on the media we have heard stories of thuggery and intimidation, arson and wanton destruction. We have been asking ourselves, What is happening to our society? Why is it that ordinary decent people have found themselves caught up in this kind of thing? Why have such passions been aroused? And what are its long-term effects going to be on individuals and on communities which have found themselves deeply divided? And what is all this doing to the general public's image of the police?

I am not going to make judgements about the rights and wrongs of the miners' strike. There are times when restraint is more helpful than taking sides, and I believe this is one of them. What I say is intended as quite general comment.

We have been watching the internal agonies of an industry. It is an industry which, as I know well from my days in Durham, has prided itself on its unity and on the high standard of care given to its members. And now, under internal and external pressures, so much of it seems to have fallen apart. The fact that miner has turned against miner, the violence, the shouting, the accusations, the vandalism, are the outward signs of just how strong these pressures are. And it is not a pretty sight.

As with all violence, others have been sucked into it. Attempts to control it have at times seemed only to increase it. The shock has been that this kind of thing could happen on such a scale, and for such a long time, in Britain in 1984.

We have had riots in the past. We have had violent industrial disputes. We have had Saltley and Grunwick and Mr Shah. But I don't remember any other example of such long and bitter internal hatred between workers in the same industry. And this is what is worrying. If an industry which has been so proud of its unity can be so disastrously turned against itself when times are hard, then what about the bonds which bind other industries and other sections of the community together? Are they equally fragile?

I begin here, in a lecture supposed to be on 'Church and State', in order to make the point that my main concern is precisely these bonds which hold us together as communities and as a nation. Discussions of Church and State can too easily be trivialized into squabbles about how Parliament treats the Church of England, or the precise method of appointing bishops, or the implications of Mr Enoch Powell's views on Henry VIII. These are merely the framework of a particular relationship between the Church of England and the English nation, and may be interesting in themselves but are not the real meat of the subject. The central question I want to consider is whether religion makes any real difference to the way a nation conducts its business.

I deliberately use the broader word 'religion' rather than the narrower word 'church', because any realistic discussion of church activity in Britain today has to take account of the fact that there are different churches, and indeed different religions, in our country. The fact that two of them, the Church of England and the Church of Scotland, have special responsibilities towards their nations as a whole, does not make the contribution of the others to national life any less important. It just makes it different. But for the purposes of this lecture it is the similarities, not the differences, that I want to emphasize.

So does religion have anything positive to contribute in face of the present stresses in our society? I do not mean pronouncements by church leaders. There is a time and place for those, but I have already suggested that in present circumstances public interference by outside parties could well serve only to make matters worse.

Nor do I have in mind the sort of individual reconciling work and efforts at mediation which professional people like industrial chaplains and local clergy and ministers, or even bishops, can try to undertake, and which has certainly been going on, but which for obvious reasons remains unpublicized.

I am thinking of the more general ways in which religion affects people's assumptions, and their reactions to one another and – in words which I used earlier – 'binds' a community together. In fact the original meaning of the word 'religion' is precisely that – a bond, an obligation. It is what binds us to something greater than ourselves. And this leads me directly to the two social functions of religion I especially want to consider.

Let me stress the word 'social'. The main function of religion is to express and deepen our relationship with God. A religion which does not make this central soon goes desperately wrong. But when it *is* central, it has, as I see it, social spin-offs. One of these concerns the unity and cohesiveness of society, a unity and cohesiveness, resting ultimately on the belief that the one God provides a common source of values. The other spin-off seems on the face of it in direct contradiction with this. Religion, at least the Christian religion, provides the basis for a radical critique of society. The God to whom Christians are bound is not a God who is content just to let people settle down into a nice stable, complacent and ultimately self-centred social structure. He disturbs, he challenges, he changes, he haunts people with a vision of something better.

So those are my themes. Unity and disturbance.

Take unity first, and look at two arguments which have been used very frequently in our present disputes.

One side says: if we take a long view of the needs of our nation, if we face the facts of world competition, if we try to be fair as between the needs of different industries and different sections of the population, then we shall be forced into taking hard decisions which may entail people losing their jobs or moving their homes or in other ways ending up worse off then they are now. Efficiency has a price tag which somebody has got to pick up, and in a free society there is no way of controlling who are going to be the unlucky ones. Unless we become more efficient we shall all suffer.

The other side says: in a humane society it is precisely the unlucky ones who need special care. We have to start, not from long term considerations about the prosperity of the nation, but from the reality of people without jobs or whose jobs are threatened. It is the disadvantaged, not the successful, who have first claim on our resources. We ought so to order our society that its burdens and opportunities are distributed more fairly. Economic policies must serve people; people must not be sacrificed to policies.

You have heard the arguments a hundred times and both are impressive. Both are put forward with utter conviction by those who advocate different policies. The difficulty is that there is no meeting point between them, and no rational way of deciding which is right. Those who start from the need for economic efficiency and realism may claim to be just as humane as those who start from considerations of human need. But they insist that human needs cannot actually be met unless we so organize ourselves that there is enough wealth to go round, and to do all those things which may be socially desirable, but which cost a lot of money.

Those who start from human needs claim that unless these, rather than efficiency, are the top priority, then they will never in practice be met anyway, and we shall create the kind of society in which all suffer because we have ceased to care.

How can one find agreement between two such viewpoints? In prosperous times maybe it is not so difficult. There is enough flexibility, enough surplus wealth to create at least a semblance of common policy. But in hard times, as we have seen, the real depth of the divisions is revealed.

I have said that there is no rational way of deciding the arguments. Let me underline the word 'rational'. There are, of course, other ways – of which brute force is one. But leaving that aside for the moment, let us look a bit more closely at this business of rationality.

The argument from efficiency and economic realism assumes that we understand the economic forces operating not only in our own country, but in the world at large. It assumes that at least as a rough approximation we can predict what the results of major policy decisions are going to be, and that we know enough about human nature and the likely future of our society to make it sensible to commit ourselves to long-term economic plans. It assumes in fact that there is an appropriate expertise which makes the large-scale management of human affairs a rational enterprise. But is there?

I am not denying that economics, and social analysis and political planning have their uses. Of course they have. But equally it is hard to deny that in practice most economic predictions turn out to be wrong, and most attempts at large-scale planning turn out, if not to be failures, at least to have some totally unexpected consequences. And this happens, and is going to go on happening, for the very simple reason that people are people and are not going to be pushed around, and much that happens in the world is unpredictable, even in principle.

Again, let me stress, I am not saying that planning is useless or efficiency doesn't matter. I am saying that in the end the rational basis of the whole enterprise is not strong enough to win the argument against the other approach, the approach that begins from considerations of humanity.

But then neither is the rational basis of that other approach strong enough to win the argument against efficiency. What is the rational basis of this so-called 'right to work' which has been added to the growing list of other human rights which are now so much part of our political currency? We are told that we not only enjoy basic human rights, the right to life and freedom of speech, but also quite specific rights which require other people to do things for us, the right to marry and have children, to be fed and educated – and to work.

I am not denying that all these may be good and desirable. Like most other people I long for a society in which most of these human needs are satisfied, even though I have to admit that this can never be complete because some of them are incompatible. But I also have to admit that every attempt to provide a rational basis for the long list of human rights has ended in failure. There is simply no way of proving, for instance, that everybody has a right to work. There are arguments in favour of it. There are strong emotional feelings about it. But the arguments and the feelings are not conclusive. That is why in the end we have to fall back on making assertions about human rights. We 'declare' them; we can't prove them.

Why is this important? Why does proof matter? All I have been doing so far is trying to explain why there is no purely rational way of winning the argument about one of the major disputes in this country. I know there are many subsidiary arguments in this particular dispute, of a more or less factual nature, in which it is much more possible to demonstrate clearly that somebody is right or wrong. I know too that in practice there is not much obvious concern to be rational about the basic questions of principle in this dispute. My point is that even if there were such a desire, it would not help much, because reasoning about these matters can only take us so far, and no further.

It is not just about miners. The differences in basic understanding and approach I have been talking about go much deeper than a single industrial confrontation, however dramatic. They underlie deeply held differences of opinion on a whole variety of topics. And because rational argument in the end breaks down, the confrontations tend to become shrill, the atmosphere embittered, and the eventual solution a botched-up compromise which only leads to a further recurrence of the dispute in some other place at some other time. That is the measure of our problem.

Alas, I have no magic formula to offer as an alternative. I think it is useful, however, to make this sweeping sort of analysis, if only to identify the particular confrontation I have been talking about as part of a larger problem to do with social fragmentation. Everybody nowadays recognizes that at least to some extent we live in a pluralist society. I say 'to some extent' because there are also very powerful forces tending to stamp us into the same mould. We live in a TV-based culture. How many millions watch Coronation Street? or Dynasty? and become emotionally involved in them? and find attitudes shaped by them?

To a quite astonishing and frightening extent we share the same experiences. The other day I met a government official from Malaysia who talked delightedly about the relevance and popularity in his country of the programme 'Yes Minister'.

Certainly there are similarities between people – even on a world scale. But the overall message of the media may be rather different, may in fact help to reinforce the social fragmentation which makes it so hard to have a real meeting of minds. It is true that the experience given us through the media may be shared between millions of people. But the experience itself, seen as a whole, contains deep inner contradictions. We are bombarded with different beliefs, different values, different customs, different interpretations. Experts give us different and incompatible analyses. We are faced with a kaleidoscope of different images. And the overall effect, I suggest, is to reduce all differences to the same level, to make us immune to real distinctions, to imply that the most we can hope for is not truth, but mere opinion. And it is *that*, that shift from the belief in secure values and valid understandings to a jumble of conflicting opinions, which lies at the heart of pluralism.

I don't blame the media for this. I simply use them as an illustration. They are only one symptom among many of this tendency to fragmentation in our society. The point is that if everything is mere opinion, then there is no meeting point between those who share different opinions. We are back where I was a few minutes ago with people shouting at one another, because there is no rational way of winning the argument.

I have been trying to describe in a very few words one of the main problems I see afflicting our society. I began by talking about religion as a bond. Perhaps a better way of putting it now would be to say that religion does, or at least *can*, provide a shared language, a common stock of values, a starting point of mutual commitment, on the basis of which genuine conversation about some of these differences can begin. I am not claiming that if everybody was Christian, or a member of the Church of England, or whatever, the differences would wither away and all our problems be solved. That would be absurd. In practice Christians disagree among themselves on all sorts of fundamental matters. There are sincere Christians on both sides in the miners' dispute. But people who share a common faith at least have a chance of finding together some fresh insights to resolve their differences. The emphasis on different values may differ as between different Christians, but at least they are part of the same family of values and are rooted in the same religious tradition. So there is something to start talking about, and a language in which to say it.

How far is this true of our nation? I have been emphasizing the differences. But of course even in our modern pluralist Britain, with its deep social and political differences, with its ethnic minorities, with its feeble hold on religious faith, with the growing gulf between comfortable Britain and deprived Britain, there are still many things which hold us together. We take pride in British medals at the Olympics whatever our ethnic origins. We take for granted the freedom to be ourselves and express ourselves and do our own thing, hardly conscious of how rare and precious, on a world scale, such freedoms are, and how costly they are to maintain. By and large we accept the institutional basis of British public life. We may criticize politicans and curse bureaucrats, but we go on electing the one and accepting the other. Despite disturbances we still live in a basically stable society.

But the roots of it, the values and assumptions which sustain it, have to be nourished and guarded. I have given reasons for suggesting that they are under threat. I have spent much of this lecture giving an example of where they seem to be pulling apart. So I come back to the main question implied in my title. Is there a sense in which these subtle, and often unrecognized factors, which create the conditions for discussion and communication, depend on some shared system of values? depend, in other words, on a common faith? And can we, without them, really hope to find agreed solutions to our problems, which entail more than one side enforcing its will on the other?

I put it vaguely and modestly because there is no point in claiming a role for the Churches which they obviously do not and cannot fulfil. For one thing, the Churches are themselves divided. For another, religion in Britain today does not just mean the Christian religion, and we have scarcely begun to work out the ways in which different faiths should relate to one another. But my aim is to locate the real heart of arguments about Church and State, and to ask why Churches should go on bothering about their relationship to the State, and why the State should feel that it makes any difference whether or not it is still officially classed as Christian. And my answer is that it *does* make a difference; and that a state is in peril if it allows a religious and moral vacuum to develop or – and it amounts to much the same thing – if it encourages such religious and moral bedlam that concern about values ceases to have any real influence at the level of public life. There are lots of people who would like to push religion into a little private corner by itself, where it need have no influence on political decisions. But I fight, and will go on fighting, to maintain in our nation the sense of its religious inheritance as part of its public and political life, because I believe that is where religion ought to be, and because I believe the nation needs it.

I said when I first introduced this theme that there are two kinds of social spin-off from religious faith. One, which I have spent most of my time talking about, is in terms of social unity and cohesiveness. The other I described as disturbance. In my last few minutes I turn very briefly to that.

Most of us want a comfortable religion, something to take the strain out of living, something to give a respectability to our prejudices. The danger in what I have been saying about social unity is that it could amount to little more than that. Let the Churches spread around a thin coating of shared values, and then we can all get on with living our own lives. Let those whose job it is, solve the problems. We can remain as we are.

But that is not the way God works. A religious and moral vacuum, if that really is what we are creating, affects everybody. And God, the disturbing God, asks questions about *us*. It is not enough just to think about the good of the nation, or the solving of practical problems, or the deepening of our sense of belonging together as one society. God asks us what we think we are creating in our own lives and in our world.

Are the practical problems soluble at all in a society dominated by consumerism? How can we possibly begin to sort out the conflicts between economic planners and the individuals affected by those plans, unless we can escape from our present obsession with individualism? unless we can begin to see the fulfilment of human life, not in terms of individual success, but in terms of our relationships with one another? How can those who are deeply divided begin to find a way of reconciliation unless there is an acknowledgement that we are all equally under God's judgement, all equally in need of his forgiveness?

Questions on this level do not cut much political ice. Yet one essential reason why the State needs the Church, and why Christians need to be in places where they have to face real political problems, is precisely so that such questions can be asked; and asked in ways which strike home.

I am sorry if I have disappointed those who expected me to speak on such fascinating topics as establishment, and ecclesiastical politics and bishops in the House of Lords. As I see it, such matters are only significant against a broader background of Christian concern for public life as a whole. I hope this broader field is one in which we can go on increasing the very considerable co-operation which already exists between Christians of different denominations. I hope, too, we can find ways of encouraging the various ethnic communities, and members of other faiths, to play a fuller part in strengthening and stabilizing the religious dimension in public life. And if our present troubles as a nation have the effect of alerting us to the need to look once more at those things which bind us together, then something worthwhile may emerge from them.

4

The Industrial Society

Sermon preached in St Mary's, Bryanston Square, London to The Industrial Society
3 June 1986

SOME STORIES ARE inexhaustible; and the story of the Good Samaritan is one of them. Perhaps I had better start by explaining that I did not choose it as the lesson for this service. It was chosen for me. I always ask bodies holding special services to choose their own lessons, because the choice says something about what such a body sees as important, and where it sees itself in relation to the gospel.

I was told that the most apposite verse in the story is the final one, 'Go and do thou likewise'. And that is not surprising in a society where action is more important than talk, and where there is a great and wholly understandable desire to get things done in a country in which it is all too easy just to carry on in the same old ruts.

Last week I noticed that in a translation from a Russian document this verse appeared as 'Go and do them likewise', which is not quite the same thing, but perhaps takes us equally near the heart of the problem.

Others look in the parable and see different things. In recent years even the political parties have brought their own interpretations. One party sees it as the vindication of a social order based on fulfilling needs and the fairer distribution of wealth. Another points out that the Samaritan could help only because he had made his money in the first place. I am still waiting for a third party to remind us that the inn where they all ended up was halfway between Jerusalem and Jericho.

For me the heart of the parable lies in verse 33, 'A certain Samaritan as he journeyed came where he was . . .' This is what the others in the story failed to do. They kept their distance. Not just because they were in a hurry, or had pressing business in Jerusalem, not just because they exhibited the hypocrisy which is all too easy in those who are professionally religious, nor for any of the other reasons which are commonly read into the story by way of explanation. The reason is there in the text. The robbers had left the traveller half-dead. If he had been clearly dead he would have posed no problem. If he had been clearly alive he would have been an obvious case for compassion. But half-dead he represented an insoluble dilemma for those who wished to avoid the ritual penalties for touching a dead body. A choice had to be made. Not a straight choice between compassion and indifference; but a much more difficult choice conditioned by imprecise perceptions and unquantified risks. Hence the temptation not to make that choice, and to keep at a distance.

It was left to the outsider, to the man who had nothing to lose in terms of his own ritual purity, to come where the victim was, and see, and act.

This is a parable, therefore, about where we are; alongside the victim or keeping our distance. And it is a parable too about our attempts to justify ourselves in keeping our distance. The lawyer who asked the original question, 'Who is my neighbour?', did it, we are told, 'to justify himself'.

At a deeper level, it is a parable about where Christ is. It is the despised and rejected helper, the outsider, who comes where the victim is. And if humanity is the victim, then the words as applied to Christ, 'he came where he was', sum up the message of salvation. Surely he has borne our griefs and carried our sorrows, and is among us as one who serves.

If I am not mistaken this too is the kind of message which the Industrial Society, in its own limited sphere, has been trying to get across: the imperative need of those who would share a common task to come where the other is. If we try to keep our distance, if we refuse to face the ambiguities and dangers entailed in actually coming alongside one another, then in the end we are left with victims on the one hand and discredited leaders on the other. This is as true of a firm which fails through bad industrial relations, as it might be of a nation which simply pushes its victims to the side of the road.

I have recently been reading some articles about the industrial scene in Japan. I assume it is the kind of material which is basic to your work as a society. As an outsider I have been struck by the contrast between a social order like our own, in which confrontation, often of the most sterile kind, seems to be the norm from Parliament downwards, and a social order in which the basic assumption is benevolence.

Trollope's Mr Bunce was always 'longing to be doing some battle against his superiors, and to be putting himself in opposition to his employers – not that he objected personally to Messrs Foolscap,

Margin & Vellum who always made much of him as a useful man – but because some such antagonism would be manly, and the fighting of some battle would be the right thing to do'.

Mr Bunce's character may be overdrawn. But isn't it the Bunces of this world on both sides of industry who howl at Parliamentary Question Time? And whose style consists more in destroying an opponent than in solving a shared problem?

Japanese assumptions that rulers and authorities ought to be, and generally are, benevolent, may belong within a very different cultural context, and may have its own weaknesses and limitations. But I find it somewhat shaming that a so-called Christian society should have to rely so heavily on conflict, whereas a Confucian one has shown itself adaptable to deep-seated forms of industrial co-operation.

We have forgotten the lesson of the Good Samaritan – the need to come alongside one another, where we are. Given our history this is a perilously ambiguous thing to do. We have to start against a background of centuries of social division, deep wounds from the past, inherited suspicions, habits and assumptions which automatically push us into different classes with different privileges, different styles, different long-term prospects and hopes. We need the outsider, the third party, the faithful friend, to set aside the divisions and cross the road to the place where help is needed. And that, if I am not much mistaken, is what your society exists to do.

Let me end with a final word on your Director's favourite text, 'Go and do . . .'. I understand that this is the last Annual Service before his retirement, so perhaps a personal text may be allowed.

The point is that exhortation is not enough. Last week I returned from Moscow where the only public advertisements in the streets show workers marching forward side by side to glorious increased productivity, with some slogan setting the next industrial target. They are very striking, very strident, but if the general poverty of the country is anything to go by, they plainly don't work. Exhortation which doesn't engage us by actually beginning where we are, ultimately provokes ridicule.

Action, likewise, which fails in this basic 'being alongside one another' may be equally ineffective. Think of all those five year plans. Think of the immense efforts in our own country to solve our industrial problems.

It is not action as such which is needed, but action of a particular kind – the action of crossing the road to the wounded brother, the action of building bridges of trust and understanding between divided interest groups, the action of genuinely sharing common goals, of moving from conflict to mutuality. The theological word for this is 'incarnation' – love seeking its own. And this is where the very practical work which some of you do every day, touches the fringe of the mystery of the saving activity of God.

5

Doorkeepers

Sermon preached in Christ Church, Oxford, to the Annual Conference of the Secondary Heads Association
20 April 1986

'See, I have placed before you an open door that no one can shut' (Rev. 3.8).

ONE OF THE hazards of cathedral Matins is that you have to accept the lessons you are given. At first sight the letter to the church in Philadelphia may not seem to have much of direct relevance to say to the majority who make up our congregation here this morning. Yet in a day when doors seem to be closing all over the educational world, the message of the open door may not be all that distant from our concerns.

It is a complex message. Everything in the Book of Revelation is complex, full of allusions to the Old Testament, exploiting symbolism, turning images back on themselves.

The central image here of Christ as the faithful doorkeeper relies on an Old Testament story about an unfaithful doorkeeper, and it was meant to speak to those who felt themselves excluded from the synagogues which had once been home to them. Christ opens the door and keeps it open. And it is through the open door of heaven that St John enters to receive his revelation.

But in the very next letter to the next church, Laodicea, the image is inverted. This time it is the shut door, where Christ stands and knocks. 'If anyone hears my voice and opens the door, I will come in . . .' The open door can be shut after all, shut by ourselves from within.

Our own century has inverted the image in an even more disturbing way. There is the famous parable in Kafka's *Trial* about the man seeking admission to the law – the law which is going to solve all his problems and bring him justice at last.

He comes to an outer door and is told by the doorkeeper to wait. Beyond the door lie other doors and even fiercer doorkeepers. But he meekly waits. And waits. For days. And years. He pleads with the doorkeeper. He tries to bribe him. He watches him incessantly, as they both grow old.

At last the man sees a light streaming out of the door, and makes one last effort to ask the question which has been haunting him all these years. 'Everyone strives to attain the law,' he says, 'how does it come about then that in all these years no one has come seeking admittance but me?' The doorkeeper replies, 'No one but you could gain admittance through this door, since this door was intended only for you. I am now going to shut it.'

I called this a twentieth-century inversion. It conveys a sense of the loose ends, and the frustrated hopes, and the undercurrent of disillusionment, which have become all too familiar in our European culture. There is the haunting vision of a door which is somehow 'ours', a threshold we alone have to cross, yet which is unattainable. Kafka's hero, K, dies 'like a dog'.

The open door; and the closed door. It is a profoundly religious theme, because religion has always dealt with what the anthropologists call 'thresholds', those periods of significant transition in life, the passing through a new door into the unknown. Womb to world, childhood to adulthood, singleness to marriage, job to job, life to death, earth to heaven.

They are potentially dangerous moments. The first story of danger in the Bible, the quarrel between Cain and Abel, uses the imagery of a demon lurking at the threshold. Doors into new stages of life can be stress points. They focus insecurity. Psychologists claim that moving house takes a bit off your life, and I can well believe it. So we make the crossing of thresholds into ritual occasions. We look for community support. And the question of who stands at the door, and whether doors are perceived as open or closed, and what we expect to find on the other side of them, is more than a nice piece of religious imagery. It has to do with our capacity to change, and with the kind of security needed to cross some major threshold.

The traditional role of the clergy has made us into doorkeepers at some of the thresholds of life. We have had to learn to work with the contradictions. The open door through which so many refuse to pass. The doors which seem to be open, and frustratingly prove to be closed. The haunting visions, the unrealized opportunities, the final threshold of death.

And what makes the role of the doorkeeper possible is the faith that the final word is said by the one who holds the keys of death and hell, 'See, I have placed before you an open door that no one can shut.'

Teachers, too, deal with thresholds, as do members of some other professions. And no doubt we all experience similar contradictions and stresses, fears and hopes, and find the role of doorkeeper sometimes an uncomfortable one. Enabling young people to grow up, and to discover themselves, and then to discover a world beyond themselves, and giving them the courage not to turn away when doors seem closed against them, and helping them to cope with a Kafka-like world which alternately affirms and denies them, all this surely is one of the most delicate and demanding of tasks; a task which has analogies with priesthood. Like religion it depends on community support and understanding. Like religion it has its elements of ritual. And like religion it depends on the ability to synthesize personal commitment with the acceptance of a public role on which people can rely during their dangerous transitions.

Let me spell this out in more direct language. Teachers are professionals in a world of professionals. The trend towards more and more specialized professional development is one of the main features of modern life. All of us rightly guard our professional integrity, seek to raise our professional standards, and recognize a certain distinction between what is proper for us in our professional role, and what we may think and feel as individuals.

All this fits in with the pattern of modern everyday life, much of which is lived in separate compartments. We go to a professional adviser for help in some particular problem, and that is what we expect of him, that and no more. A bank manager who kept on regaling customers with his personal philosophy would soon lose them.

But what about a doctor? A good deal of recent discussion about medical ethics carries the message that professionalism by itself isn't enough. The separate compartments of life keep breaking into one another. Personal qualities and judgements cannot in the end be detached from professional ones. Doctors stand at transition points in life where elements of a more priest-like role may sometimes be required. And so do teachers. And perhaps other professionals as well.

We all have our expertise, our status, our rituals, but these are only part of what is needed. Threshold experiences have a community dimension to them. And that is why those who try to help others pass through them and make sense of them, must never overlook the wider community. Teaching is never just 'me and the children'. The whole question of public acceptance, public esteem, is central to the task.

Even more important is the personal dimension. There is an alarming sense in which a good teacher also needs to be a good person.

Professional values and moral values cannot in the end be separated. The transition periods in life are times of personal exposure and vulnerability, when those who stand beside us need to be whole people as well as skilled people, people whose own lives are not shut into the compartments which otherwise fragment our world.

To be this kind of a doorkeeper is a demanding vocation. It is all the more difficult for those who are beset by professional problems, and who feel undervalued. The changes through which our society is going to have to be helped to pass are enough to daunt anybody. It is tempting just to close the door and sit tight.

That is why my text is so necessary: 'See, I have placed before you an open door that no one can shut.'

No one. Not even faithless doorkeepers who fail so often, like ourselves. There is no need to be crushed by the weight of our own inadequacies. Because another part of this complex imagery is the picture of Christ himself as the door, the door of the sheepfold, the door kept open by his own presence for the greatest transition of all, the passage between earth and heaven. And we who are called to be helpers at the thresholds here on earth are not alone. We do it in him and with him and for him. And we renew our faith and our hope by looking to that other open door – the stone rolled away for ever from the mouth of the tomb.

6

The Christ-Centred Public Square

Sermon preached in St Michael's, Cornhill, London, at the City New Year Service
12 January 1988

'God is the source of your life in Christ Jesus whom he made our
wisdom, our righteousness, and sanctification and redemption'
(1 Cor. 2.30).

I WAS DRAWN to preach on this text when I read that St Michael's stands
on the site of the Roman forum; here was the focal point at which the
whole of the city came together. Rightly or wrongly I like to imagine St
Paul mentally placing himself in the forum at Corinth, surveying all
the activity of that busy cosmopolitan city, with its difficult people, its
divisions, its moral lapses. And in his mind's eye he sees on one side of
the forum, perhaps, a school or library, a place of human learning, a
symbol of wisdom. On the other side, the law court, the place of
justice, a symbol of righteousness. On the third side, a temple or two,
symbols of the persistent human search to make contact with the
sacred. And on the fourth side, the slave market, the place where
human lives were bought and sold – and if they were lucky, redeemed;
the ultimate kind of commerce. And somehow he saw all this human
activity, all this busyness, as finding its fulfilment in Christ . . . 'Christ
Jesus whom God made our wisdom, our righteousness, and sanctification and redemption'.

Maybe my picture of the forum is fanciful. But at least it can remind
us that wisdom, righteousness, sanctification and redemption don't just
belong in some private religious sphere, but have their counterparts in
the market place.

Wisdom is not just a personal quality. It is the sum of human
knowledge. Paul has just been writing about the wisdom of the Greeks.
Wisdom is the principle which holds all things together. 'By me,
wisdom, kings reign and princes decree justice.'

Righteousness, too, is more than personal rightness with God,
essential though that is. It has to include the rightness, the justice, of
men's dealings with one another.

Sanctification has its public face as well as its inner spiritual reality. Religion is a public phenomenon. The cult is not just for individuals, however much individuals may benefit from it, but is a vital part of the fabric of society – 'the sacred canopy' as it has been called.

And redemption – again it is a mistake to think only in terms of individual salvation. In the Old Testament it was the nation which was redeemed from slavery in Egypt. And in many parts of the world today the hope which keeps Christian faith alive is the hope of release from some equivalent kind of corporate slavery.

St Paul claimed all this for Christ. And he did it at the end of a famous description of the weakness and foolishness of Christians. This is not some monstrous Christian imperialism. It is not a take-over bid by the Church, which in any case at that time was tiny, insignificant, and in deep internal trouble. Paul is doing something more profound, and more far reaching. He is saying that at the centre of all this human activity, this search for wisdom and justice and holiness and freedom, and the key to its ultimate meaning – is Christ.

It is a claim our world finds hard to accept, for a multiplicity of reasons. I want to concentrate on just one of them. To claim that the market place as well as the human heart ought to belong to Christ is to threaten one of the fundamental assumptions of the modern world, the assumption that different spheres of life and different disciplines each have their own autonomy. The modern world became what it is through specialization, through fragmentation, through the setting of limits to what belongs properly to different kinds of activities. So science is science, and commerce is commerce, the law is the law, philosophy is philosophy, and religion has its own separate and diminishing area of relevance in a world divided up between the experts.

In a sense this had to happen. The stranglehold of theology in the medieval world had to be broken. New enterprises, new developments in thought, could never have succeeded as long as the feeling persisted that all the answers had somehow already been given, or were to be settled by the ecclesiastics.

The part of the story which has always interested me most is the development of science. There is a strong case for saying that science in its modern sense could only have been conceived and born in a Christian culture, against the background of a Christian doctrine of creation. But it is also true that in its early years, and still in some circles today, science had to fight hard to insulate itself against theological explanations. If the explanation of the variety of animal species is simply that God made them that way, then the search for biological explanations comes to a full stop. Part of the battle over Darwinism was a battle for the autonomy of biology. Biologists, it was claimed, must look for biological explanations of biological phenomena, and if they wander outside these into theology then they have betrayed their calling. This is not to say that they cannot be Christians, only that their Christianity ought not to influence their biology. There is no specifically Christian biology – only biology.

And so with mathematics, and physics and economics, and commerce, and stockbroking and sport and a hundred and one other activities which make up the modern world. Each has its relevant skills, its experts, its methods and procedures, its body of knowledge, its devotees, and for much of the time it can function in a closed world of its own as if the rest of the world were of no account. And the same can happen to religion. Religion can become a specialist activity for those who happen to like it. It is relegated to a lowly category in the modern world – as unproven opinion. And when it breaks out of these limits, as in the Middle East or in Ireland, or in different ways in North and South America, then the consequences can be world-shaking.

I have been exaggerating, of course. The world is not quite as fragmented as I have been suggesting. And in any case different kinds of expertise can meet in the same person. A stockbroker may also be a father, and may even be a churchwarden. But we are a long way from being able to stand in the market place of the modern world, and claim it for Christ.

Yet that is what we are here for, and I want in this second part of my address to suggest how we might begin. William Temple once said that it was not the job of Christian spokesmen to tell engineers how to build bridges, but simply to encourage them to build good ones. Far be it from me to criticize a great Archbishop, but it has always struck me as a rather feeble remark. Any engineer worth his salt doesn't need encouragement to build good bridges; it is part of his proper pride and professional expertise to do so. But he may need reminding that decisions about bridges are not purely engineering ones. Questions about why a bridge is needed, and where it should be, and what its impact is likely to be on the communities it serves, and who pays, and how well it fits into the landscape and other questions of that kind are all part of the total operation in which the engineer is only one element. In other words, he has his expertise, and his expertise belongs to him alone. But his autonomy is, or ought to be, limited. A bridge has to fit within a total context. It is more than a piece of engineering.

So with other specialities. We have chopped up our world into fragments. And maybe this was necessary if we were to create the ranges of expertise needed to cope with such a complex reality. But we have confused expertise with autonomy. Our task now is to start putting the fragments together again, seeing the connections between things, allowing different types of insights to influence one another. And our encouragement for doing so is Christ – 'whom God has made our wisdom, our righteousness, and sanctification and redemption'.

We have been learning again the hard way that there can be no sound commerce without deep roots in morality. Those who deal in money as a commodity need constant reminders that somewhere these billions of pounds, which ebb to and fro across the world, touch the lives and livelihoods of actual people. Some of the most difficult and contentious legislation facing us over the next few years is difficult precisely because it arouses strongly held feelings about justice and personal worth and dignity.

Even science is discovering the limits of its autonomy. I do not mean that theological explanations are beginning to creep in by the back door, but that science as a total enterprise cannot survive in a philosophical vacuum, any more than it can survive in a society which regards it as a useful adjunct to industry. Science needs some vision of ultimate truth, a truth worth pursuing simply because it is true. And so does theology. By a curious turn of history, science and theology need each other today more than they have ever needed each other since the very beginning of the scientific adventure.

Christian faith assures us that there is a single reality at the heart of things, a connectedness, a single light which shines, refracted into many colours, reflected off innumerable surfaces, a still point at the centre of all our busyness, a single life which comprehends all life.

He is our wisdom, because all the lines of knowledge run back into God. Much may be utterly incomprehensible to us, but the human quest for knowledge, the human concern for honesty, integrity, truthfulness can be maintained against all the attacks of cynicism, because there is something real to be truthful about.

He is our righteousness, the source of rightness and the judge of it. Our world may be faced by many ethical problems which are baffling in their complexity – how to use our knowledge wisely, how to relieve suffering and injustice, how to encourage enterprise while restraining greed. It is tempting sometimes simply to ignore them, or to dismiss them as somebody else's problem, or to give up in despair. To see the righteousness of God in Christ is not a recipe for easy answers. But it is the guarantee that there *is* a righteousness, and that the struggle to do right ultimately matters.

He is our sanctification. Religion can go terribly wrong. There are times and places, past and present, when religious emotion has unleashed hatred, violence, bigotry, fanaticism. Prejudice, more often than not, dresses itself in religious clothes. This is one reason why public rows about religion, particularly in its social role as the guardian of public values, can sometimes get so rough. Our religious up-tightness needs to be healed by the touch of real holiness, the holiness of self-giving love.

He is our redemption, the touchstone of true freedom. This is not the freedom to trample on one another in some self-serving frenzy, but the freedom of a world in which all are free to value themselves and each other at their true worth, the worth God places on us. We are bought with a price.

The message of the gospel belongs in the market place, belongs wherever human beings think and dream and work and make judgements and try to reach out beyond themselves, often not knowing what they seek. 'God' is the word which carries the terrifying weight of all this hope and longing and aspiration. And the message is that 'God is the source of our life in Christ Jesus . . .'

7

Order and Law

Sermon preached in York Minster at the Annual Legal Service of the North Eastern Circuit
5 October 1986

'Your statutes have become my songs . . .' (Ps. 119.54).

THE IDEA THAT law might be something to celebrate and sing about is not, I suspect, immediately obvious these days, even to lawyers. No doubt for those with eyes to see one statute differs from another statute in glory. But in a service of this kind, the thought uppermost in our minds is likely to be the weight of responsibility carried by the legal profession, and the need for all those qualities of wisdom, integrity and insight required to fulfil your role.

Yet there is something to celebrate. For the psalmist the statutes, judgements, precepts and so forth which appear in every verse of this immensely long psalm, were a revelation of the mind of God. They were the assurance that underneath the tensions and ambiguities of everyday experience there is an underlying order, a God-given order. We human beings are not left to our own devices in trying to find a decent way of life together. The law is seen not just as a set of obligations imposed on unwilling people who would rather be left alone. Nor is it arbitrary. It is our guide, our mentor, our friend, a pointer to reality, a proper subject for song.

The Old Testament perspective comes in for some hard knocks in the New Testament, but it is not superseded. We are told that the spirit of the law is more important than the details of it; it has to be internalized, the law of the heart rather than the law of external observance. We are told that law by itself is not enough; as a way to God's righteousness it fails, because *we* fail, and that is why we need the gospel of grace. We are reminded that though law is essential, love is greater.

But when all the criticisms are made, there is still something to celebrate, still an underlying order which expresses the mind of God, and which it is the task of the law to spell out and safeguard. We can still sing Psalm 119, and mean it.

I have begun in this rather abstract way because it seems to me that in popular usage the phrase 'law and order' is frequently misinterpreted. Order comes to be thought of as if it were the same as orderliness, not doing things in the street which might frighten the horses, keeping people 'in order'. The notion of 'God's order' has been weakened. There is no obvious association in many people's mind with the deep underlying order of society, with the network of assumptions, conventions, values and expectations which make a society what it is. 'Order', in the sense in which I am using the word, is about the way a society understands itself, about the way it is structured, about the quality of relationships and the norms of behaviour. And the law stands round this like a ring of buttresses round a cathedral, supporting it, and also shaping it.

The 'supporting' function is easy to understand. But I have found that our legislators are often none too keen to recognize the 'shaping' function of the law. They are happy to see the law reflect changes in social behaviour, and a great deal of liberalizing legislation in recent decades has been of that kind. They are less happy to ask of any particular piece of legislation how far it is likely itself to change people's attitudes, and to change the character of society. One of the obvious crunch questions in the last twenty years has been the question of abortion. The present law fulfilled a social need which was felt to be more and more pressing. But how far has it also changed attitudes to unborn life, and so increased the size of the problem it was meant to relieve?

My point is simply that the relationship between law and order is a profound and subtle one, which needs a great deal more reflection than it usually gets.

There is a chapter in the Report of the Archbishop of Canterbury's Commission on Urban Priority Areas, *Faith in the City*, called 'Order and Law'. The phrase is turned on its head largely to make this same point. In the urban priority areas with which the report is concerned the forces of law are under strain, so the argument goes, not just because people are misbehaving, but because there are fundamental cracks in the social order. Indeed in extreme cases there is a rejection of the social order as such. The report speaks of the loss of respect for people and property, the mood of sullen apathy, the sense of being trapped in a hostile environment, which undermines the assumption that there is an order worth preserving.

Maybe the picture is overdrawn but one doesn't have to go far into some of our most difficult housing estates or inner city areas to see some truth in it. And when this kind of thing begins to happen, the mere toughening up of the law can simply accelerate the disintegration of the underlying social order.

I suppose the extreme form of this process ends in terrorism. The terrorist rejects the social order he is fighting against to the point of dehumanizing the people who make it up. They are seen as belonging to an alien order, victims, hostages, pawns in a game, passers-by in a street, whose suffering is of no moral significance to the terrorist because they are not really thought of as people.

In our justifiable horror and revulsion at terrorism we go through the same process of depersonalizing the terrorists. The words which come spontaneously to mind are 'animals', 'not fit to belong to the human race'. The most successful strategy against hostage-takers lies in refusing to allow this depersonalization to take place, by building up some minimal kind of social order between hostages and captors. It then becomes harder to kill people you have actually talked to and acknowledged as people.

I take this extreme example of terrorism because I believe it can help us to spot much smaller but also much more widespread symptoms of the breakdown of a fundamental sense of order in our society. In our complex stressful world most of us have deeply divided political allegiances. It is only the most committed or the most acquiescent who can say 'My party right or wrong' – or 'My nation right or wrong'. The rest of us have reservations, disagreements, sometimes downright antagonism to what goes on. Modern societies consist of multitudes of different interest groups, pressure groups, action groups which sometimes screw themselves up to standing outside the accepted social order. Why else should solid respectable citizens demonstrate, however ill-advisedly, against nuclear test-drilling? For me the most disturbing aspect of these last incidents was the apparent inability of the contending parties to talk to each other. What TV showed us, and I realize that the camera usually lies, was people simply concerned to get their slogan broadcast. Even bishops, these days, are tending to get closer to the line at which illegal action is justified in the name of conscience.

These complex groupings and antagonisms and divided allegiances at the root of our modern society are responsible, I believe, for a certain fragility in our present social order. I have already suggested that mere strengthening of the law will not heal it. We have to rediscover a deeper order still, a moral order within which our divided allegiances can be contained. Indeed I believe that one of the most urgent tasks facing our society today lies in this rediscovery of its moral roots.

'Your statutes have become my songs . . .'

Mere assertion of the moral principles is not enough. Telling people to be good is one of the surest ways of provoking a counter-reaction. But celebrating goodness, rejoicing in it, presenting a vision of the loving purposes of God, reaching out for our ultimate unity in God, can be like water on a thirsty ground, nourishing the roots from which better things can grow.

8
Freemasonry and Christianity

*Speech at the General Synod during the debate on the Synod report
'Freemasonry and Christianity: Are they compatible?'
13 July 1987*

LET ME START by putting my cards on the table and saying that I regard
Freemasonry as a fairly harmless eccentricity. I am sorry the Churches
have started getting so solemn about it and I hope Christian
Freemasons will not be too distressed by the highly selective
quotations from this Report headlined by the press. On the whole I
think it is a good Report, which has tried to be fair, and is a delight to
read. I shall certainly vote to receive it.

I regret, though, that it was ever commissioned, and I see certain
danger signals in this kind of attempt by the General Synod to lay
down criteria about what is or is not compatible with Christianity.

No doubt there are many cases of people being unhealthily absorbed
in what is by any standards a rather odd society. No doubt some
masons become religiously confused. But this is not unique to masons.
No doubt there have been Masonic Lodges whose members have been
tempted to become introverted, conspiratorial, self-seeking and
manipulative. But this is not entirely unknown in churches. However,
to use words like 'heresy' and 'blasphemy', is to judge it by standards
which are inappropriate for this kind of body. I am much more
disturbed by prying Christians who want to make everything conform
to their own standards of truth than by groups of well-meaning and
charitable men who enjoy meeting together and dressing up, or down,
as the case may be.

I have described Feemasonry as a fairly harmless eccentricity. That
is not meant to sound superior. It will be a sad day when there is no
room for eccentricity in the Church of England.

I must add that it is an eccentricity with which I find it hard to feel
any personal rapport. I can see how some people's lives are starved of
meaningful ritual. I can see a certain antiquarian interest. I can see a
value in banding together to do good works secretly. I can see a definite

value in the close friendships which can develop in such circumstances. I can see how it is possible to get a frisson from pretending to possess secret knowledge. I can even see that men gain a certain pleasure in doing things together which they wouldn't do in front of their wives.

But these are all harmless pleasures. And if people enjoy them, why shouldn't they?

As for the secret name of God, I am reminded of the Arab story that God has 100 names of which man knows only 99. The camel knows the 100th, and that is why his expression is always one of ineffable superiority.

There are, of course, questions to be asked about religious syncretism. I have already made the point in another context that there is much work to be done by Christians in discerning where the true meeting-points lie. I deplore the implication in para. 112 of the Report that one can make simplistic judgements about what is going on in an inter-faith service; and it seems to me that the hint that the Assisi meeting of leaders of different faiths might be 'just an exhibition of spiritual sleight of hand or ecclesiastical hypocrisy' is unworthy of a church document.

We badly need good contexts in which people with different religious convictions can work together without abandoning those commitments, or ignoring them. Freemasonry has tried to provide such a context. We may not like its style. I would certainly have some difficulties about worshipping an architect, and despite what some people say I am not greatly attracted by Deism. But I think the craft needs to be commended for at least *trying* to solve an exceedingly difficult problem.

I have referred to Freemasonry as 'fairly harmless'. Let me in conclusion explain why I use the word 'fairly'. I think there is a slight danger of masons doing harm to themselves – not by the rituals, certainly not by the charitable giving, but by the aura of secrecy, however trivial the actual secrets and however unreal the privacy in actual practice. If something looks like a conspiracy, people will treat it as one, whatever the disclaimers. And the conspirational atmosphere is infectious. There was a feeling of great things at stake in the publication of this Report. The secrecy surrounding it was much better than anything the masons have themselves achieved. I even received my draft copy in *two* sealed envelopes and very nearly ate it after a first reading.

The danger in all this is not so much in any actual underhand dealing, favouritism and connivance, though doubtless some of it goes on, as in any comparable organization. The danger lies in the suspicions of it, and this is why I think those who occupy public roles are well advised to be cautious. It is possible to give the impression of being one of a clique while in fact behaving entirely honourably.

Hence I am glad that most modern bishops have avoided the Craft. I want in no way to condemn those who belonged in the past or who belong today. My answer to the question posed in the report is Yes, Christianity and Freemasonry *are* compatible. But while all things may be lawful to those who love God, not all may be expedient.

9

Public and Private Morality

Presidential Address at the York Diocesan Synod following an address by Mr Douglas Hurd, the Home Secretary, to members of the General Synod 12 March 1988

I WANT TO reflect a little this morning about the role of the Church in public life. In recent months we have been exposed to an extraordinary amount of publicity, with numerous voices telling us what is wrong both with the Church and with the nation, and what we ought to do about both. Some of what has been said has been vicious and inaccurate and it is as well to remember that there are some people in the media, as well as in public life, who have no love for the Church of England as it now is and who seek actively to do us harm. That is why it is important not to take everything at its face value.

Nevertheless some of the publicity derives from the fact that there are real worries about what is happening to our society, real conflicts which the Church can to some extent articulate, and real divisions within the Church itself which can be exploited by those who have a mind to do so. We ought not therefore to expect an easy ride or be too worried when headlines scream at us that we are on a downward spiral, or that nothing can save the Church from disintegrating. This is rubbish and we know it is. We know that the gospel is unchanged. We know that the life of faith and worship goes on. We know that in many, many places the Church is strong and healthy and growing, though we know also to our shame that in many other places there seem to be immovable obstacles against developing a real living Christian community.

If we are wise we will see the peculiar challenge of our times as a sign of life, as a reminder that the quality of our Christianity actually makes a difference, and that our task as Christians takes us deep into the divisions and conflicts and insecurities of our society as a whole.

And so to my theme – our public role as a Church. When Mr Hurd addressed members of General Synod last month he spoke about the limitations of the Government, indeed of any government, in attempting to tackle some of the major social problems of our day. He instanced the crime rate, particularly crime among young people, and the apparent insensitivity of some young people to other people's feelings. He urged the Church to concentrate on personal morality and so to create a firm basis for social cohesion in the nation. One of his implications, though he did not put it as crudely as this, was that if we kept out of politics and taught individuals to be good, we would be more true to our calling than in pursuing unrealistic, and ultimately confusing attempts to involve ourselves in the ordinary political rough and tumble. Those who live by politics are judged by politics, but the Church ought to stand for something more.

He had a point. I do not myself believe that the Church as Church should take political sides, unless an issue is so overwhelmingly clear as to demand particular Christian response. I also, of course, accept that we have a major duty to teach personal morality in the light of the gospel, and I believe that a great deal of this goes on week by week in our parishes, though it never hits the headlines. In fact, I recently tried an experiment by sending the full scripts of some sermons on basic moral values to some sections of the media which had already shown an interest in the occasions on which I was to preach them. Not a word was published. Perhaps they were rotten, dull sermons, but I suspect the truth is that goodness isn't news.

Up to a point, as I say, I agree with Mr Hurd, but we need to be aware of two complications. The first is a complication within Conservative philosophy itself and I think it underlies part of Mr Hurd's message to us. The current dominant philosophy within the Conservative party seems to some commentators to be made up of two strands. One of these we can label neo-liberalism – belief in the central importance of individual freedom, coupled with the further belief that the central condition for securing this freedom lies in the free market. It follows from this that justice will be better secured by multiplying opportunities and by increasing prosperity than by artificial attempts to impose greater equality, and that therefore the role of Government should be minimized as far as possible to allow individual competitiveness to have its maximum effect.

That is one strand. We all recognize it and I have tried to describe it as uncontroversially as possible. The other strand can be labelled neo-conservatism. This is a return to an older, more familiar Conservative philosophy, rooted in a view of society as a complex and coherent whole, which evolves organically; it entails an elaborate system of checks and balances which should not be tinkered with more than absolutely necessary. In particular, neo-conservatism is suspicious of grandiose plans for putting society to rights because these are bound to be less balanced in their effects than the wisdom already built into the system over many generations. Thus, neo-conservatism, like neo-liberalism, also values low profile government, though the motive for it is different. Neo-conservatism looks for consensus and stability, for firm but non-interfering government, based on traditional values. Neo-liberalism is a formula for undirected change, subject only to market forces, and it welcomes individual diversity and enterprise.

I oversimplify, but I believe we can see both strands in present Conservative political thinking, and the tension between them is to a large extent unresolved. It need not be destructive, but in some instances it can be. There is a good example of it in the field of broadcasting which we debated at our last meeting and which the General Synod endorsed in February. Neo-liberalism wants to open up broadcasting to more and more competition. Our main argument in our debate here was that this can only be done at the expense of the high standards and basic values of public service broadcasting. Neo-conservatism wants to preserve these values, and the two philosophies are thus in direct conflict. It can be sidestepped by falsely equating quality with efficiency. Competition can certainly raise efficiency in a financial sense, but there are areas of life, and broadcasting is one of them, where competition squeezes out the space available for the development of excellence. If everything has to be judged in terms of the ratings, then there is overwhelming temptation simply to pursue the well-tried and popular formula with the dreary results which are all too familiar to us. It remains to be seen whether the same principle applies to education.

The basic conflict, let me repeat, is between a philosophy which roots freedom in competitiveness and a philosophy which wants to sustain traditional values. One way of resolving it is to divide roles; to say that it is the role of government to maintain the freedom of the market place and the role of other bodies, notably the Churches, to provide the necessary moral stability and backup. Again, I am oversimplifying, but I suspect that some such division of roles follows inevitably from a divided philosophy, and that it accounts for a good deal of the confusion about the direction in which our society is heading and who really bears responsibility for it.

The first complication then in this programme of simply making the Churches responsible for private morality is that it rests on a confusion of aims which needs to be brought out into the open and looked at much more searchingly. The second complication in this neat division of roles is that life does not actually divide up into public matters which are primarily political and private matters which are primarily moral and spiritual. I very much doubt whether young people are led into crime because they haven't heard enough sermons about morality from bishops, or because they weren't taught about honesty and encouraged to be honest at school. A whole complex of social factors, individual experiences and peer group pressures, contribute to the making of the criminals, and more so in days when individual conscience tends to be weak. And why is conscience weak? Here again, we have to recognize the influence of major social changes over the last forty to fifty years. Strong consciences develop in societies, families and churches which place a high premium on authority. In our modern world authority is one of the great problem areas. It is making a comeback in some highly authoritarian forms of religion, but in society at large external authorities tend to be suspect, particularly among those who have been brought up to distrust and oppose the mysterious 'them' who seem to dictate the conditions of their lives. In such circumstances conscience doesn't develop as a strong internal compass. People develop antennae to sense what they can get away with.

I say this not as an excuse for the failure to develop appropriate forms of authority in our society and appropriate moral teaching in the Churches, but as a reminder of how impossible it is to disentangle personal morality from its social environment, or to establish it on a firm base unless the social dimension as well as the individual dimension is recognized. The debate about violence on television is a case in point. We just do not know how individual attitudes are affected by the programmes which people watch day in and day out. But to say that they have no effect at all would seem to fly in the face of all experience.

What I am saying is that public and private attitudes are inextricably intertwined. There are, of course, those in the churches who would welcome a retreat into a purely private morality. This is one reason why the churches have so often been obsessed with sex. There are certain very intimate matters which seem to be wholly under individual control and to touch some inner realm of personal value where the pressures of individual conscience can really get to work.

Conscientious people tend to feel more guilty about sex, and more angry about other people's sex, than about greed or envy. But even in sex, perhaps especially in sex these days, we cannot escape the fact that private acts have public consequences.

There is in fact no way of carving up morality into a private sector and a public sector. We are social beings and we who find the major liturgical expression of our faith in communion ought to be the last people to forget that. It means that for the foreseeable future we are going to be involved in the stresses and strains of public life, as well as in that all-important and personal commitment and personal moral growth without which our role as Christians in public life would be merely fraudulent. Most of the quiet task of developing and applying Christian insights within the workaday world has to be done by lay people, and they need constant encouragement and help, especially in discouraging times when all they stand for seems to be under attack. Much of the publicity, though, falls inevitably on the clergy, especially when we fail and make a mess of things, as we frequently do. So clergy too need help and encouragement and understanding as we try to respond to the complex pressures to which we are all subject.

Finally, for those who may be tempted to feel a bit bewildered and long for some never-never land in the past when all seemed so much simpler, let me reassure you that despite all these complexities the gospel is essentially simple. It is about following Christ and finding our life in him. Where he leads us we are not told in advance. Some are called to live lives of simple faithfulness. Others have to become immersed in the compromises and uncertainties of public life. But we are all followers together and, as such, I pray that we shall find strength through one another.

PART II

CONTROVERSIES ABOUT BELIEF

10
Obedience and Faith

Sermon preached in St Paul's Cathedral at the Annual Festival of the Corporation of the Sons of the Clergy 22 May 1985

'If anyone chooses to do God's will, he will find out whether my teaching comes from God, or whether I speak on my own' (John 7.17).

IN OTHER WORDS, there is a practical test of faith in the shape of obedience. Those who do, know. Obedience is not just the sign that we have faith. It is the condition, the context, the frame of mind, which enables faith to be established. To know the truth of a teaching, we have to live it.

This was the answer Jesus gave to those who criticized him for teaching without authority. 'How did this man get such learning without having studied?' As so often, he turned the question back on his questioners: 'Do you who give such reverence to your teachers, actually obey what they teach?'

The passage we have had read to us this evening is only a snippet from a much longer series of conversations in St John's Gospel centering on the questions 'Who is Jesus?' and 'Where does he come from?' With typical irony the point is made again and again that those who are most certain that they know are the most likely to be mistaken.

It is easy enough to say that the origin of Jesus is a mystery. But what the world calls a mystery, what the crowds gossip and speculate about, is not true mystery at all. Human beings, St John is telling us, constantly reduce and demean the mystery of God's action by trying to bring it within the limits of the world's own criteria. 'He is a good man', say some. Others reply, 'No, he deceives the people'. But the knowledge of God is not like that. The author of the Cloud of Unknowing got it right – 'of God himself can no man think . . . by love he can be caught and held, but by thinking never'. When the depth and truth of our relationship with God is at stake, knowing, being and willing are inseparable.

This may seem a strange theme for a Festival of the Sons of the

Clergy. The Corporation is a marvellously practical body which now distributes nearly £900,000 a year. It is involved in down to earth ways with huge numbers of clergy at their point of need.

It must save many clergy families from near disaster and despair. Trying to do the will of God is an essential dimension of its task, and that is why it is right that we should come together in this splendid service to thank God for its achievements, and for the hard work and the continuing generosity which sustain it. But why go on from this essentially practical celebration to raise the large issues of obedience and faith?

Let me give an embarrassingly direct answer. It is because many good lay people in today's church are increasingly making the connection between their support of the clergy and their expectations of them. The expectations have not for the most part, thank God, taken the form of tests of faith. But there is a deep rooted, and surely wholly justifiable expectation that the clergy, despite all our humanness, all our faults and failings, will somehow manage to convey to those to whom we minister some sense of the reality and presence of God.

I learnt this right at the beginning of my ministry, before I went to teach in a theological college, when I asked a group of people I had been working with what they expected of a priest. The only atheist in the group gave the best answer. She described childhood experiences in Scotland when the minister used to call. The feeling had never left her that here was somebody different, somebody rooted in a different, more mysterious, more important reality. Doing, being and knowing all converge in this impossible, glorious, demanding, grace-full vocation.

This is why it is sad that in the public mind recently questions of intellectual belief seem to have become detached from the whole nexus of prayer, action, commitment and community to which they properly belong.

The point was made to me with brutal directness by a TV interviewer who was quizzing me in preparation for a possible programme on the theme, 'What is a Christian?'

I started explaining to him the many dimensions of religious commitment; an intellectual dimension certainly, but also large components of feeling, deep rooted symbolism, stories which echo in the subconscious. Then there is the ethical dimension and the social one; the realm of ritual action, public and private, and those inner experiences which differ so startlingly from one person to another.

I started to spell out some of the complex interactions between those different dimensions; how some people find the most compelling spiritual reality in sacramental worship; how for others it is the sense of intimate personal relationship with Jesus which is all important. For some the content of religion is largely ethical. For others it is social, a question of belonging rather than being or doing. The permutations are endless, which is why there is no one simple answer to the question 'What is a Christian?'

'That's all very well', said my interviewer, 'but what viewers really want to know is whether a Christian has to believe in the Virgin Birth.'

How can one explain that this narrowing down of the manysidedness of faith to a single issue about the precise form of certain doctrinal statements, is to do precisely what the crowds in Jerusalem wanted? 'Give us a simple answer to a simple question . . . tell us whether your teaching is true.'

Of course, plain answers and simple truths are important. Of course, the controversies of recent months have been about substantial issues. The point needs to be made again and again that the Christian faith is rooted in history, in what God has actually done, and there can be no valid faith which discounts or undermines this historical dimension.

But there can be no valid faith either if we lose sight of what all our expressions of Christian belief are actually for – not to fill our minds with a certain style of mental furniture, but to relate us to God. 'If anyone chooses to do God's will, he will find out whether my teaching comes from God . . .'

What St John's Gospel describes for us is a search, an adventure, an argument which moves first this way, then that, a respect for actual experience out of which emerges, often slowly and painfully, deeper knowledge of God. It is not the kind of knowledge which can somehow be read off from an authoritative formula. Its authority emerges with it, through the process of questioning and hearing and responding.

One of the greatest contemporary expositors of St John, C. K. Barrett, has described the Gospel's theology as dialectical. It is full of contrasts, oppositions, paradoxes. Those who think they see, are blind. Blessed are those who have seen the risen Christ. But blessed also are those who have not seen, and yet believe.

This constant moving between affirmation and denial is not just a peculiarity of St John's method. It is an authentic insight into the nature of Christian truth, in which being and doing, responding and questioning, are an essential part of knowing.

So how do we convey this reality in an age which finds it hard to believe? I have already said that directness, simplicity, certainty, straight answers to straight questions, are not to be despised. But I suspect that the fundamental disagreement in our Church today concerns the amount of simplicity and directness it is right to expect. Controversies over the precise historical interpretation of particular doctrines may sway the argument this way or that. But the root difference lies between those with a questioning exploratory faith, and those who hold that essentially all the answers have already been given.

Even that is putting it too simply. Even the most questioning faith is more than a list of questions; it has to be a response to and an exploration of what God has actually done, a dialectic between yes and no. And even the most unquestioning faith has to allow room for discovery unless it is to lose all sense of the life-giving work of the Spirit. As always we are faced with a spectrum of attitudes, not two utterly opposed viewpoints.

Nevertheless there is a difference and it is important to recognize it. And it is important for those who have expectations of the clergy to ask themselves what in the end they want from them. Do we want to be made into explorers or into recipients? And which approach is likely to lead us deeper into the knowledge of God?

If we answer, as I believe St John answers, that we have to be explorers, then maybe we can go on from there to see the differences between Christians as all part of a larger dialectic which will eventually bring both sides to a more authentic faith.

Please God we shall tackle our differences in that spirit. Thus in listening to one another, and in loving one another, and in working with one another, and in common obedience to our Lord, we shall know whether our teaching comes from God, or whether we speak on our own.

11

Letters on Belief

Archbishop's Letters in the York Diocesan Leaflet
July 1984 – March 1988

Christian Believing

THEOLOGY IS IN the news. Discussion of fundamental Christian doctrine on TV or in the press has revealed yet again how difficult it is for the general Christian public to appreciate what theologians are doing, or to understand how this relates to the ordinary business of believing. It may be helpful, therefore, if I use this letter to reflect briefly on the nature of theology, taking the doctrine of the Virgin Birth as an example of the subtle interplay between various levels of belief.

The starting point for understanding any theology is the frank recognition that theologians are trying to do the impossible. Human language, however sophisticated or exalted, is inadequate to describe the mystery and splendour of God. This is why various types of language have to be used – straight historical narrative, poetry, parable, exhortation, complex symbolism, in fact every available device for stretching words and images far beyond their normal meaning. To confuse these different types of language, to treat poetry as history, say, or vice versa, is to create unnecessary difficulties. But even if that pitfall is avoided, words in the end must fail. All true theology culminates in the prayer of silent adoration. And it is in such prayer that different expressions of theological truth may come to be seen as not necessarily in conflict, but complementing and correcting one another.

The creeds, which try to catch in words the essence of the Christian faith as it was defined in relation to particular historical conflicts, stand as permanent signposts of Christian orthodoxy. But in interpreting them the same principle applies as in interpreting the Scriptures on which they are based. Each generation of Christians has to use the best scholarship available to get back into the minds of those who first experienced the impact of Christ's coming, and endeavoured to put it into words, and then ask the question, 'What must the truth have been if it appeared like this to men who thought and spoke like that?' The terms in which the truth is expressed may differ in different generations. The essential thing, and the true test of orthodoxy, is not whether we would use this or that precise form of words if we were writing the creeds today, but whether through them we can discern the authentic vision and experience to which they bear witness.

So with that as a preliminary, and very compressed, warning about what to expect of theology, let me turn to the doctrine of the Virgin Birth. Why is it in the creed, and what is its importance?

The first essential is to be clear about the logical relation between this doctrine and the doctrine of the incarnation. Many people mistakenly suppose that belief in the incarnation somehow depends on belief in the Virgin Birth. In the New Testament, however, the overwhelming emphasis is on the resurrection of Jesus, and the continuing evidence of his presence, and his fulfilment of the purposes of God as Christians came to understand these from the Old Testament. It is the whole impact of his life, death and victory over death, which drives forward the belief that here indeed is the ultimate revelation of God's presence. The Virgin Birth came to be seen as a fitting expression of this truth, but it can hardly have been central to New Testament thought, since the majority of New Testament writers make no mention of it. It follows that doubts about the Virgin Birth do not necessarily imply doubts about the incarnation, though obviously the fact that it occurs in the creed means that it came to be regarded as having a special importance. What was this?

There are many possible explanations. The emphasis on the birth of Jesus from a human mother was a safeguard against a heresy known as 'docetism', the belief that Jesus was not really a man at all, but merely God 'appearing' as man. The emphasis on the work of the Holy Spirit in the conception of Jesus highlights the new beginning for humanity, the new work of God promised in the Old Testament, now inaugurated in the coming of Christ. There is a more subtle theological point being made also in terms of the transition from Judaism to Christianity. Judaism, though potentially a universal religion in its scope, was and is heavily dependent on actual physical heredity. Most Jews are born Jews. Christianity broke out of this mould to become truly universal, and the breaking of the physical heredity in its origins is a powerful symbol of this universality.

These are some of the theological reasons why those who first experienced the newness of life in Christ felt it appropriate to express it through this article in the creed. There may also have been less desirable theological motives, among them the revulsion from current attitudes toward sex, and the consequent exaltation of virginity. Some would question the doctrine as threatening belief in the true manhood of Christ. There is also a dangerous streak in all new and exciting religious experience which accentuates marvels and tries to use these, often unwisely, as if they were the main evidence for the experience itself.

Some contemporary theologians are more concerned about these negative aspects of the doctrine than its positive value in symbolizing God's new initiative. Inevitably this affects their interpretation of the historical evidence.

I come to the question of history last because, in the nature of the case, the historical evidence is bound to be very slender. Apart from a few possible, and disputed, hints in St John's Gospel and two Pauline epistles, the sole evidence is in the nativity stories in Matthew and Luke. The fact that these differ from one another, while agreeing on the fundamental point, is an indication that the tradition on which they are based is older than both of them; this is a fairly strong reason for believing that they are witnessing to a real historical event. But the most important point is that, for the purposes of Christian faith, it is what a doctrine tells us about God that matters, rather than whether it is possible to make firm historical judgements about an event which is by its nature inaccessible to ordinary investigation.

In summary, therefore, the structure of theological thinking on the subject is something like this:

As Christians we believe that God has done a new thing in Jesus Christ, revealing himself in a human life, subject to the ordinary conditions of humanity. The historical reality of this new thing is attested by the New Testament and by two thousand years of Christian experience.

The doctrine of the Virgin Birth is a powerful symbol of this truth, but is not the only means by which the truth can be expressed or safeguarded.

Evaluation of the doctrine has to rely more on judgements about its theological appropriateness than on historical study.

This is only a very small sketch map of a large territory, but I hope it may help some of those who are puzzled by recent public discussion of these matters.

July 1984

How does God Act?

A few months ago I had about an hour and a half in front of TV cameras in discussion with a philosopher of religion on that most difficult of topics – how God acts in the world. Excerpts from this conversation appeared in a programme last month, and it has been suggested by some of those who watched it that it might be worth summarizing a few points on paper. So here goes.

I was told by the producer that one of the clergy interviewed for the programme had described how, when he drove to London, God always kept him a parking space, because he knew that he wasn't a very good driver. Other Christians have an intimate sense that God is organizing every detail of their lives, and point to the Bible as evidence that God is always, as it were, adjusting the system to take account of the special needs of individuals. Why pray, indeed, unless you believe that God hears each prayer, and that it makes a difference?

Yet viewed from a different perspective the picture of the world implied by such beliefs is full of difficulties. It is not just sceptical scientists or unprincipled liberals who see something odd about a world in which the traffic arrangements in central London are at the mercy of thousands of individual Christian prayers. What would happen if you tried to park in a space reserved for one of God's favourites? Would you find yourself pushed on further down the street? Or do we have to imagine God orchestrating countless responses of this kind into some huge parking plan which we all unconsciously obey? But in that kind of a world, what happens to morality and choice?

The point is that special actions by God which may seem entirely appropriate in the context of an individual life, become a recipe for chaos when seen as a whole. The difficulty is not, repeat not, a new one cooked up by science. It has been apparent for centuries, and is inherent in the notion of God's action itself. I have illustrated it by a slightly facetious, though genuine, example, but the problem itself is a general one in the philosophy of religion. How can we think about God acting in the world, as the Christian faith requires us to do, without undermining belief in the world's orderliness and regularity? If everything keeps changing, as Alice discovered when trying to play croquet with live hedgehogs and flamingoes, intelligent play becomes impossible. But if nothing changes, if regularity is the last and final word, why talk about God at all? How can we come to understand God as neither inactive nor capricious?

It is a tough question. But I believe the answer lies in asking how *we* act in the world.

Though it is hard to describe exactly what we mean by it, most of us assume that by and large we are free agents. What we choose to do actually makes a difference to the way things are. Yet this free action takes place in a world, and through bodies and brains, which operate according to the ordinary laws of nature. We do not break the laws of nature every time we act freely or create something new. But neither do the laws, the regularities, say everything that is to be said about freedom and creativity. The universe, in other words, seems to be open-textured. Each of us knows at least one place, in our own hearts and wills, where what happens is open to be influenced by personal decision.

If this is true of us, may it not also be true of God? What I am suggesting is that we should think of God as working through the regularities of nature in the same kind of way that we work through our own bodies and brains. The fact that things *are* regular no more means that God isn't there, than the fact that someone has a reliable brain means that he isn't a person. And just as we sometimes reveal new depths in our personality by doing something unexpected, so God sometimes surprises us into a new understanding of himself by actions which, as it were, break the pattern. Whether they break it in some absolute sense, or whether they break only our inadequate grasp of the pattern, doesn't really matter. The point of such actions is not precisely how they happen, but what they reveal to us of God.

This month we celebrate the greatest of all those 'breakings of the pattern'. The resurrection is for Christians the supreme sign that God does indeed act in this world to bring life out of death, hope out of despair, victory out of defeat, and vindication to those who trust him. It is an invitation to live hopefully and to pray faithfully, because it shows us that just as we are free to 'do a new thing', so is God.

Prayer is the exploration of that freedom, both God's and ours. It is the sending of our spirits beyond the realm of calculations, necessities and regularities, to the realm of openness with God and openness to God, where God's freedom to give or to withhold is openly and gladly acknowledged.

There is a whole world of spiritual discovery in unpacking this grossly over-compressed summary. But it is more rewarding, I suggest, than looking for parking spaces.

April 1985

Six-sided Christians

The other day I was being quizzed by a TV interviewer about a possible programme on the theme, 'What is a Christian?' I launched into a long description of the six dimensions of religion – doctrine, ritual, myth, ethics, social institutions and personal experience – and was just about to explain how they applied to Christianity, when he interrupted me.

'What our viewers really want to know is whether you have to believe in the Virgin Birth.'

'I wonder what Gregory of Nyssa would have said to that', I replied rather desperately. Gregory was one of the great fourth-century theologians who saw clearly the danger of trying to distil religious truth into precise propositions and turn faith into mere intellectual assent. The idea that doctrine is the only dimension in religion which matters was for him the essence of unbelief. In his own words: 'To believe that true religion consists only in dogmas – what is this but the special characteristic of the pagans.'

Alas, Gregory of Nyssa counts for nothing with the Great British Public who, according to our media pundits, are only interested in the Christian faith when somebody appears to deny it. But Gregory had hold of an important truth, easily trivialized into the pulpit platitude that religion is about the whole of life. Perhaps our six dimensions can help to give that platitude some freshness.

The first of them, doctrine, is important because Christians need to think about faith, to relate it to tradition and to a general understanding of the world, and to make sense of it in terms of the other dimensions of Christian living. Thinking implies learning, and that essentially is what doctrine is. It is what is given to believers as our Christian intellectual heritage, not to stop us thinking, but precisely in order to give us the basis from which to start. This is why a mixture of receptiveness and criticism has always been part of the Christian way of doing things.

The second dimension, ritual, is one of the primary means of expressing faith in a religious, rather than an ethical, context. The word can cause some misunderstanding because it is easily confused with 'ritualism', which is often used to describe particularly elaborate forms of ritual. But in essence ritual can be very simple, the formal and repeated use of certain words, gestures and actions which gradually become charged with deeply symbolic meanings. Everybody who has sung a well-loved hymn, or worshipped through the Eucharist, or knelt to pray, knows how such actions can help us to relate more openly and explicitly to God.

Myth, the third dimension, is the inner side of ritual. It is the technical term for the stories, whether historically based or not, which give ritual its meaning. Without the Easter stories there could be no Easter ritual. But the stories are not confined to their ritual context. The great religious stories, from the story of creation to the story of the last judgement, go to work on our feelings, they shape our perceptions, they mould our unconscious. The word 'myth' is used here to draw attention to this deep emotional level on which religion operates, filtering through to us both consciously and unconsciously in culture, art, language, symbolism, not limited to bare facts and intellectual truths.

Ethics, the fourth dimension, brings many people onto more familiar ground. Everybody knows that Christians ought to behave in a certain way. If asked to spell this out, they might find themselves mostly describing a certain basic goodness and decency. But even in the flattest descriptions of Christian behaviour there are hints of mountain ranges where the saints have pioneered their difficult paths. And there are expectations that somehow Christians ought to be different, hand in hand with wry disappointment that so often we are not. What is harder for many people to grasp is that such difference as there might be, can spring only from the fact that truly Christian behaviour is rooted in a loving worshipping relationship with God.

Mention of social institutions as the fifth dimension of religion can easily raise hackles. Here comes the Church! The brute fact is, though, that unless a faith is embodied in some social group, and unless there are deliberate institutional means of maintaining it, it ceases to exist. The reason for the Church is as simple and as basic as that. No matter what doctrinal or ritual overtones we add to our concept of the Church, and no matter how far the Church in practice fails to live up to its calling, as a bare social reality it remains indispensable.

Finally, personal experience. At some point or other religion has to link into our own inner lives. The ways in which this happens and the inner realities of religious faith are hugely different for different people. This is why it can be so tedious and unproductive when people try to impose their own form of religious experience on others. But what can legitimately be done is to share experience, to encourage one another in the actual business of being Christian, and to hope that one experience may help to illuminate another.

All six dimensions belong together, like the six faces of a cube. But different individuals and different traditions put the emphasis in different places. This is why Christianity is such a marvellously complex and varied phenomenon.

Some lean on ritual; others centre their faith on an intense personal relationship. Some find their main Christian experience in an ecclesiastical context; others outside it. Some wrestle with intellectual problems; others are activists, busily pursuing good causes. Six-sided Christians manage to have something of everything, but even the most balanced of them look lopsided to those who build their cube a different way.

That is why anyone who seeks to answer the question, 'What is a Christian?', needs first a good dose of humility and charity. It is unfortunate that these are not the virtues which make for 'good television'.

June 1985

'Whatever it is – I'm against it'

'If you believe the doctors', wrote a former Lord Salisbury, 'nothing is wholesome; if you believe the theologians, nothing is innocent; if you believe the soldiers, nothing is safe.'

Give or take a bit for changes in the last hundred years, it still rings true. Indeed it is capable of extension . . . If you believe the politicians, nothing is honest; if you believe industry, nothing is fair; if you believe the farmers, nothing ever prospers. And so on.

Denials are always easier than affirmations. Yet paradoxically people are usually nearer the truth in what they affirm than in what they deny. We tend to affirm things we know about. 'Cricket is a wonderful game', says somebody, 'even in the West Indies.' And the odds are that he either plays it or reads about it or watches it; cricket is part of him.

'Snooker is dreadfully boring', says somebody else, and the first obvious question to ask is, 'How much do you know about it?' Ignorance is a great generator of dislike.

It is not only in comparatively trivial matters that this principle applies. We live in a critical and sceptical age. Criticism is one of the great tools of modern understanding. It is a rule of science that everything, even one's most cherished beliefs and assumptions, have to be available for questioning. And like the rocks and mountains which have withstood the erosion of wind and rain and sea, the things we can claim to know are the things which have survived the critical onslaught.

But we also have to face the paradox that we do not really know things if we are *merely* critical. Some truths can be known only from within; some knowledge gained only by those who love what they are seeking. The solid core of rocks and mountains may be revealed by erosion, but there has to be something there in the first place. And for seekers after truth the 'something' may be mostly inarticulate, felt on the pulses rather than analysed in the head. In comparision with what is known in the heart, clever criticism can sometimes seem dreadfully superficial.

All this is leading us to philosophical deep water into which I shall venture no further. But it has a practical point.

Think of our Anglican faith. The principle that people are nearer the truth in what they affirm than in what they deny is central to Anglican self-understanding. Our comprehensiveness, our attempts to hold together both Catholic and Protestant, both liberal and conservative, can only be justified if we are prepared to recognize each other's truth. This does not mean agreeing with everything everybody says, and putting it all together in some glorious mish-mash. But it does entail respecting and being willing to hear those who speak of what they know from within, and accepting that our, perhaps negative, reactions to it may spring as much from ignorance and misunderstanding as from our keen critical intellect. The different versions of truth may not have to be seen as alternatives, but as opposite sides of some greater whole.

In the providence of God it seems to be the special task of our Church to live with the uncomfortable tension this understanding of truth creates for us. It is sometimes hard to affirm each other, much much easier to dismiss what we have not yet learnt to appreciate. Indeed there are already disturbing signs of otherwise good Anglicans rushing to man the barricades.

Or take another hot subject – feminism. There is a positive side to this, a wholly admirable affirmation of the rights and dignity of women, an assertion that differences of gender need make no difference over a huge range of human activities. But some forms of feminism – mostly, I am glad to say, confined to the United States – adopt a much more negative and critical approach, even to the ludicrous extreme of refusing to use the word 'woman' because of its unsavoury association with the dreaded word 'man'. 'I kid you not', as the saying goes. It is all in a new Feminist Dictionary which charmingly defines marriage as 'Chief vehicle for the perpetuation of the oppression of women'.

This is negativity gone mad. It shows what happens when the balance between denial and affirmation is destroyed by frustration, anger and contempt. It could happen in other spheres, not least in the Church.

The modern world is full of 'anti-' movements, anti-racism, anti-fascism, anti-this, anti-that, all no doubt started with the best of intentions to fight some obvious evil. The trouble is that movements born in hatred very quickly take on the characteristics of the thing they oppose. Violence creates violence. Rejection breeds rejection. And the old adage that truth is the first casualty in war applies just as much to the war of ideas as to wars between peoples.

I am not, of course, for one moment suggesting that we should cease to regard evil things as abhorrent. But they need to be fought with affirmations, not with negations. The counter to racism is the assertion of human dignity and equality. The counter to fascism is the assertion of human freedom. The counter to sexism is the affirmation of womanhood. And the counter to religious divisiveness is the joyful celebration of our oneness in the mystery of Christ.

May 1986

Lessons from History

1889 saw the publication of a volume of essays, called *Lux Mundi*, which marked the beginning of Liberal Catholicism in the Church of England. Its aim was to bring together the best fruits of modern scholarship, particularly biblical scholarship, and relate them to Catholic tradition. As Charles Gore, editor of the volume and later Bishop of Oxford, put it: 'The real development of theology is the process by which the Church, standing firm in her old truths, enters into an apprehension of the new social and intellectual movements of each age, and because "the truth makes her free" is able to assimilate

all new material, to welcome and give its place to all new knowledge
. . . and so to witness under changed conditions to the Catholic
capacity of her faith and life.'

The then Archdeacon of Taunton, a famous Catholic diehard,
would have none of it. He described *Lux Mundi* as 'another symptom of
the decadence of England under Mr Gladstone, to be classed with
universal suffrage, Welsh disestablishment, secular education and
schemes for a Channel Tunnel'. He was only one among many who
regarded the whole enterprise as dangerously subversive.

The controversy raged for several years, and opened the way for the
entry of the Church of England into the modern world. *Lux Mundi* is
now old hat, and a present-day reader might wonder what all the fuss
was about. But in its day it was crucial in defining the belief that
Christians should be free to think, free to respond to change, free to
come to terms with the world as it is, and not be shackled by all sorts of
misapprehensions, unnecessary assumptions and spare intellectual
luggage from previous ages.

The good Archdeacon came to mind the other day when I was
shown a list of what some faithful Church of England members dislike
about their Church, as they see it, in the latter part of the twentieth
century: its association with the British Council of Churches, and the
World Council of Churches; its trendiness and left-wing attitudes; its
opposition to the present Government; its attitude to South Africa, to
the Falkland Islands, to the inner cities and to the miners; new
liturgies; and the Bishop of you-know-where. Perhaps it is as well that
the Church has not yet declared its mind on the Channel Tunnel!

But though the list differs in detail, it has basically the same
characteristics as the Archdeacon's opposition to *Lux Mundi*. Religion
ministers at a very deep level to our sense of the orderliness of things, to
our longing for continuity, to our unspoken assumption that all right-
minded people think as we do. Change, therefore, tends to be
perceived as threatening, destabilizing, a betrayal of something felt to
be precious.

I am exaggerating, of course. Most people recognize that there are,
or ought to be, disturbing elements in religion, and Christians rejoice
that their faith has been a major force for change in the world. But it is
easy to accept this in theory, while not wanting it to make any
difference in practice. So unwelcome changes are seen as emanating
from a kind of conspiracy, the 'trendy vicars' of Peter Simple's column
in *The Daily Telegraph*. If only the leadership had not been seduced by

the desire to appear modern, runs the argument, the Church would now be flourishing in the good old ways it has inherited from the past.

Lux Mundi can remind us that 'the good old ways' had themselves to be fashioned through painful controversy. If the battle had gone the other way the Church of England would at some stage have had to go through the deep intellectual traumas later faced by the Church of Rome, or found itself locked in the intellectual ghetto from which the Evangelicals have only recently extracted themselves. The Church, any Church, has in the end to live in the world as it is, and face the intellectual, moral and social challenges which actually come to it, if it is not to become a detached and irrelevant sect.

Take that bogey-man, the World Council of Churches. As one who is deeply involved in it, I frequently criticize it from within, and believe that I have the right to do so because I care about its ultimate objective of witnessing to our oneness in Christ. I stick to it, despite disagreements, because whether we like it or not, the world actually contains Christians of different denominations, races and nations, who do not all perceive their Christianity in the same way as members of the Church of England. Unless we are prepared to listen to them, and learn from them, and work with them, and when necessary argue with them, we are denying the universality, the catholicity, of the Church. And there is no other instrument for doing this but the World Council of Churches.

Again take the Church of England's shockingly new flirtation with so-called left-wing politics. Anybody who knows anything about the history of Christian socialism, or the work of William Temple, will know what an absurd misunderstanding underlies this kind of complaint. Two quotations from *Lux Mundi* may be enough to make the point: '. . . the recognized and traditional duty of the Church to maintain the cause of the weak against the strong, of the poor against the rich, of the oppressed against the oppressors'. That is not a quotation from *Faith in the City* but appears as a platitude in 1889.

And secondly, a sentence worth reading with the Falklands war in mind: '. . . deep and penetrating as has been her influence and manifold her consequent implications with the existing national and social life of mankind, the Church is essentially Catholic and only incidentally national.' In other words, an international perspective is not a betrayal of the Church's character, but basic to it.

I suspect that the impression of a Church moving leftwards owes more to the polarization of present-day British politics than to any actual change of position. Anglicans tend to be attracted by consensus politics, and when this was broadly represented by the political right, this is where the Church felt most at home. Confrontational politics generates unease, and confrontation.

It would take more space than I have at my disposal to go through the list of discontents as it was represented to me. In any case I am not in the business of providing excuses, or knock-me-down answers, or trying to belittle the genuine feelings of concerned people. It is important, though, to gain a sense of historical perspective, and this is why I have gone back to a controversy nearly a hundred years old. History may not solve our twentieth-century problems for us, but it can show us that things which seem new and threatening may perhaps not be so new after all, and things which seem like immemorial traditions may perhaps not be so old.

Since the Bishops' Report on *The Nature of Christian Belief* will be published by the time this letter is circulated, I end with a reminder of an incident which occurred thirty years before the publication of *Lux Mundi*. Frederick Temple, later to become Archbishop of Canterbury, as did his son William, had written an essay which shocked his contemporaries by its liberal views on the Bible. When faced with a petition against his appointment as Bishop of Exeter, he refused to make any other declaration of orthodoxy beyond that required by law. There were protests at his consecration. The Church of England was threatened with schism. The bishops were themselves divided. The upshot of much frantic debate, pamphleteering and political manoeuvring was that the Church gained a bishop who did not think it wrong for clergy to engage in the reverent search for truth through biblical criticism. It seems obvious now. But Lord Shaftesbury writing in his diary in 1869 described it as 'the turning point in the ecclesiastical and theological history of England'.

July 1986

Bible Christianity

We hear a lot of the phrase 'Bible Christian' these days. I want to suggest in this letter that it is not a particularly helpful one.

Sometimes it is used as a label to distinguish between so-called 'real believers' and those who merely conform outwardly. Fair enough. The distinction contains an important truth. Anyone with half an eye can see that for some people Christian faith is little more than a matter of habit. For others it is the focus of a deep commitment, enthusiasm and an impressive Christian life-style. True, there are many shades of grey between these two. There are also many possibilities for misjudging the depth of other people's commitment. But by and large the different expressions of faith and the different degrees of commitment are recognizable, and have been recognizable throughout Christian history.

But why *Bible* Christians? Why does a particular depth of commitment, as I have been describing it, have to be linked so often in people's minds with a particular way of regarding the Bible?

'Ah, because only Bible Christians take the Bible seriously.'

Do they? Is it true that other types of Christians are merely 'Church Christians' or, worse still, 'liberals' whose supposed lack of a certain kind of enthusiasm simply reflects their failure to respond to the Bible message?

I put the question sharply because it seems to me that one of the deepest and most destructive modern divisions between Christians is developing along the line between 'Bible Christians' and the rest. And this is both mistaken and unnecessary. The truth is that there are different ways of taking the Bible seriously, and all of them may have something to learn from each other.

The self-styled 'Bible Christian' can be relied upon to know the actual contents of the Bible through constant study, and this is a priceless asset not shared by everybody. There is a word for every occasion. If the Bible says something, that is the end of the argument. What is written in it is simple truth, and its application to life is direct and immediate. It is a source of power.

Such an attitude to the Bible can be held with great depth and subtlety. But it has its difficulties. Some of the more obvious ones become apparent when the Bible is thought to be a reliable guide on matters in which its authors were not basically interested. On evolution, for instance, or ancient history, or communism, or the precise ordering of the Church of England.

There is a more insidious problem, though, which occurs when the Bible is treated as a kind of compendium of facts and instructions, wrenched out of their historical context, and presented neat as if they had been newly minted for 1987. The 'word for every occasion' can become detached from the circumstances and environment in which the word was actually spoken. In being cut loose from history and applied too directly to 1987, it can lose its original meaning. Genesis 1, for example, can be forced to give answers about modern cosmology, irrespective of whether that was its author's intention or not. There is a paradox in all this. The attempt to read too many modern meanings into an ancient text in a curious way devalues it.

But what is the alternative? 'Scholarship', says somebody. 'Away with fundamentalism. Let the scholars wrestle with these complex documents, and tell us what we can really believe!'

This approach has the merit of removing many of the more hackneyed objections to religious belief. There is no need to worry about Cain's wife, because characters in myths don't need wives anyway. Some of the moral enormities of the biblical story fall into place as primitive stages in a developing faith. The puzzlements and the contradictions are now seen as products of their historical contexts, where they make more sense. Scholarship can strengthen faith by demonstrating how it has arisen and where its deepest roots are to be found.

But it can also confuse and undermine. Its greatest problem is that for many ordinary believers it makes the text seem less accessible and immediate in its impact on them. To be too conscious of the varied and sometimes curious things scholars have said, can create a kind of nervousness. Can we really say that Jesus is the light of the world, unless we can back it up with half a dozen learned footnotes? Scholarship certainly takes the Bible seriously, very seriously indeed. But the results can be ambiguous.

What both pure scholarship and pure 'Bible Christianity' frequently lack is any strong sense that the Christian believer's relationship to the Bible belongs within a developing tradition of worship. And this, I suggest, is where we can begin to bridge the gulf between attitudes which often seem poles apart.

We most characteristically 'hear the word of the Lord' in church. The worship of the Church provides a tradition within which the Bible stories can be heard, assimilated and interpreted. It is possible in that context to receive them – as stories. We hear them as they were written, and the scholarly questions, Who? How? Why? When?, are not at that moment our main preoccupation.

But nor are direct personal revelations. True, the words may sometimes strike home with great sharpness. But they belong within a community of people, a tradition of liturgy, a history of scholarship in which they have been brooded over and lived out for two thousand years. If this is not to take the Bible seriously, I do not know what is.

I hope, therefore, that those who differ on these matters may learn to respect each other more. In the final reckoning we may find that we are all Bible Christians.

March 1987

Hear the Word

Last month I tried to explain how it is possible to take the Bible seriously, and care deeply about its message, without becoming entangled in arguments about fundamentalism and the role of biblical scholarship. I suggested that we 'hear the word of the Lord' as we worship within the context of a living tradition.

Bible and Church, in other words, need to be held together. The Bible is the Church's book, spelling out, correcting and providing the basis for the Church's tradition of faith. And the Church's tradition acts as the interpreter of the Bible, enabling us to understand how this very varied collection of literature can be read as having its central focus in Christ. The Church is the community of study, prayer and commitment which under the guidance of the Holy Spirit has the task of making this biblical truth alive and available for each succeeding generation.

Sometimes the process can get bogged down. People look to the Bible for answers to inappropriate questions, or parade as infallible truth answers to contemporary problems, which are clearly naive and insufficient. Others give up in disgust on discovering how hard it is actually to apply biblical insights with integrity to the issues which face us in a world so different from that in which the biblical books were written. It is worth stressing again and again, therefore, that the Bible is primarily and fundamentally about God. It provides a perspective on a particular slice of human history in a way which enables God to be perceived at work in it. And it witnesses to a particular human life, the life of Jesus, through whom God is uniquely revealed in human personal terms.

All this comes to us through the witness of a community, which experienced these things in a particular time and place and through a particular culture. Our own Christian community is continuous with this earlier one, but is conscious of living in a very different time and place and culture. Our understanding of what the world is like has changed rapidly and radically, especially during the last three hundred years. To grasp the central message of the Bible, there is no need to put ourselves back into a vanished world. The most fruitful questions are: If those people saw God at work like that then, how should we see him at work now? and if God required people to do that then, what does he require of us today?

Let me illustrate, using a well-known New Testament story. Accounts of Jesus' feeding the large crowds in lonely places occur no less than six times in the Gospels (twice each in Matthew and Mark, and once in Luke and John). The use of that amount of space in ancient manuscripts clearly implies that the incident or incidents were important in the minds of the early Christians.

Yet for us, accustomed as we are to reading stories of this kind as if they were newspaper reports, there are obvious problems. Quite apart from the miraculous element, the sheer mechanics of feeding five thousand men (not to mention women and children) from a single distribution point, must surely raise questions in the mind of anyone who has organized even a modest-sized parish picnic, especially when, as we are told, it was already late in the evening and presumably just about to get dark.

Matthew, Mark and Luke are not interested in such details. They are not even particularly interested in the miracle, and give no sign that the crowds recognized what had been happening. They focus on the compassion of Jesus, on the fact that Jesus fed people when they were hungry, and on the huge crowds involved. Mark and Matthew record some obscure comments on the actual numbers themselves (Matt. 16. 9-10; Mark 8. 19-21) and Mark also uses the image of a shepherd gathering a scattered flock (Mark 6. 34). All three evangelists stress the action of Jesus in giving thanks and breaking the bread, and for Christians whose community worship centred on 'the breaking of the bread' the reference was unmistakable. The story was valued and repeated because Jesus was still visibly feeding his followers, now brought together by the one true shepherd, in a constantly renewed act of thanksgiving – the Eucharist.

John makes all this explicit. In chapter 6 he tells the story in rather more detail, draws out the contrast between the boy with his dinner and the vast numbers fed, describes how the crowd responded to the 'sign' (a favourite word with John) and totally misunderstood it, and then uses the incident as the basis for a long conversation on the Bread of Life. Couple this with the earlier sign described in chapter 2 where, instead of huge quantities of bread, we find huge quantities of wine, and the eucharistic interpretation of the stories is unavoidable.

Nowadays when we read one or other version, as we frequently do, in the context of the Eucharist, the story highlights for us one element in the whole complex richness of eucharistic theology. We are reminded that the Eucharist is about feeding together on the Bread of Life, a feeding which owes little to our own meagre resources, but which nevertheless requires us to give them up. It is only when we are empty that we can be filled, as a darkening world closes in about us. But what God gives, he gives abundantly, and he gives it not just to the disciples but to the crowds.

There is a great deal more in this story than I have had space to indicate. In fact John goes on uncovering layer after layer of meaning. But none of this helps to answer the question, What actually happened? The reason is simple. It was not a question which, in that particular form, the evangelists had any real interest in answering. It owes more to our own peculiarly modern obsession with literal-mindedness. If we get stuck on it, then we miss the main point.

The Bible, remember, is fundamentally about God. What the evangelists are here telling us about God is that his creative generosity flows through the life of Jesus, and is made explicit today within the community of thanksgiving. To 'hear the word of the Lord' is to be brought face to face with this God, and to realize to our shame that the crowds are still thronging to be fed.

There is nothing particularly modern about such an interpretation, but neither is it fundamentalist. It takes seriously the fact that a community treasured these words because they were able to point it to God. And they can do the same for us.

April 1987

Tell me the Old Old Story

'Tell it again', whined the insistent child. Grandma launched into Little Red Riding Hood for the umpteenth time.

'No! You've got it wrong. You should have said, "What big ears you have!" You're stupid. You've spoilt it all.'

Grandma sighed, and started yet again. Parents and grandparents will know the feeling.

Some stories bear constant repetition. And it is not just the stories but the actual words which are important. Words and phrases from well-loved stories linger deliciously in the memory, and to recall and repeat them can help to affirm some of our deepest feelings.

To change them induces a sense of shock. 'God is my herdsman' may mean exactly the same as 'The Lord is my Shepherd' but it rings no bells in the imagination. Some people become understandably angry when on Christmas morning, 'Fear not; for behold I bring you good tidings of great joy . . .' becomes 'Do not be afraid; I have good news for you.'

I say this, not to make a cheap jibe at modern translations of the Bible. We need them, and we need their unfamiliarity to make us think about what we are reading. But we also need to remember that much religious feeling runs in well-worn channels, and may easily be lost if these are too brutally disrupted. Our Christian faith is full of stories, sayings, poems and prayers which can and must be heard over and over again without growing stale. It is an old old story with the power to become new every morning.

But some stories do not bear much repetition. Cousin George's joke about the Englishman, the Irishman and the Scotsman can be guaranteed to empty the local well before closing time. Even some ways of telling the gospel story can induce a sense of being trapped at sermon time. A liberal sprinkling of 'in' words – reconciliation, ongoing commitment, mission, solidarity and the like – may have the reverse of their intended effect on those who hear them. Familiarity, in other words, is not everything. Boredom is one of the most widespread of ecclesiastical diseases.

There is, in fact, a delicate balance between saying things too little and saying them too much. There are some circles in which certain trigger words – 'justice and peace', for instance – will always raise a cheer; but the more thoughtlessly they are repeated the more emptied of meaning they become. There are other circles in which constant mention of the name of Jesus and reference to the work of the Spirit, are the badges of 'sound spirituality'; but these, too, are subject to the same law of diminishing returns. Christmas every week would be intolerable.

This is why alongside the telling of the old old story there has to be a search for radically different ways of expressing the same truths. Indeed one of the signs of the enduring vitality of the gospel is its power to take innumerable shapes and to remain itself within surprisingly unfamiliar portrayals.

People who accuse clergy of playing with politics when they ought to be preaching the gospel, often fail to see that a concern about some contemporary political issue may spring precisely from a desire to bring fresh understanding and commitment to some aspect of Christian faith. It is possible to discover a lot about the Christian meaning of communion, for instance, by looking at what is going wrong in some of our community relationships. Conversely, it is also possible to deceive ourselves into thinking that this is what we are doing, when we are in fact just 'playing politics'. Preaching the gospel in unfamiliar forms is no easy task, and those who attempt it are all too liable to fall flat on their faces.

The attempt has to be made, however, not just in the field of politics, but in the arts, in literature, at work, in family life, in every field of human endeavour, because a gospel which is not illuminating all these areas has contracted in on itself. It has become narrowing to those who believe it, rather than broadening. The unfamiliar portrayals of the gospel are a necessary part of its being a gospel for the whole world.

I am tempted into these reflections by comments I occasionally hear from readers who would prefer these diocesan letters to have 'a more directly spiritual content'. I respect what is being said. But I do not accept the advice for reasons which I hope are now becoming clear. These are letters, not sermons. I do not aim to repeat in them what every Christian ought to know, using the kind of language which fits the context of worship.

Every one of them is rooted in the old old story of Jesus and his love. But they try to explore its meaning in a variety of secular contexts, national, local and personal. The familiar affirmation, as in the words of the liturgy, can reassure us and deepen our security in God. The unfamiliar slant can wake us up and provoke new responses. Both are necessary. Even little Red Riding Hood may be able to show us some new facet of eternal truth.

October 1987

Traditions and Trends

'Just like his father!'

'Yes, that nose! and the look in his eyes, and the way he drags his feet. Smokes like a chimney, too.'

Like father, like son. But why are they like each other, and how is the likeness transmitted? The shape of a nose would seem almost certainly to be a matter of genetic inheritance. A distinctive nose can survive in a family for generations. Smoking, on the other hand, is more likely to be learnt by example, bad example in this case, but there may be peculiar family stresses which predispose to it.

What about the other resemblances? It is hard to say. A particular way of walking may be partly inherited and partly learnt, and it would be impossibly difficult to unscramble one factor from the other. Most of our characteristics fall into this mixed category. We are shaped by many influences, some internal and some external, and these react on one another in ways which are usually too complex to analyse.

Sometimes there are big public rows on the subject, as in the famous controversy some years ago about whether intelligence is inherited or whether the failure to perform well in intelligence tests is a mark of social deprivation. The answer is probably – both. But where the emphasis is put makes a difference to educational and social policy.

To put the point in technical language – most things have multiple causes. Causes and effects are not like a chain with one link leading on inevitably to the next one. They are more like networks where each strand and knot is where it is because of the forces acting in many other parts of the net.

If this is true of things in general and human beings in particular, then it is likely to be even more true of societies. A society is what it is for millions of reasons, some of which derive from its own inner dynamic (its genetic inheritance, as it were) and some from its history (the various events and influences which have impinged on it). And just as it is impossible to unscramble these in the case of a human being, so it is impossible to say precisely what belongs to what in the case of a historical institution. The Church, for instance.

Our own Church belongs to a family tree of Churches which have the same genetic inheritance. We have all sprung from the same basic beginnings – the history of Israel, the life, death and resurrection of Jesus, the impact of his teachings, and the earliest decisions about the shape and character of the Church. We all have the Bible in our bloodstream and treat it as normative. But we have developed as Churches under different social and historical pressures, in different parts of the world, and in response to different, but sometimes crucially significant, decisions.

Up till fairly recent years the different branches of this tree have looked at each other as if they did not really belong. Some have claimed to represent the only true line of descent, the real blue-blooded aristocracy. Others have denied that anything of any significance, other than the gospel itself, has had any influence in shaping them.

Others may have seemed to imply that branches look more decorative and attractive without the encumbrance of roots. The truth is, though, that all are shaped *both* by the inheritance they have received *and* by the influences to which they have been subject. And it is very hard to be certain which is which.

When people throw words like 'traditionalist' and 'liberal' at each other it is worth remembering the family tree. No doubt cousin George went off the rails because he fell into bad company and forgot who he was. The family genes were not of much use to him when his veins were full of heroin. But can Aunt Mildred be quite so certain that it is breeding which has raised her to the pinnacle of respectability, rather than the fortunate circumstance of having ten thousand a year? In just the same way we might perhaps be able to pinpoint a few of the causes of some ecclesiastical disaster. There is such a thing as faithlessness to the gospel. But we are less likely to be able to say for certain why some Churches flourish and others do not. Nor can we say for certain what is an authentic development of tradition and what is a deviation from it under the influence of the spirit of the age.

Of course, we can try. Much of the work of theologians and religious leaders entails trying to distinguish the authentic from the deviant. But there comes a point at which the distinction begins to blur. Did not God who made the root of the tree also make the soil in which it grows and the winds which shape it? Our human inheritance is not just in our genes. Our development depends on countless influences, including other human beings. Why then should we expect God to shape his Church only in terms of what it has inherited from its origins?

The Spirit of God is in the Church, so we devoutly believe. But the Spirit is also at work outside the Church. In fact the Bible is full of indications that this is so, from the Old Testament consciousness of God's hand in world political movements, to Jesus' preaching of the Kingdom. It is a tragic mistake to think of holy Church and secular world as if they were totally divorced from one another. In Britain what we call the 'secular world' has to a considerable extent become what it is under Christian influence. The spirit of the world may in many respects be worldly. But it may also sometimes convey some part of God's truth which those who suppose themselves to be uncontaminated by the world may need to take on board.

Simply to talk in terms of 'tradition or trend', therefore, is not particularly helpful as we try to discern how God is leading us. To say this is not to deny that there is a real and vital difference between the effects of our Christian inheritance and the effects of our somewhat mixed and muddled secular environment. But we do not learn much about ourselves and God's will for us by setting up false oppositions, when the truth is that both elements have, under Providence, made us what we are, and can point us to what we should become.

March 1988

12
The Crockford Preface

An account of the 1987 Crockford affair specially written for this book
May 1988

WHEN DR GARETH Bennett had finished writing his Preface to the 1987/88 edition of *Crockford's Clerical Directory* he expressed the hope that 'it might do some good'. In agreeing to write it he had sought assurance on two stringent conditions: first, that whatever he wrote would be published unaltered; and secondly that his anonymity would be completely safeguarded. In the event the manuscript was delivered two months later than promised, during the July 1987 meeting of the General Synod, was scanned hurriedly by the Secretary-General, one of the only two people who knew his authorship, and passed straight to the publishers.

The possible implications of what he had written only became apparent in mid-November, about a fortnight before the publication date, when a few typewritten copies began to circulate. I received my own copy at this time, and while saddened by much of its contents, hoped that the media would give it no more attention than was usual for such prefaces – a few sober paragraphs in the quality press.

It was, as I feared, a false hope. The intensity of the publicity, and the extent to which the media concentrated on personal denigration of the Archbishop of Canterbury, was unprecedented. He had already made it clear to me privately that he was not intending to reply. It seemed to me that if I, as one of the few people close enough to him to know the truth, was also to say nothing, the impression might be given that the Preface's verdict was accepted and its accuracy unquestioned. So, under considerable media pressure myself, I issued a statement which, because it has been widely misquoted and misinterpreted, I reproduce here in full:

There is a sourness and vindictiveness about the anonymous attack on the Archbishop of Canterbury which makes it clear that it is not quite the impartial review of church affairs which it purports to be. At the heart of the attack is a claim to know what goes on at private meetings of a key sub-committee and of the Crown Appointments Commission which recommends the names of bishops to the Prime Minister. If the anonymous author is a member of these bodies then he or she is guilty of deliberately distorting the truth. If not a member, then he or she is writing with assumed confidence on the basis of guesswork. Either way the cloak of anonymity puts those who try to answer scurrilous charges in an impossible position, and I hope the public will treat this abuse of privilege with the contempt it deserves.

Accusations about lack of leadership are easy to make, but in a body where there are few effective sanctions and which depends upon consensus, a widely embracing style of leadership may in the long run be the most effective. A recent church report said 'Clergy, particularly bishops, are familiar with the call to "give a lead" in circumstances where it is quite clear that a lead in only one preferred direction would be welcomed.' The anonymous author is careful to say nothing about the direction in which he himself is looking for a lead. In fact the entirely negative tone of his whole Preface is one of its most disturbing features. I think the Church would be wise to regard it as an outburst from a disappointed cleric who manages to pinpoint some of the real problems which face the Church of England and the Anglican Communion, but has nothing constructive to offer about the way ahead.

As a response to what the media were then saying this statement naturally concentrated on the attack on the Archbishop of Canterbury. It was not, however, a hasty response. I had had the text for a fortnight and was aware, as some commentators appear not to have been, of the extent to which much of the Preface's argument was cumulative. In trying to pinpoint the central defect in Anglicanism the author explored and rejected a number of possibilities, and in the end focused on the leadership, and in particular on the way in which Church of England bishops are appointed. A central criticism of the Archbishop of Canterbury was an allegation that he, and to a lesser extent myself, manipulated the Crown Appointments Commission. Although the media concentrated on his alleged indecisiveness, it was obvious to me that the most destructive criticism concerned this supposed lack of integrity in the conduct of the Commission. Other prefaces have said rude things about individuals, and in cosy ecclesiastical circles a certain amount of backbiting among friends can easily be tolerated. But this particular charge, crucial to the argument of the whole Preface, was not only untrue, but if left unchallenged was likely to diminish confidence in the work of a vitally important body.

The proceedings of the Crown Appointments Commission are strictly confidential and all its members make a solemn declaration to maintain this confidentiality. The reason for this is simple. The Commission can only do its work properly if its members feel free to discuss the lives and characters of well-known clergy with total frankness, and if those who provide information can be similarly assured that nothing will be disclosed outside the actual meeting itself. It follows from this that if an anonymous author claimed to write knowledgeably about the Commission he must either be a member of it, in which case he was both abusing confidence and to my knowledge wilfully distorting the truth, or he must be speculating on the basis of gossip; in either case his general argument about lack of integrity was groundless. My statement to the press made this as its major point, and I believe it is irrefutable.

In fact Dr Bennett was not a member of the Crown Appointments Commission at the time he wrote his Preface. He was subsequently elected to it, and attended one meeting at the end of October 1987. How far the experience shook his confidence in what he had written we shall sadly never know.

Death changes things. Dr Bennett's totally unexpected and deeply tragic suicide changed media reaction to his Preface overnight. He began to be presented as a misunderstood prophet who had dared to criticize an all-powerful establishment, been savaged by it, and died in despair at a Church which had rejected him. One curious twist to the story, as far as I was concerned, was a newspaper speculation that I would be leading an investigation into the affair at a meeting of the General Synod Policy Sub-Committee which was to take place a few days after the publication of the Preface and which Dr Bennett had been himself due to attend. (He had in fact sent his apologies before the Preface was published.) The implication of this speculation was that fear of this confrontation was one of the factors which had led him to take his life. The story was pure invention.

My own feeling about his suicide at that time was that the suggested explanation was psychologically implausible and failed to do justice to Dr Bennett. He was well used to ecclesiastical controversy, and knew how to handle archbishops. He can hardly have been so naive as to suppose that what he had written would provoke no response. But it seemed to me very probable that he had misjudged the media reaction, underestimated the intensity of the search to uncover his authorship, and been overwhelmed and disorientated by pressures which were unfamiliar to him and which he had to bear alone. He also suffered the unpleasant experience of having to lie repeatedly to the media about his authorship and, worse still, to some of his closest friends.

Two pieces of evidence confirmed this view. The first was an informal remark by a leading member of the press that they would not rest until the author was found. In fact I am told that one well-known journalist spent over half an hour in a telephone call to Dr Bennett. Such intense press interest in him may well have aroused fear that his identity was about to be revealed. The second was a statement by one of Dr Bennett's close friends whom he had told about a £5,000 offer from an unnamed newspaper for an article on the Preface, with a promise to increase it to £10,000 if he would admit his authorship.

Given an invitation to comment on the matter on a live radio programme, I decided to refer to the £10,000 and to question the current explanations of Dr Bennett's suicide, which were by then hardening into a widely canvassed orthodoxy. It was obvious that the media would not welcome a view which laid much of the blame on pressure from within their own ranks, but I expected that the inquest would follow swiftly and vindicate what I had said. Unfortunately there were long delays, so long that the General Synod held its debate on the Preface before the inquest findings were known. When the inquest eventually took place, its main source of evidence was Dr Bennett's own diary which revealed clearly his agitation about the publicity he was receiving, his regrets about what he had written, and his fears of exposure. The last entry written the day before his death, records a rumour passed on to him by a *Daily Mail* reporter that his identity would be revealed within forty-eight hours. Without actually ascribing blame, the Coroner drew attention to the role of what he coyly described as 'the fourth estate'.

In some mitigation of the press it also needs to be said that the hapless Dr Bennett was caught in a trap, partly of his own making, and partly caused by the failure of the publishers to anticipate the pressures to which he might be subjected in an age eager to flaunt scandals and to use any stick with which to beat the Church.

But that is to anticipate. The immediate response to my broadcast was a denial from the *Daily Mail* (which had not been mentioned) that it was the paper referred to in my remarks. A reporter from the *Mail* sat in my drive for most of a day in order to pass me the message, as I left for an evening engagement in Lancashire, that I had made 'a very serious charge', and to elicit the reply that I had said nothing about the *Mail* at all. The *Mail* was formally correct in saying that a letter sent to Dr Bennett had contained no financial offer. The offer had in fact been made by telephone. What neither they nor I knew at that stage was that Dr Bennett had recorded it in his diary. This was subsequently mentioned at the inquest but whereas newspaper reports of the inquest curiously referred to an offer of £1,000, the diary states explicitly, 'A reporter from the *Mail* rang to offer me £5,000 if I was the author and wished to go public with them.'

No doubt there is much more to be said. My aim so far has simply been to put on record what I know so that that when the whole story is told some of the more obvious mistakes and misinterpretations can be avoided. The whole episode was a tragic one which released deep, and sometimes not altogether charitable, feelings and which destroyed a good and gifted man.

. When the ugliest passions and distortions have been cleared out of the way the question still remains, Why did this donnish and predominantly negative analysis of the state of Anglicanism arouse such a response? Unkind cracks at the Archbishop of Canterbury can produce media headlines, but there has to be something more substantial if an essay is to be labelled 'prophetic' and 'profound'.

I find these adjectives puzzling. Dr Bennett wrote well and much of his analysis was acute and touched on real, if familiar, problems. For many readers such a trenchant exposure of them was clearly new and exciting, but for those of us who had been wrestling with these same problems for years there was disappointment that the author had gone no further than making complaints, and had failed to use his considerable theological skill in advancing the arguments constructively.

The Preface had three main strands:

1. A critique of the Anglican Communion for avoiding hard questions about authority;
2. Criticisms of the General Synod and its committee structure for failing to provide a coherent policy for the Church of England;
3. The identification of a powerful liberal establishment determined to upset the traditional balance of the Church.

Together they provided a focus for many people's apprehensions about unwelcome changes, the perceived ineffectiveness of much Christian effort, and above all for the fears of a minority about the possible consequences of ordaining women to the priesthood and episcopate.

I do not wish to underestimate the seriousness of these issues. By the time this is published I hope the 1988 Lambeth Conference will have gone some way towards tackling the problems of authority. It will not lack well-prepared and searching documentation on the subject, but it will also be aware, I hope, that the issues which have to be faced arise, not from some peculiar Anglican aberration, but from fundamental questions, common to all major Churches, and many secular bodies as well, about how genuine local diversity can be held together within a coherent structure. It is true that Anglicanism, with its somewhat haphazard history, suffers from the tension between diversity and cohesion in a particularly acute form. But like the Church of England itself it also has a unique opportunity to explore the nature of communion and community, and to pioneer methods by which diverse groups and individuals can affirm their sense of belonging together – methods from which the world at large desperately needs to learn.

Dr Bennett's preferred solution was a committee one. He advocated a strengthening of the Anglican Consultative Council, coupled with a self-denying ordinance that certain matters would not be decided by separate Provinces of the Communion without the establishment of a common mind among all. This is one of a number of suggestions which had been canvassed before he wrote, and it has its attractions, but it was clear from the start that only very limited movement was possible in that direction.

My own belief is that the best way forward is by strengthening the theological coherence of the Communion. A start was made in 1978 by setting up an international Doctrine Commission, and much useful work was done in the pre-Lambeth '88 period in trying to spell out the substance of a Communion-wide Declaration of Assent. This is not the place to argue the merits of different approaches since this essay is being written too late to make any difference to the Lambeth Conference, and too soon to refer to its decisions. My only comment on this section of the Preface (which I regard as the best part of it) is that it managed to put sharply and succinctly what many people knew already, but failed to offer any real help in suggesting viable alternatives.

Criticisms of the General Synod and its machinery never fail to strike a responsive chord. I tried to analyse some of the reasons for this in *Church and Nation in a Secular Age* (Darton, Longman and Todd 1983) and there has been no shortage of other commentators. Dr Bennett's own comments would have been unremarkable had he not used his direct knowledge of two central committees, the Standing Committee and the Policy Sub-Committee, to highlight the extreme difficulties of policy-making in such a widely dispersed organization as the Church of England. What he omitted to mention was that the main problems had long since been identified by both committees and a major review set in hand to try to remedy the organizational defects. This has subsequently been published as the *Infrastructure Review* and if implemented will for the first time give the Standing Committee adequate information by which to determine priorities, and adequate financial power to carry them out.

A body like the Synod always tends to hover uneasily between wanting to give everyone their say and wanting to demonstrate its importance by actually doing things. It contains those who think that policy is made by sitting down in front of a blank piece of paper and spelling out some long-term aims. And it contains others (like myself) who think that policy decisions usually emerge out of an analysis of actual situations, and who see policy-making as a reflective exercise always closely allied with practical administration. What counts as policy-making may therefore itself be a matter of controversy and a source of frustration.

Dr Bennett drew attention to the powerlessness of committee members. It has to be said that the sense of powerlessness was greatly exacerbated by the 1985 elections to the Synod, which increased the polarization of opinion both within the Synod itself and in its main committees. Committees in which there are sharp differences can work effectively provided their members exercise reasonable restraint in not jockeying for advantage on every possible issue. Dr Bennett saw the supposedly rigged power structure as the main cause of the Standing Committee's troubles. But what can be just as damaging to effective participation is overzealousness in finding fault everywhere, coupled with a desire to do every sub-committee's work for it, and compounded by lack of a sense of proportion. He was right to express a sense of dis-ease. I believe he was wrong in his diagnosis. And, as in his description of the Anglican Communion, he omitted to mention what was actually being done about the problems he identified.

His characterization of the so-called 'liberal establishment' for obvious reasons attracted the most attention. Everybody loves a conspiracy. And at a time when it is undoubtedly true that some members of the Church of England, especially some Catholics, feel threatened and marginalized, there is a good deal of mileage to be had in hinting that this marginalization is being actively promoted. The Preface released a huge reservoir of disaffection which it would be dangerous and wrong to ignore.

I believe there are simpler and more convincing explanations of this phenomenon than those Dr Bennett put forward. But first let me challenge the dubious contemporary use of the word 'liberal' as a synonym for disbelief, irresponsibility and irresolution. If this book does nothing else, I hope it will help to expose this interpretation for the travesty that it is. Polemics conducted in such terms only serve to reinforce prejudice.

I accept, nevertheless, that there are elements of truth in Dr Bennett's own analysis. There are fashions in churchmanship as there are in theology, and it should not come as a surprise to anybody that those whose minds were formed in the sixties are now reaching positions of leadership in the eighties. It is already obvious that this pattern is going to change as the full impact of Evangelical recovery makes itself felt, and there is no need to invoke deliberate manipulation as the explanation of it. It is also true that at certain times certain theological colleges have attracted the most able and lively ordinands who subsequently make their presence felt in the Church, but this bunching is found in other spheres as well. A recent study of suffragan bishops revealed that no less than eight had been undergraduates at Queens' College, Cambridge.

The setting up of the Crown Appointments Commission, to which I have already referred, has itself had an unintended and unexpected effect on the types of bishop appointed not, as Dr Bennett suggested, because the Archbishops will it so, but because democratic bodies tend towards the middle of the road. This tendency is far more obvious in those overseas Provinces which have a wholly electoral system for appointing their bishops, and which give less weight to the needs of the national church and the nation itself than the present English system. But even in the Church of England the weight given to a diocese's own choice biases the eventual decision in the direction of safety, broad pastoral experience and wide acceptability of opinions. This bias is accentuated by the main weakness of the present system, namely the virtual impossibility of planning a long-term and national strategy of appointments. Each meeting of the Commission changes its composition since it includes representatives of the diocese to which an appointment is to be made, and those representatives are understandably concerned with that appointment and that only. Even if a particular Commission wanted to, it could not influence the decision of the next meeting which would contain a fresh set of diocesan representatives, again concerned with only the one appointment. There is a further hazard in that even if some appropriate patterning is achieved, there is no guarantee that the Prime Minister will endorse it.

Under the previous system whereby direct advice from the Archbishops to the Prime Minister played a much larger part than it does now, the need for balance in the bench of bishops could be, and in some cases obviously was, a main factor in the making of an individual appointment. Today's Archbishops are no less concerned to secure a proper Anglican spread of opinion and churchmanship. They simply have less power.

There are problems, therefore, in the appointment of bishops, but they are not the problems identified in the Preface, nor can the charges about gross imbalance be sustained when the evidence about appointments is actually examined. Canon Craston published an analysis in the *Church Times* which clearly refuted the basis of Dr Bennett's argument. But it also needs to be recognized that there are weaknesses in contemporary Anglo-Catholicism which makes it hard to see how those who at present feel themselves marginalized can quickly recover a more significant position.

This is sad and ironic, because in the long-term the future lies with Catholicism. It must, because only Catholic tradition is rich enough and stable enough to be able to offer something distinctive to the world without being captured by the world. But it must be a Catholicism which is true to its highest vision, and hence broad enough, hospitable enough, rooted sufficiently in sacramental reality, confident enough in its inheritance to be able to do new things, diverse enough, and yet passionately enough concerned about unity, to be genuinely universal.

At the moment neither Roman Catholicism nor Anglo-Catholicism measure up to this standard. If Dr Bennett's Preface sidetracks his Catholic colleagues into further recrimination and introversion it will simply have done harm. A parish in my own diocese has, as I write this, advertised a Mass for 'the maintenance of Catholic Faith and Order in the Church of England' complete with a 'procession to the crowned statue of our Lady Queen of Heaven' and 'veneration of the relic of Saint Pius V'. I do not wish to carp at what is doubtless a sincere intention, but it is plain that the Catholic future cannot possibly lie in that direction.

Nor can it lie in the belief that there is some unchanging and unchallengeable core of tradition which, if only it can be preserved, will somehow guarantee true catholicity. Catholic fundamentalism is no more viable than biblical fundamentalism, and no more capable of being validated by historical enquiry. True catholicity belongs as much to the future as to the past. It entails the creative development of tradition as well as humble respect for it.

Dr Bennett wrote his Preface as if he had an alternative pack of cards up his sleeve, but his argument revealed all too clearly that there isn't one. We have to play with what is on the table already. His sharp sense of historical reality and acknowledgement of ecclesiastical failures carries its own message. He leaves us therefore with a tension, a gentle critical scholar longing for the Church to be something other than it is, yet driven by his own integrity to recognize that it never has been. The Church always lives uneasily between its transcendent ground and its all-too-human membership.

If what he wrote, despite its shortcomings and its attendant traumas, can help Christians to go on facing that basic paradox, if it can be read with discrimination and with growing understanding of the true nature of the issues he identified, if it can stimulate the recovery of a Catholic vision which embraces today's necessities and tomorrow's hopes as well as yesterday's glories, then in the long run it may indeed 'do some good'.

13
Faith and Intellectual Integrity

Sermon preached in the University Church of St Mary the Virgin, Oxford 18 October 1987

'Only the spirit of God knows what God is . . .' (1 Cor. 2.11).

I QUOTE THAT verse as a warning. It is a warning which runs through all profound religious traditions. Don't pretend to know more about God than it is possible to know. God is the ultimate mystery. To define, to pin down God, to describe him in human terms, within the limits of human language and human imagination, must be to describe something less than God.

It is a warning which reverberates through the Old Testament. To see God in ancient Jewish thought was to die. There is a marvellous story about Moses just being allowed to glimpse the backside of God as he passed by. 'To whom will you compare me, or who is my equal?' says the Holy One. That's Isaiah. And again Isaiah, ' "My thoughts are not your thoughts neither are your ways my ways", declares the Lord . . .' And my favourite from Ecclesiastes, 'Do not be quick with your mouth, do not be hasty in your heart to utter anything before God. God is in heaven and you are on earth, so let your words be few.'

God is different, other, hidden. Whole traditions of theology have been built on this insight: the so-called negative way – the description of God in terms of what he is *not*; the claim of Eastern Orthodox theology that God is unknowable in his 'essence' and revealed only in his 'energies'; Luther said much about 'the hidden God'.

Again there are whole traditions of spirituality which centre upon the stripping away of the various images and accretions and supports for the mind which otherwise tend to hide God from us. It is not for nothing that one of the most enduring books on contemplative prayer is called 'The Cloud of Unknowing'. Another is 'The Dark Night of the Soul'.

'Only the Spirit of God knows what God is.'

But Paul goes on, 'This is the spirit we have received from God . . .'

In other words, there *are* other things to be known. Against this background of the ultimate mystery of God, we are not simply reduced to silence. Isaiah may have said to God, 'My thoughts are not your thoughts'. But Paul dares to say, 'We have the mind of Christ'.

I make this contrast because it pinpoints the relation between two basic strands in Christian faith, the relation between knowing and non-knowing. And that is what I want to explore with you this evening.

There are some Christians who seem to know everything. I remember a stage in my own life when the meaning of the Bible seemed so luminously clear and its implications for life so straight-forward, that I felt there were really no problems about knowing God. There it was all written down in a book. There in the testimony to Christ was a revelation so complete that any merely human worries and criticisms seemed trivial by comparison.

This claim to know, and to see, to have the certainty of direct experience, is not to be despised. If we are to know God at all the knowledge has to have this sense of compulsion about it, of being given to us, not constructed by us. And we won't get far in reading the Bible either unless we begin to glimpse something of this luminous quality. According to Matthew Arnold revelation is what *finds* me.

The trouble is, though, that knowledge with this degree of certainty can easily turn into a kind of knowingness, into illegitimate claims to know too much. This is what is so tedious, and ultimately so irreverent, about fundamentalism. If it is all there in the book, then we really have got the measure of God, and of everything else too. All that is needed is to proclaim it. And if the whole edifice of sure and certain beliefs seems a bit crumbly sometimes, then shout the louder. There is no actual need to listen to what is going on in the rest of the world of thought and experience.

George Orwell annoyed his socialist friends by saying that the trouble with orthodox Marxists is that, possessing a system which appears to explain everything, they never bother to discover what is going on inside other people's heads. There can be similar versions of Christianity, a knowingness which devalues other knowledge and other experience, and ignores the stresses and weaknesses and inconsistencies within its own system.

It is possible to claim too much. But it is also possible to claim too little. Alongside a proper sense of the mystery of God can go a nervousness about saying anything at all. And this is powerfully reinforced as we try to exercise the kind of intellectual integrity which ought to be central in the life of a university.

Go into the Bodleian, look at the index, and think of all the books you have never read, and never will read. Think of the vast oceans of human knowledge and speculation and critical thought, and compare this with the claims we cheerfully make to know the very secret of the universe and to speak with its author.

Or think of the movement of critical thought itself, away from certainty about anything into an all-pervading kind of relativism. On such a view, what we think we know is relative to who we are, where we are, and the culture we have assimilated and the society we belong to. There can be an African or Chinese understanding of reality, say, which is just as valid as the one which seems natural to us as part of Western culture. And even science which tries so hard to leap over these cultural differences and to find a universal language and universally agreed results, runs into difficulties. There are the radical critics of science who claim that what counts as a scientific explanation is just as much socially conditioned as any other kind of commitment. I think that is going a bit far.

But even the mildest philosophers of science have to admit that what scientists are doing is to build little islands of rationality in a universe which is still deeply mysterious. These little islands of rationality, the things we think we know most clearly, the basic concepts of physics and chemistry, the insights into the nature of things which have given us telephones, and satellites, and antibiotics, even these have their limitations, especially the telephones. Our islands of rationality are far more successful at predicting the flight of a space craft than they are at predicting the weather. And they have hardly yet begun to help us understand human beings. Even in the heartland of physics itself it has become clear that 'reality' is not just something lying out there waiting to be studied by some totally detached observer. It is all much more complicated than that. The very act of observing affects the reality; and so the idea that there can be some totally objective knowledge independent of who we are and where we are and what we do doesn't work even in the area of knowledge where one would most expect it to work.

There are good secular reasons, therefore, as well as good religious ones, for not claiming to know too much.

But where does that leave us? I find it useful first to distinguish between what I call 'necessary agnosticism' and 'pernickety or fearful agnosticism'. 'Necessary agnosticism' is what I have just been talking about, a proper recognition of the ultimate mysteriousness of God and the universe and the limitations of knowledge and the relativity of our standpoint.

'Pernickety or fearful agnosticism' is the use of this sense of mysteriousness and human limitations as a means of escape from the deepest questions about being human.

This came home to me some thirty years ago in a remark made by a scientist – a man I much admired. He said that after much wrestling with religious and philosophical questions he had given them up, and decided to concentrate instead on problems which could actually be solved. This sounds fine. For academic purposes it is an excellent strategy. But as a strategy for life it doesn't work. It can lead to a shrinkage of the imagination, a narrowing of interests, a fragmentation of knowledge.

And in any case the big religious and philosophical questions refuse to go away. Human beings can't simply abandon the search for meaning in life without losing something essential to our humanness. And that is why the kind of agnosticism which tries to put these questions to one side is in my view a form of escapism. Agnosticism as an excuse, impoverishes life. Agnosticism as part of a proper approach to mystery, can enrich it.

Given that distinction, can we go further? I called this address 'Faith and Intellectual Integrity'. The word 'integrity' itself has two meanings. The first is 'honesty', and it is really about honesty that I have been talking so far. We have to be honest in facing our limitations, in facing the sheer complexity of the world, honest in facing criticism even of things which are deeply precious to us.

But integrity also means wholeness, oneness, the desire for single vision, the refusal to split up our minds into separate compartments where incompatible ideas are not allowed to come into contact. I am sometimes amazed by very naive Christian believers who, outside their church-going life, are engaged in highly sophisticated jobs and ways of thinking, but are almost childish in terms of faith. They seem to live in two worlds. Most of us, I hope, look for something better than that.

An undivided mind looks in the end for an undivided truth, a oneness at the heart of things. And this isn't just fantasy. The whole intellectual quest, despite its fragmentation, despite its limitations and uncertainties, seems to presuppose that in the end we are all encountering a single reality, and single truth. It may be incredibly mysterious or wonderfully simple. But ultimately, beyond the imperfections of our knowledge, beyond all the relativities, it is what it is. I think if we gave up believing that there is some ultimate truth, ultimate reality, in this sense, then we would be in danger of losing the notion of truth altogether. There would be my truth and your truth and somebody else's truth and the one which prevailed would have more to do with power politics than with honest search.

I am not trying to construct an argument for the existence of God. But I am saying that this search for a oneness at the heart of things forces itself upon us if we want to be one with ourselves. In this second sense of the word 'integrity', faith and intellectual integrity find themselves walking side by side. And where better to do it than in a University which once was dedicated to the task of bringing all knowledge to its focus in God?

People sometimes react to faith in God as if it were a narrowing thing; as if amid all the rich complexity of the world and all the huge variety of knowledge, the mind suddenly shut tight on some little fraction of truth and proclaimed it to be the whole. I hope it has begun to emerge from what I have been saying that faith in God can actually be a liberating thing, a breaker down of barriers, a refusal to accept fragmentation as the last word, a stimulus to look beyond our own relative, partial, blinkered standpoint, an encouragement not to be frightened and overwhelmed by mysteries beyond our understanding, a promise held out to us that truth is one, and truth is great, and will prevail.

The dangers of giving up, of claiming to know too little, are just as real as the dangers of claiming to know too much. 'Only the spirit of God knows what God is', nevertheless 'we *have* received the spirit of God'.

There *is* a kind of truth which hits us – not necessarily all of us, and not necessarily all in the same way. But the experience of being grasped hold of by some religious reality, of being upheld, strengthened, challenged, purified, integrated, is astonishingly widespread.

Here is an example from the writer Monica Furlong: 'I was sitting at a bus-stop on a wet afternoon. It was opposite the Odeon Cinema, outside the station, and I was surrounded by people, shops, cars. A friend was with me. All of a sudden, for no apparent reason, everything looked different. Everything I could see shone, vibrated, throbbed with joy and with meaning. I knew that it had done this all along, and would go on doing it, but that usually I couldn't see it. It was all over in a minute or two. I climbed on to the bus, saying nothing to my friend – it seemed impossible to explain – and sat stunned with astonishment and happiness' (*Journeys in Belief*, ed. B. Dixon, Allen & Unwin 1968, p. 81). It was an experience which took her many years to work through into full Christian commitment. But it was life-changing.

Religious vision when it comes seems inescapable. But it doesn't have to be mystical vision. Most Christians who discover a new depth of faith do so, not by some personal revelation nor by argument, but because the story of Christ has captured them, or because the difference made by Christ in the lives of other people has challenged and attracted them, or because some personal crisis has awoken a faith which was there in embryo, but ineffective.

To respond to this kind of truth is not a violation of intellectual integrity. In fact it may be the only honest thing to do. It entails choice. It entails commitment. But so does every way of life except pernickety and fearful agnosticism. 'In the process of commitment', says the believer, 'I discovered my true self. For the first time I really knew who I was – a child of God.' So the two meanings of integrity can come together. An honest response to what religiously hits us can integrate us, make us one with the oneness at the heart of things.

But mystery remains; and profound differences between people of different cultures and traditions. The sense of being grasped by ultimate reality which lies at the heart of religion, need not spill over into the kind of knowingness which I was describing earlier. True religion makes us humble; but also humbly confident, with a confidence which derives, not from knowing all the answers, but from seeing in a glass darkly the source and focus of all our searching and all our longing. Now we know in part. But then when knowledge ultimately passes away we shall see face to face.

14
Creation and New Creation

Sermon preached in Great St Mary's, Cambridge
12 October 1986

ARTHUR KOESTLER IN commenting on the story of the Tower of Babel imagined the builders to consist of various groups of experts. Such a huge and ambitious structure would need a whole range of skills and specialisms, each with its own interests, technical language and restrictive practices. Different understandings of the task would meet and conflict with one another, and there would be constant bickering about everything from financial allocations to the ultimate aim of the whole monstrous enterprise.

It would be impossible for the engineers to understand what the priests were talking about, for the brickmakers to share the architect's vision, for the philosophers to agree on the function of the tower, and for the conservationists and poets to overcome their revulsion at such a desecration of the environment. The more the work progressed the sharper and more violent would be the disputes, and whatever purpose they started with would vanish into thin air.

Koestler went on to suggest that whereas the earlier stories in the Book of Genesis described humanity's *moral* predicament – the stories of the Fall, the first murder and the flood – this one, the story of the Tower, described its *intellectual* predicament: 'We seem to be compelled to shape facts and data, as we know them, into hard bricks, and stick them together with the slime of our theories and beliefs' (*Bricks to Babel*, Hutchinson 1980). And in the end the whole edifice cracks and topples and, in the words of the story, the people are 'scattered over the face of the whole earth' . . . no longer understanding one another or able to communicate.

There are other ways of reading the story. Profound myths have this quality of being able to take many different interpretations. At its simplest what we have here is the reaction of a nomadic people coming into contact with ancient Babylonian civilization, staggered by its huge temple mounds, shocked by its arrogant self-confidence, confused by its cosmopolitan style. It is the reaction of a simple, direct, deeply religious people, to a sophisticated, ambitious and fragmented society.

At a deeper level the myth exposes the ambiguity of all human achievements. Whether we are talking about bricks and mortar, structures of civilization, or the whole edifice of human knowledge, there are dangers in being too pretentious, in failing to recognize human limitations, in claiming powers we do not possess. There is a deep unease about going too far. Witness some of the current problems in medical ethics.

Yet we *do* go too far. The attempt to do so is a basic characteristic of our humanity. And history is littered with people who believed they had achieved some kind of ultimacy, some final form of community, or some unassailable kind of power, or some absolute version of truth, at the very moment when the whole thing began to crumble.

Only last week the papers described the geneticists' dreams of being able to map the whole human genetic structure, a bargain at a mere $1000m. What they will *do* with the map when they have it was not so fully reported.

The story of the Tower of Babel is as up to date as on the day it was written. But you may be wondering what it has to do with the start of a new academic year, or with the remains of harvest festival which so obviously surround us, or with the advertised theme of this sermon – Creation and new Creation.

Let us start with the university, where perhaps Koestler's picture of the building bricks of knowledge may have rung some bells. In a modern university everybody is an expert; everybody concentrates mainly on their own expertise; and more and more of the real business of gaining knowledge involves the use of specialist languages which become more and more incomprehensible to each other.

Those of you who have just arrived will be finding your way round a Faculty, where you will be learning a discipline. The assumption behind what goes on there is likely to be that what you do is relatively independent of what goes on in all the other faculties and disciplines. Biochemists, for instance, do not need to bother about historians and theologians, and vice versa. And engineers need only be marginally concerned about English literature. Knowledge, in other words, comes in relatively self-contained blocks.

These are held together, if at all, by a rather feeble mortar made up of common aims, beliefs and assumptions. The mortar is gradually being eroded over the years by neglect. And now the whole structure is under new pressure from gale force political and economic winds which have the effect of setting different disciplines in conflict with one another. We live in times when the cracks are starting to show.

I don't wish to depress any of you at the start of what I hope is going to be a marvellous three years. But it is worth trying to get the measure of the problem insofar as it affects, not just universities, but the whole huge edifice of knowledge. We live in a a world where knowledge is fragmented, but the problems we have to face are *not*. The problems are all interrelated. Scientists can no longer duck away from ethical issues. Engineers have to consider the environment. Historians can't ignore economics. Theologians have to come to terms with biology. And so on, and so on. And the most pressing political, social and economic problems of today's world have all these dimensions and more. Knowledge conceived of as isolated blocks of material is not only ineffective but false to reality.

There is no way of solving environmental problems, for instance, without getting the science right, and the ethics, and the economics, and the politics, and understanding the history, and gaining the confidence of the people whose lives are going to be affected, and being sensitive towards the beliefs by which they live. Different disciplines are simply different approaches to a single complex world. And it is a world whose problems have to be tackled with a proper sense of our ignorance. Towers built with too great self-confidence only divide us.

I was talking a few months ago with a Minister of State in a communist country which prides itself on planning meticulously for a Utopian society. To my surprise he said to me: 'The older I get the more conscious I am of our ignorance.' It is not a bad insight with which to start a university career.

But a few moments ago I made an assumption. I spoke about a single complex world. But it is just *this* assumption that there is an underlying unity to things which is nowadays so often denied. Why should the separate bricks of knowledge fit together in a single structure?

The story of the Tower of Babel is presented to us in the Bible as part of the story of creation – a sequel to it, a distortion of it. And fundamental to the idea of creation is the belief that we are dealing with one created reality, an ordered reality springing from one creative mind, a world which ultimately makes sense. Our human vision of it may be partial and distorted and fragmented. But it makes sense in relation to God. And its ultimate unity is rooted in his unity. That is a paraphrase of Genesis 1.

To believe in creation is to see the world this way. This is not to diminish the importance of more familiar ways of celebrating creation – giving thanks for marrows and corn and chrysanthemums and a million and one other things which can all be seen as somehow part of God's overflowing creativeness and goodness towards us. But it is the belief in God as the source of all these things, as their underlying unity, which holds the whole picture together. A tower held together by mere human mortar must fall apart. Human beings held together by mere lust for achievement must eventually scatter and become incomprehensible to each other. But a world acknowledging its createdness knows that beyond all our ignorance, and beyond all conflict and division, there is a single reality. 'In the beginning, God . . .'

This is an alternative vision, a biblical vision, to set in contrast to the fragmented kind of knowledge which inevitably involves most of us for most of the time. Whether it is believable, whether it offers real hope of pulling our human experience back into some kind of unity, depends upon the third element in this pattern I am trying to put before you. I have spoken about our original unity in God's creation. I have spoken about the distortions and fragmentations which seem to be an inevitable part of human achievement. The third element is new creation.

It follows on from the story I have just been telling. The first eleven chapters of Genesis come to an abrupt end. Humanity is seen as discredited and scattered. We are presented with a few odd genealogies. And that's it.

Chapter 12 begins a new story, a new kind of story, the story of God's call of Abraham, and Abraham's response in faith. It is a story which leads to Israel, and then to Christ. And running all the way through it is the discovery that in the midst of human folly and division and despair God can do new things.

Sometimes these seem small and insignificant in comparison with the great destructive forces operating in the world around. The call of an old man to leave his home and found a nation. The faith and vision of that tiny nation as it managed to survive, loyal to its God, through more than a thousand years of tumultuous history. The new hope born in the hearts of a handful of disciples in the discovery that crucifixion had not spelt the end of their Master. And flowing out of these events, the new life experienced by countless millions of believers who have found God at work in themselves, healing, restoring, unifying, giving fresh purpose.

This is not the moment to pursue the details of this new story, the story of new creation. I simply want to make the point that in our fragmented world the Christian gospel tells us not just to look back towards the one source from which it all comes, but also to look forward to that ultimate unity in God to which it all points.

It has often been said that the Bible begins with the story of a garden and ends with the vision of a city. The unity of the old creation, the unity of the new. And in between struggle, confusion, folly, heroism, achievement and disaster, and through it all constant signs, reminders, foretastes, of that ultimate unity in love and harmony which God has prepared for us.

Let me end by going back to all those faculties and disciplines, and fragmented activities and partial truths, which make up the life of a university. There is no escape from them. There is no magic religious formula which can draw them all together into one overarching vision; and if we think there is, we are likely to be building our own Tower of Babel. Nothing is more infuriating than Christians who think they know everything.

But we do know something. We know that there is a power of resurrection life in our world; a power which shows itself in love and unity; a power which has nothing to do with cleverness or worthiness or human powerfulness, but which can flow through the lives of those who have begun to live in Christ. The Bible speaks of Christ as the only sure foundation. So for those setting out to explore the huge, and somewhat shaky, edifice of human knowledge, that is a good place to begin.

15
Science and Dogma

A conflation of two articles published in The Times
22 September and 6 October 1984

It is the adjective dogmatic rather than the noun dogma which creates the problems. Many scientists if pressed would recognize a sense in which it is proper to speak of scientific dogmas. There are basic forms of scientific understanding which, while not beyond criticism, are so entrenched in the whole scientific enterprise, that to abandon them is not seriously contemplated. Evolution is a case in point. While there is plenty of room for detailed discussion about the how and the why of particular evolutionary developments, most biologists do not doubt the key concepts of biological interrelatedness and competitive adaptation. These have become the given assumptions, the dogmas, from which research begins.

Few, however, would admit to holding such assumptions, or doing their research, in a dogmatic spirit. Dogmatism, in the adjectival sense, is held to be anti-science, and the arrogance, blindness and intransigence with which it is popularly associated, have spread a blight on the concept itself, and clouded the relationship between science and theology. Yet there are striking parallels between the use of dogmas in both disciplines. In a book with the uninviting title *Axiomatics and Dogmatics* (Belfast, Christian Journals, 1982), an American mathematician and philosopher, J. R. Carnes, explores the relationship with some subtlety. His thesis may help to set current debates about theological liberalism and conservatism in a broader context.

A scientific theorem, according to Carnes, contains two elements, the formal and the empirical. The formal element, the axiomatic system in his terminology, provides the skeleton of the theory. It defines the logical relationships between the basic terms in which the theory is expressed. The more this can be stated in mathematical terms, the more consistent and complete the formalism. But mathematics by itself is not enough. At some point the axiomatic system has to rest on terms which cannot themselves be further defined. Newton's theory of gravity, for example, simply accepts gravity as a datum without attempting to explain it further.

The empirical element in a scientific theory interprets the formalism in relation to actual experience, tests it, and may in the long run lead to its modification or replacement. Without the formal element empiricism would have no ordered data on which to work. Without the empirical element formalism becomes abstract and irrelevant. It is the combination of both which proves to be scientifically fruitful.

In much the same way, argues Carnes, dogmatic and apologetic theology depend on each other for the fruitful exploration of religious reality, the first as representing the essential formalism, and the second as grounding the whole enterprise in actual experience.

Key features of dogmatic theology are its coherence, its completeness for the task in hand, and its economy in the use of a limited number of concepts to relate a very wide variety of phenomena. Dogmas form a system. They are not unrelated truths to be discussed, modified, accepted or rejected one by one, as if change in one part of the system made no difference to any other. Admittedly the interrelationships are nothing like as logically tight as in a good scientific theory, partly because the concepts are inherently difficult to define, and partly because the basic data in Bible, Church and Creed are diffuse and capable of different interpretations. Nevertheless dogmatic formalisms exist, however disputable their details, and most Christians know perfectly well what is meant by a reference to 'central Christian dogmas'.

It is the threat to the formal completeness of such structures which gives rise to cries of pain and charges of heretical unbelief when individual dogmas are questioned. What may seem small and of no consequence to an empirically minded questioner, is experienced as a shock wave through the whole system by those concerned to protect dogmatic coherence. Revelation, incarnation and salvation, for instance, are not separate items on a list of theological topics, but different facets of a single truth about God's activity. To change the interpretation of one is to change them all.

Apologetic theology, by contrast, proceeds in a more piecemeal fashion. It is not content to assess individual dogmas simply in terms of their place within the whole tradition, but begins from the other end with the actual data of religious experience. Its criteria are consistency with the rest of experience, its power to illuminate and explain, and the degree to which its hypotheses can be tested against the evidence.

Inevitably some features of a dogmatic system survive better under this treatment than others, and in the long term the formalism has to be adjusted to take account of empirical reality. But this is likely to be a slow and uncertain business, which does not always operate to the disadvantage of the formalism. Good theories are not lightly abandoned in the face of uncomfortable facts if their loss is going to have wide repercussions. Sometimes it is the facts themselves which turn out to be mistaken, or misinterpreted, or overlooked until theoretical constraints draw attention to them. Who would have thought of looking for the planet Pluto, had there been no theoretical reason for supposing it ought to exist? And who would worry about the precise mode of the conception of Jesus were there not an elaborate theological framework in which it plays its part as an expression of the new beginning in Christ?

Apologetics and dogmatics should thus be regarded, not as two separate disciplines, but as two movements within a single process. If pursued in isolation they lead inevitably towards theological liberalism and theological conservatism, and one of the sad features of much recent popular theological comment has been precisely this polarization. To say that both are needed is not to indulge in a desperate attempt at compromise, but to state a vital truth about the character of theological knowledge, a character it shares in some measure with science. It is both empirical, in that it has to relate to life as it is actually experienced and lived; and it is also dogmatic, in that it is rooted in traditional data and understandings which in turn shape the way present experience is interpreted.

This ought to be the merest platitude. But since current disputes suggest otherwise, I have thought it worthwhile to expound Dr Carnes at some length. He manages to bring a new terminology and a freshness of detail to what are essentially old thoughts about the relationship between fact and theory. The question is whether such an analysis can actually help in resolving the disputes.

I believe it can, if only by blunting some over-sharp distinctions. The distinction between 'real historical facts' and 'mere symbolism' in relation, say, to the doctrine of the Virgin Birth instantly polarizes conservatives and liberals into those who believe 'the real thing' and those who adhere, if at all, to a watered down symbolic version of it. But what is this 'real thing' of which conservatives speak? Nobody surely wants to claim that an inaccessible gynaecological event is of huge theological significance, unless it can somehow be seen as fitting into a framework of symbolism and consistent interpretation which enables it to point beyond itself to God. The symbolism, in other words, far from being 'mere', is the key to the whole thing. The dogma is seen to be important because it is part of a dogmatic pattern.

The dispute between conservatives and liberals is not in fact over the importance of symbolism, though they may disagree about the value or appropriateness of particular symbols. The main difficulties are felt to lie on the empirical side of the theological process, and the extent to which each element in the symbolism needs to be empirically grounded.

Clearly there need to be adequate general empirical grounds if the whole theological enterprise is not to collapse. But I have already suggested how in the scientific world a formalism, granted its general stability, can 'carry' some recalcitrant facts and may itself become a basis for questioning the received empirical view. In the case of the Virgin Birth, where the empirical evidence is for obvious reasons minimal, the argument about how far this particular dogma is or is not essential and/or appropriate to the Christian dogmatic structure as a whole, has to carry the main weight. It is the formal rather than the empirical criteria which predominate.

The same point is made in a much more subtle way by Karl Rahner with his important distinction between the ground of faith and the content of faith. In discussing the historical basis of beliefs about Jesus Christ, he grounds the whole dogmatic structure on two assertions: first that Jesus saw himself as somehow in his own person expressing the definitive action of God: and secondly that this claim was vindicated by his resurrection. Everything else said about Jesus belongs to the content of faith, once these grounds have been accepted in faith as the irreducible empirical anchorage.

By this means he manages to stay within the formal dogmatic structure of orthodox Roman Catholic theology, while allowing considerable latitude in judgements about the historicity of particular New Testament narratives. The following quotation from *Foundations of Christian Faith* (Darton, Longman and Todd 1978) gives a fair summary of his position:

> We do not have to presuppose in fundamental theology that the New Testament testimony has to be found equally reliable in each and every detail. We are justified in not getting ourselves into the dilemma that either an account has to merit belief in all its details, or it is to be absolutely rejected. The answer to the question in fundamental theology about the

reliability of the sources for the life and self-understanding of Jesus and for the justification of his claim obviously cannot reach any more than a judgment of 'substantial' historicity' (p. 246).

I quote Rahner by virtue of his reputation as the most weighty and widely respected modern theologian, whose orthodoxy is unimpeachable. He clearly understood what he called 'the relationships of mutual conditioning' between historical knowledge and faith. As far as I can discover, his sole comment on the Virgin Birth in the huge volume from which I have already quoted is: 'It can be the case here that the assertion about a mere content of faith without its own ground of faith does refer to an historical event, but one whose historicity, however, is no longer accessible to us as an element in the ground of faith' (p. 244).

Reflection on theology at this level might work wonders in the debate between conservatives and liberals. Differences would remain, but there would be fewer accusations of unbelief on the one hand and of historical naivety on the other. The story of the Virgin Birth, the miracles and all other difficult details could be seen more clearly for what they are, pointers to the mystery of Christ's person and to the newness of God's saving activity.

PART III
ETHICAL THEORY

16

The Relevance of Christianity

Inaugural Southwell Lecture in memory of Bishop F. R. Barry, delivered in Southwell Minster. I had been invited to reappraise Bishop Barry's best-known book, 'The Relevance of Christianity'. 19 June 1984

It is a great responsibility to inaugurate a new lecture series, and I am conscious of the honour you have done me in inviting me to become the first Barry lecturer. I am also acutely aware of my limitations in that I never met Russell Barry, and know of his reputation only at second hand. I must be speaking to many who knew him personally, and know his books far better than I.

Yet there are compensating advantages in coming to a subject fresh. The advantages for me have been obvious and I am glad to have been forced to read his books. There may be advantages for you, in that I look at him with a fairly innocent eye – insofar as an Archbishop's eye can ever be innocent.

The Relevance of Christianity was published by Nisbet in 1931 and became one of the most popular serious theological books of that decade. It influenced a whole generation. It gained Barry his reputation as a forceful, intelligent, well-informed Christian writer at the forefront of the liberal/prophetic tradition. I will return to that label later on. I am not sure Barry would have liked it – I suspect he distrusted labels as much as I do. But it will serve for the moment.

The book earned Barry his nickname, 'Relevance Barry'. Relevance itself became a cult word and then inevitably fell into disfavour, a disfavour from which it has not quite recovered. Michael Ramsey's phrase, 'this lust for relevance', did a good deal of damage to it. Critics stressed that there is an important sense in which religion can be significant precisely when it is not relevant. The point was brought home to me very forcibly some years ago when I was travelling with a young Israeli on a bus going up to Jerusalem. We had been together for a week and I was becoming more and more amazed at the way in which Jewish culture is dominated by the so-called milk/meat rule. An orthodox Jew can either have a meat meal or a milk meal, but not the two together; and so rigidly are these separated that many Jewish households even have two kitchens. The whole thing is based on an obscure verse in the Old Testament about not seething a kid in its mother's milk. I said to this Israeli, 'Isn't it all rather absurd to build a whole culture on something so irrelevant?' I shall never forget his reply: 'It is only when God asks you to do apparently ridiculous things', he said, 'that you find you cannot ignore him. If everything in religion is rational and sensible, there is no need for God at all.'

I was reminded of the story of Abraham's sacrifice of Isaac. And the story of G. K. Chesterton, who used to say when getting up early in the morning to worship, 'only God could bring me to this pass'. A religion which is *all* relevance is a religion in danger of being brought under *our* control. *We* decide what it includes. There is an irrationality, an awareness of 'otherness', which cannot be omitted from religion without serious loss.

But an even greater danger in placing the emphasis on relevance is that relevance can become a criterion for truth. It can seem as if to prove relevance is to prove truth, whereas the opposite must surely be the case. Christianity is relevant because it is *true*. This is, I believe, what Barry himself was saying. And if he put the emphasis on the word relevance, it was not through any lack of regard for truth, or any lack of appreciation of the ultimate mystery and otherness of God, but simply because if truth is to be communicated it has to be *interesting*. His book was an evangelist's book. And he wrote of relevance because he saw the desperate need of his generation.

Why was it so popular?

First because it was urgent. Consider the opening words: 'Incomparably the most imperious challenge which today confronts Christianity is the moral chaos of our generation.' Nothing mealymouthed or half-hearted there.

Again, it was an honest book. He honestly tried to face the objections to Christianity which were current in his day, and he had the intellectual equipment to do it at the right level – on the same sort of level as the critics who caught the public ear.

Thirdly, he wrote concretely. The book is full of good concrete examples. It is about issues which for the most part are close to people's actual experience. Indeed the book was 'relevant' to anybody who could read Bertrand Russell, or Julian Huxley or R. H. Tawney.

Fourthly, and perhaps most important, he had style. The book flows. It is full of delicious phrases. I like his thanks to Julian Huxley whose vision of an evolving universe delivers Christians from trivial ideas of God. 'It offers escape from the trying people who talk as though they were [God's] private secretaries knowing his plans in every detail.' Or listen to this on divorce: 'History does not encourage us to believe that Christian standards are made more effective by the exercise of ecclesiastical discipline . . . We are to have the salt "in ourselves" – not to sprinkle it on one another's tails.' Or this: 'The Englishman's home used to be his castle. In modern life it is coming to be regarded as somewhere to sleep next door to the garage. How can it be made into a home again?'

I have said enough, I hope, to indicate the peripheral reasons why *The Relevance of Christianity* was deservedly popular. But it was primarily its theme which won attention. And to that I must now turn.

Before I opened his book I had no idea *where* Barry saw the relevance of Christianity. But the sub-title spells it out: An Approach to Christian Ethics. His thesis was essentially that Christianity has a unique and irreplaceable contribution to make to ethical thinking; that it does this by holding together a liberal Christian humanism with a proper sense of other-worldliness; and that although Christian ethics has to be rooted in Christian belief, the ethical questions are much more urgent than credal ones. Though he was called liberal/prophetic, he preferred liberal/traditional, because this was no watered down gospel adapted to 'modern man'. He went for what he saw as the main tradition. But the word 'traditional' does not convey the sense of sharpness in a sentence like this, taken almost at random: 'Christian values are frankly incompatible with those which our civilization takes for granted.'

He stood clearly in the prophetic tradition. He influenced a whole generation. Yet in a sense he was unfortunate in his timing. Reinhold Niebuhr's *Moral Man and Immoral Society* was published in 1932 and so was the English edition of Barth's *Commentary on Romans*. Those were the origins of two theological revolutions. I am told that Barry could never abide Barth, whose apparent irrationalism he deeply distrusted; nevertheless there were lessons to be learnt in Barth about human limitations and human sinfulness which could have made all the difference. Barry learnt them instead from Niebuhr, who later become one of his heroes. But to put *The Relevance of Christianity* and *Moral Man and Immoral Society* side by side to compare them before this influence had begun to be felt, is to be aware of a huge gulf between them. Barry at that time was still high on the tide of liberal optimism. Niebuhr had looked into the abyss. Barry wrote about transforming values. Niebuhr wrote about political power. Barry later looked back on *The Relevance of Christianity* as a young man's book, which somehow missed the reality of sin. Niebuhr taught him about it.

But it would not be fair to press the contrast too far, because Barry was certainly conscious of the ills of contemporary society. In fact his diagnosis could have been written today, which I suppose is some comfort to those who think that all our problems are modern ones. The list of symptoms is all too familiar: uncertainty about truth, conflicting moral claims, secularization, the fragmentation of culture, the loss of religious roots in home and society, this-worldliness. These are some of the characteristic twentieth-century problems which we may feel have grown immeasurably worse in our own day, but which I suspect were felt just as acutely fifty years ago. In fact it seems to be the rate of change in values and the rate at which former securities are eroded, which creates religious and moral difficulties, rather than any standard amount of defection from some previous – and highly idealized – condition of faith and morality. The present and future always look more threatening than the past, and no doubt always have.

In trying to tackle these problems Barry wanted to steer a middle course between stressing the offence of the gospel and encouraging a fake other-worldliness. He was very critical of what he called 'barren forms of asceticism' or any kind of faith which stood aloof from the actual struggles of real people. Above all he abhorred churchiness and sectarianism.

'The clergy are apt to invite the laity to turn aside from the office or the golf course, the laboratory, garage or consulting room, at the end of the day or maybe in the lunch hour, in order "to give part of your time to God"! But what do we think they have been doing all day? If God is not present in the enterprises, the scientific research, the "city" life, the school, the home, and even in the pleasure of this richly coloured and absorbing age, I cannot conceive where in the world he is.'

In contrast with this open attitude enabling religion to relate to the whole of life, the church often seemed like an ancient walled city. Since he used York as an example, I hope you will forgive another quotation: 'The city walls still remain standing amid the confusion of modern shops and dwelling-houses. In the past these walls encircled the city, guarding the lives of its inhabitants, defining their activities and relationships, marking out the pattern of communal life, and holding together in an organic unity its richly diverse projects and purposes. The modern city has spread beyond their boundaries. It extends for miles outside the "city" area, with its ever expanding population, its industries constantly developing, its schools, cinemas and playing fields. The more the community develops its life the further it moves away from the centre. The ancient walls are still preserved as honoured relics of an historical past, but they no longer embrace the life of the people. The expansion, the movement, the novelty, the developing purposes and creative planning, all lie away beyond the old citadel. I have sometimes thought that this is a parable of the plight of religion in the twentieth century . . .'

In line with this he saw the creative edge of religion more and more in the hands of the artists and novelists, dramatists and broadcasters, a prophecy which was strikingly fulfilled in the generation which saw T. S. Eliot, Charles Williams, C. S. Lewis and Dorothy Sayers. These were the four most influential Christians of the war-time period, none of them professional theologians, all of them lay.

False other-worldliness, churchiness, narrowness, these were the pitfalls on one side; ethics has to relate to the world as it is, and point the way to the fulfilment of human nature, not to its denial. On the other side was the danger of mere populism. Somehow he had to make the case that Christian ethics is not only relevant, but distinctive and challenging – indeed relevant precisely because it is distinctive. And it is on his success or failure in achieving that, that his book must in the end be judged.

He turned to the New Testament and it is here, I think, that the modern reader becomes most conscious of the huge changes which have taken place since 1931. It is interesting, first of all, that the Old Testament is hardly mentioned throughout the entire book. The need to interpret Christianity against its Jewish background, the role of the early Church in shaping the forms in which the New Testament stories and sayings come to us, the detailed attempts to understand the Gospels as fundamentally theological documents, all this was scarcely on the horizon when he wrote. Instead we have an uncompromising rejection of the setting in which Jesus lived and taught, and a concentration, almost to the exclusion of everything else, on the quality of his life as a revelation of the heights and depths of moral and spiritual possibility.

The New Testament is not a source book of Christian ethics. Nor is Jesus our example, as if the Christian life could be in any literal or detailed sense an 'imitation of Christ'. The teachings of Jesus belong to his world, not to ours. The Jewish background is irrelevant. 'A real incarnation in history involves real historical limitations.' 'The eternal value of the sayings [of Jesus] is primarily the witness they bear to the quality of his thoughts and intuitions. They are precious because they manifest him, in his characteristic self-revelations. They are the expressions of his spirit and are thus normative of the Christian life, but rather by way of redeeming our attitudes and lifting us into a world of new insights, than by giving us positive guidance in detail about the moral demands of Christian living.'

In other passages he goes even further. The significance of Christ lies primarily in his creativeness in the lives of others. It is primarily religious rather than moral. It is the opening up of a new dimension in ethics by revealing God in the midst of human life, and Christian ethics is therefore distinctive for its quality rather than for its content. Why has St Francis been such a creative force in Christian living? Not because many people have been able to do what Francis did, but because he, like Christ, though in a much lesser degree, embodied this same transcendent vision and orientation. Christian ethics is 'ethics thought from a new centre', a religious centre. Its differentia, in Barry's words, is 'the vision of God's holy love, seen through the windows of Christ's mind and mediated by his spirit'.

That is a fine statement but when it is translated into practice it tends to look a bit weaker. Later on in the book where Barry is trying to relate this distinctive Christian goodness to the goodness of non-believers, it comes out like this: 'We have contended that what is truly implied in the demands and claims of the moral consciousness is only fulfilled in the Christian religion; and that, within the Christian experience, goodness itself is so clothed upon with new richness and delicacy of colour as to be invested with a changed significance and to evoke new ways of response to life.'

Here the difference is a difference in colour, colour partly provided by consciousness of sin, which sharpens and purifies the moral sense; and colour also provided by worship which expands horizons and enlarges affections. The whole picture is one of growing onward and upward as religious insights add momentum to the growth of natural goodness. Barry quotes with approval a passage from A. E. Taylor whose Gifford Lectures delivered a few years beforehand had clearly had a profound influence on him. It is a passage which captures the whole feel of the philosophies of progress which were still in the ascendant when Barry wrote: 'As we rise in the moral scale, under the drawing of conceptions of good more and more adequate to sustain intelligent aspirations, living itself steadily takes on more and more a "form of eternity". For, in proportion to the level we have attained, each of our achievements becomes more and more the reaction of a personality at once richer and more unified to the solicitation of a good, itself presented as richer and more unified.' I do not quote this in order to mock it. There is a proper sense in which morality advances, in which 'a man's reach must exceed his grasp', and in which ethical standards constantly have to be transcended. But what is missing from all this is quite simply the cross.

It suddenly hits you when you read books of this period and in this tradition that the kind of significance which it is now commonplace for Christians to see in the cross of Christ as the very heart and centre of the Christian faith, scarcely finds a mention. The only reference to salvation in the whole of Barry's book is derogatory. He dismisses the tradition which sees Jesus as 'a theological lay-figure in a half-mechanical scheme of salvation, rather than a real man among men.' He accepts that Christianity is a religion of redemption. Progress is not inevitable. Barry knew enough about the consequences of human wickedness through his distinguished war service to have no doubts that things could go terribly wrong. But redemption is 'by God's power and presence in Jesus'. It is the transfiguration of our values. The word 'transfiguration' is itself significant. What needs to happen is the fuller revelation of a glory that is already there. But what is missing from this picture is the descent from the Mount of Transfiguration to the squalid scene below, and then the painful road to that other Hill where love seemed to be defeated and hope extinguished.

I think it would be impossible nowadays to write a book on the relevance of Christianity without once mentioning suffering. It is here that the contrast with Niebuhr is so instructive. Let me stress again that later on Barry was quick to learn Niebuhr's lessons. But it is sad for him that the book by which he is most remembered should have failed so disastrously at this particular point.

An individualistic religion can concentrate on moral aspiration. Individuals may learn to transfigure their values. Individuals may cope with personal suffering, and even to some extent transcend the distortions of human sinfulness. Niebuhr would accept all this. In fact he said of the cross, 'the devotion of Christianity to the Cross is an unconscious glorification of the individual moral ideal. The Cross is the symbol of love triumphant in its own integrity . . .' And then he went on 'but not triumphant in the world and society. Society, in fact, conspired the Cross. Both the state and the church were involved in it, and probably will be so to the end.'

This is the point. An ethic which claims to be about the whole of life has to come to terms with the evils and the sufferings, the distortions and the limitations of our lives together in society. And an ethic which is weak in its treatment of personal sinfulness and suffering, is lost when it tries to tackle the much more intractable social and political dimensions. I hope I am not being unfair if I say that Barry got half way towards spelling out the significance of Christian ethics for social and political life, but failed at the precise point where Niebuhr's political realism took over. Let me illustrate from passages where they are both writing about the religious dimension in justice.

This is Barry: 'Christianity clothes the term Justice with an immeasurably enriched significance. It will not be content with the overthrow of privilege and a real respect for the rights of backward peoples, though both of these are ahead of current standards. It will rather insist that if God so loved the world, if a man is worth that in the sight of God, if the Spirit can evoke such qualities out of very average human nature as are the commonplaces of human history, then a man's due has never been rendered him till Society has helped him to realise all the goodness for which God designed him. On that level Justice is so transmuted as to be more truly described as redemptive love.' Note the onward and upward. And note the transition from personal aspiration to social action.

Here, in contrast, is Niebuhr: 'Religion will always leaven the idea of justice with the ideal of love. It will prevent the idea of justice, which is a politico-ethical ideal, from becoming a purely political one, with the ethical element worked out . . . there must always be a religious element in the hope of a just society . . .' So far he is with Barry. But then he goes on: 'Without the ultra-rational hopes and passions of religion no society will ever have the courage to conquer despair and attempt the impossible; for the vision of a just society is an impossible one, which can be approximated only by those who do not regard it as impossible.' In other words it is not a question of onwards and upwards, but of a radical ideal which inspires and corrects and judges societies which are, and will remain, inherently imperfect. Niebuhr summarizes, 'The full force of religious faith will never be available for the building of a just society, because its highest visions are those which proceed from the insights of a sensitive individual conscience.'

Religious aspiration can take one so far. To that extent what Barry was trying to do in spelling out the social as well as the personal implications of Christ's transforming vision, was valid. But it was Niebuhr's greatness also to see the other side of the coin, to recognize the inherent limitations and dangers of religion when used to justify particular political and social policies. Religion absolutizes: 'Human vice and error may thus be clothed by religion in garments of divine magnificence and given the prestige of the absolute.' We have seen some of the terrible fruits of this absolutizing of political policies in our own day. It bedevils the politics of the Middle East. It lies at the root of the problems of Northern Ireland. And one can see it happening in the present miners' strike, in which quasi-religious mythologies are developing which are going to make the conflict harder and harder to resolve.

To be fair to Barry, he never seems to have fallen into this particular trap. He was far too generous and open and responsive to the actual complexities of life. Thus on economic affairs: 'Christian teachers are apt to observe that if everyone would accept Christianity our economic difficulties would solve themselves. Such assertions may be quite true [Are they?] but unless the Churches show themselves capable of constructive and realistic thinking to vindicate these enormous generalizations they are bound to appear futile and almost meaningless.' Even that statement, though, holds out the hope that given enough realistic thought the problems could be solved.

I have felt it right to spend all this time contrasting him with Niebuhr, precisely because he was not an easy target for Niebuhr's scorn of liberal-minded Christian moralists. He knew the pitfalls. Yet at this stage in his life he seemed to lack the radical sense of evil which was soon to dominate the theological stage. And the different styles of the ethical thinking of these two men, the broad Christian humanism of the one and the prophetic and paradoxical political realism of the other, are still relevant in discussions of religion and politics today. I must now turn much more briefly to one or two of the actual moral issues which Barry tackled.

On many of them he was surprisingly modern. Having recently done some writing myself on the relationship between the state and voluntary organizations, I was intrigued to find him reflecting about the Church Assembly, which was then only nine years old, in a way which is still worth pondering. His theme at that point was the growth of the state, the centralization of responsibility and the inherent conflict between what he called 'Freedom and Community'. He saw in the Church Assembly a fruitful precedent for what we might now call 'bodies with relative autonomy'. The Church of England is a voluntary association, but not simply a voluntary association. It has its recognized place in the life of the nation, and its members have direct access to the Crown in Parliament, which in turn guarantees its autonomy and sets limits to the extent to which its legislation can infringe the rights of other citizens. Here then, in the very status of the church vis-à-vis the nation, is a complex balance of freedom and responsibility, which might well have wider implications. In the event it did not. But it was perceptive to see the possibilities. And there might still be something in the idea for the future.

On big questions of the day, like peace and disarmament, his views were much as one might expect. He was not totally pacifist, but as near as possible. 'The Christian Church has not yet recovered from its humiliating surrender in blessing the arms of all the late belligerents . . .'; there is the echo from his war experience. 'An open door now stands before it – the greatest opportunity yet vouchsafed to it – to recover its hold on the world's moral allegiance and to lead the nations into the way of peace.' Nothing surprising about that. But then interestingly he went on to deplore the development of national Churches and to remind his readers of the real meaning of catholicism. 'If Christendom must remain divided, let the lines be denominational rather than national.' We could go beyond that today, but the fact that he focused so quickly on what the Churches might do in their own life, is to my mind the mark of a true prophet. And what he said then is just as relevant now.

But it was on the subject of women, sex and the family that he was most radical. To read him on marriage and divorce, in the light of our present preoccupations in the Church of England, is to realize that the argument has not advanced much in 50 years. He was ahead of his time on contraception. And he urged the Church to take seriously the question of women's vocations – not only vocations to ordination, but to useful spheres of service and professional work in general. Nowadays when we agonize over the ordination of women there is a certain value in putting oneself back mentally into the world Barry faced, seeing the way in which the Church seemed to connive at the business of keeping women in their place, and then pondering his final remark: 'The question of the ordination of women should be re-examined, not merely as one of ecclesiastical order, but as part of a large problem of Christian morals. What value do we actually give to people and their aspirations?'

It would not, I think, be useful to pursue any further his actual moral policies and recommendations. Time has overtaken them, not least his prescription for ending the economic crisis of the thirties by a policy of voluntary austerity, put forward on the eve of the Keynesian economic revolution. But who has ever got economics totally right? The important thing about Barry was that he thought, and took the trouble to inform himself, and had a genuine vision of the infinite possibilities of human life in God, and was able to set it all out with clarity and passion. And that was why so many people read him.

I end with a postscript. Suppose one was writing a book on the relevance of Christianity today, where would the emphasis be different? I have already suggested one difference in the central place given in modern Christian thought to the realities of sin and suffering. Our God is a crucified God, and his glory has first to be seen in his cross before it can be seen in his triumph.

I think another difference might lie in a shift away from problems of ethics to the problem of meaning. This is not to say that ethics is irrelevant today; far from it. There is huge public interest in major issues from politics to peace and from medical ethics to third world economics. But we have large numbers of ethical pundits of all shapes and sizes. I suspect that the main religious concerns of people lie beneath all this public debate. Is there any way of deciding these things? Is there any authority in terms of which one could decide? What meaning can be given to the process of deciding, and indeed to life itself?

A third difference might lie in the kind of equipment available to us for tackling such problems. In some ways doing theology is harder now than it was then. But in other ways I believe there has been some recovery of theological nerve. A modern approach to the New Testament would place much greater emphasis on the theological intention of its writers; and a modern approach to ethics would try to root particular practical insights much more firmly in theological principles. I think we might also place greater value on the diversity of theological approaches, and see this as itself providing a source of insight into the complexity of ethical problems.

I am glad I do not have to write the book. It is exceedingly hard to capture the mood of a generation, to meet its questions, to distil a tradition in ways which fire the imagination, and to do it all with integrity, scholarship and energetic insight. Having contemplated the task, I salute even more fervently the man who achieved so much of it at the age of only forty-one, half a century ago.

17
Making Moral Decisions

*A lecture to the Ecumenical Consultation for Northern Church Leaders at Scargill House
29 February 1988*

Our growth together as Churches raises questions about how well we are going to be able to work together on moral issues, particularly those with an obvious public dimension. Are we likely to agree? Does it matter if we do not agree? Are we fulfilling a useful role as Churches if we simply demonstrate creative disagreement? and can such creative disagreement be faithful to the gospel?

A first step to answering such questions must be to ask how in our different traditions we actually make decisions. I am thinking not so much of ecclesiastical processes as of the methods and assumptions which underlie the business of decision-making. Furthermore this lecture is not about specific moral decisions, though I shall be using homosexuality as an example of how the same issue can be approached in a variety of ways, all of which can properly be described as Christian. The emphasis rather is on the different approaches themselves. Different Churches have their own characteristic methods and assumptions, but the differences are not merely denominational nor are the methods mutually exclusive. Most actual decisions probably employ a combination of them. What follows, therefore, is an over-simple analysis of methods, but one which may help to pinpoint similarities and differences between us more clearly.

1. The first method of moral decision-making is by the appeal to direct authority. The authority may be biblical, ecclesiastical or personal, but for the moment I want to put the emphasis on the word 'direct'. Its implication is that answers are simply 'given' once the authority is recognized and accepted. The authority is regarded as unchallengeable and the expectation is that it will in fact provide a clear and binding answer to all appropriate doctrinal and moral questions.

Biblicism falls into this category. The assumption on which it operates is that the Bible is the equivalent of a maker's handbook. Scripture contains the complete instructions for being human, and although these instructions may not always be easy to unravel, the experienced practitioner can always throw light on virtually any problem and expects to find firm authoritative guidance on most of them. Thus questions about homosexuality are settled beyond dispute by reference to the appropriate proof texts in St Paul and the Old Testament. Arguments against them on the grounds that St Paul's attitude towards homosexuality belongs within a particular social setting are to be discounted as dangerous attempts to water down truths which Scripture has clearly stated.

The main difficulty with biblicism is that it falsifies the nature of the Bible. To think of the Bible as a set of timeless instructions is to overlook the fact that, like it or not, it is a historical document written over many hundreds of years, reflecting many different points of view, and deeply embedded in the culture of different eras. This is not to devalue it as revelation but to take it seriously as God's revelation of himself through the ambiguities of history.

Biblicism also misleads through being selective. To claim that there is clear biblical teaching on this or that contemporary problem is to ignore the lengthy process of interpretation which has led to the conclusion that these particular biblical texts, and these only, are relevant in our day whereas other injunctions, like stoning adulterers, can safely be ignored. All our readings of Scripture are interpretations, and to assume that there is something identifiable as pure unadulterated biblical teaching is to be self-deluded.

Even more foolish and deluded is the opposite extreme which would deny any moral authority to the Bible at all. Christianity inescapably requires acceptance of the Bible as authoritative, but this is not the same as biblicism. Biblical authority is encapsulated in the events it describes and in what successive generations of believers have made of those events. Of supreme authority for Christians are the teachings of Jesus, but these are themselves often complex and ambivalent, given more in hints and parables than in direct commands. Furthermore none of this can be separated from the ways in which churches have responded to it in different times and places. Just as the Bible is historically conditioned so is the Christian response to it.

Ecclesiastical authority at its best gathers up and transmits this constantly developing tradition. The great landmarks in theology are the authoritative interpretations of Christian events and teachings which have stood the test of time. At its worst ecclesiastical authority assumes the same direct and domineering role as biblicism and becomes a new law standing between the believer and the basic Christian events. This is always one of the great temptations of the Church. The more it perceives the importance of its own role as interpreter and guide, the more it is in danger of magnifying its own authority as the only direct and certain means of access to God's truth.

A church-centred approach to questions of authority runs into a further problem, namely, who speaks for the Church? In churches where a particular group or individual takes on the role of authoritative interpreter then the question has to be asked, how does this ecclesiastical authority harvest and use the insights and experience of the whole people of God? An ecclesiastical authority perceived as standing over against the whole body of the faithful would have to rely on a very strange theology of the Church. Yet unless some can speak for all, nothing is going to be said. Questions concerning 'the mind of the Church' are not easy to resolve, except in relatively small self-contained churches.

For some people, and perhaps a growing number, the authority of direct personal encounter with God outweighs all other considerations. Prophetic vision carries a sense of its own authenticity. Conscience can make an individual immovable. 'Here I stand, I can do no other.' Such claims to direct encounter often go hand in hand with an individualistic, not to say idiosyncratic, variety of biblicism.

It is difficult to argue against such conviction. Neither is it possible to escape awkward questions about how it can be distinguished from illusion and prejudice, unless somehow the vision can be shared and criticized. The mailbags of church leaders all too often contain lengthy manuscripts from lonely and unbalanced 'prophets' who have managed to solve all the world's problems to their own, but no one else's, satisfaction.

A question which arises from what has been said so far is whether any unmediated encounter with the divine will is possible at all. Does our knowledge of God's will always have to be through the distorting lens of human fallibility? The Bible has to be interpreted. The Church shares the limitations of its time and place. Individual conscience can go astray. All appeals to direct authority receive answers conditioned, at least in part, by our own history and circumstances. We see in a glass darkly and it should not surprise us, therefore, if from our different perspectives we sometimes see different things.

2. The second method of decision-making I shall call 'penny-dropping through story telling'. This is the parabolic method. It takes seriously the way Jesus actually taught, mostly through telling stories. It also takes seriously the nature of the biblical revelation as being largely narrative.

The phrase 'penny-dropping' comes from Ian Ramsey who made much use of the idea in his own pioneering work with interdisciplinary working parties. The essence of the method is that, confronted with a particular moral issue, different experts tell their stories; the theologian too tells the stories out of his own tradition; from this mutual story-telling a new perspective can emerge. New connections may be seen; the light of genuine Christian insight begins to dawn; the penny drops.

It is a powerful method. A great deal of moral education depends on it. Moral insights are often conveyed much more powerfully through stories, whether biblical, personal or fictional, than through spelling out moral precepts. When Dickens wanted to expose the moral evils of nineteenth-century England he wrote novels about it. When E. M. Forster wanted to explore the moral implications of his own homosexuality he wrote a novel, now made into a film, *Maurice*. The implications of nuclear testing in the Pacific have been conveyed far more powerfully to me by hearing the testimony of a Marshall islander than by reading statistics in a book.

Stories and case histories allow for greater subtlety of analysis than the straightforward application of rules. Stories with a moral point also leave space for the hearer to make a creative response. The meaning of Jesus' parables does not lie on their surface; in fact they go on being endlessly powerful and illuminating as different people respond in their own terms and out of their own situations.

There is a drawback in story-telling, though, in that the method can be somewhat hit and miss. The right story at the right moment can have huge prophetic power, but the actual selection of stories can be arbitrary or even manipulative. In the end story-telling is no substitute for systematic analysis. But how is this analysis to be made? If the appeal to direct authority ultimately fails us, and if it is wise to be suspicious of story-tellers, what other basis can there be for true moral discernment?

3. The third method of making moral decisions entails deducing the answers from generally accepted principles. It rests on the assumption

that it is possible to specify clear rules, principles and values, which are seen to have universal validity and from which particular judgements may then be deduced. In its classic form this approach to morality, the so-called natural law approach, rested on the belief that there is a given order in nature which, despite the limitations of human sinfulness, can still be discerned by reason and which must be obeyed as the expression of God's will. The great strength of this approach to morality is that it is essentially rational. Hence its prescriptions are, at least in principle, accessible to anybody, whether Christian or not, who takes the trouble to follow the argument.

This does not preclude an appeal to Scripture. In fact a Christian might well want to derive his starting point from some basic principles seen as summing up the essence of the scriptural message. But the method of proceeding would then be the same. The argument moves from general principles to particular cases, and the traditional claim made for the method is that the end result is the same whether the starting-point is Scripture or natural law. In terms of basic human morality Scripture confirms what a rational understanding of God's order in nature is seen to dictate.

The natural law approach to homosexuality argues from the given constitution of the human body. Certain organs are clearly intended for certain actions and not for other actions. Curiously this argument overlooks the given constitution of the human mind which may not always correlate as expected with bodily function. Natural law theory has not yet come to terms with the fact that some five to ten per cent of people are born 'naturally' homosexual. There are even more fundamental difficulties in this understanding of the order of nature as something simply 'given' by God, and thereby seen as possessing a kind of moral authority, in an age which is trying to take seriously a vastly increased knowledge of the natural world as a hugely diverse, evolving and open-ended process. Nature does not stay still in the way that a traditional understanding of God's 'order' requires it to.

A major difficulty in the attempt to derive clear moral deductions from general principles, is that the more specific the deductions the more controversial they are likely to be. Any move from the general to the particular entails an increasing dependence on the interpretation of empirical evidence the further one moves away from broad platitudes. Conclusions derived solely from general principles become more and more difficult to justify rationally without introducing all sorts of individual judgements, each of which may be disputed. In a nutshell the whole method runs the risk of trying to deduce too much from too little. In practice weak arguments presented to the faithful as if they were conclusive have generally had to be buttressed by an appeal to authority.

And how rational is morality anyway? Christians with a strong awareness of sin may legitimately doubt whether human reason is up to the task. On the other hand if grace alone can bring true moral insight, why should we have to think of grace as working on us only through irrational means, rather than as illuminating and guiding reason itself? The argument from human sinfulness is not to my mind conclusive against a deductive approach to morality. The greater danger, as I see it, is that such an approach can too easily lose its anchorage in facts and so become remote, irrelevant and unreal.

4. A fourth method of moral decision-making takes the empirical facts as its starting point and tries to bring theological insights to bear on them. The emphasis is on the word 'theological'. The assumption behind this method is that Christianity's main contribution to ethics is not a new set of rules, or even a new set of general moral principles, but theological understanding. What distinguishes Christian ethics from secular ethics is doctrine. It is insight into the nature of the world as God's world, and humanity as finding its ultimate fulfilment in relationship with God. The claim underlying this method is that we do not truly know ourselves, or our circumstances, unless these are seen in the light of God. But such knowledge has to assimilate and, where necessary, build on the best that secular analysis can provide.

Thus utilitarianism is not to be despised. Most public policy rests on utilitarian foundations because public policymakers cannot, and should not, avoid trying to calculate the consequences of their decisions, nor will they retain their positions if they ignore human happiness. But utilitarianism is not enough. Its great defect from the start has lain in unanswered questions about the true nature of human happiness, and the felt need to justify some forms of happiness as intrinsically more valuable than others. It is a moral theory which desperately needs an injection of theology. Other secular theories of moral obligation, most of them variants of Kant's appeal to human rationality, usually cry out for a deeper understanding of what it is to be a person. If with Kant we are always to treat persons as ends rather than as means, then it is not enough simply to root their value in human reason. For Christians personhood is a far richer concept than this, bound up with the theology of the personhood of God. In a similar vein, secular theories of what human societies are, or could be, can be enriched and illuminated by a Christian understanding of communion.

The point is that both in terms of secular ethical theory and also in terms of the analysis of concrete problems, there are resources of Christian understanding available, and these constitute the distinctive Christian contribution to morality. They may not make it any easier to arrive at clear and simple answers, but at least they ensure that we do not rest content with superficial ones.

I return for the last time to the question of homosexuality. The method of bringing theological insight to bear on the best and most thorough empirical analysis cannot start with the assumption that particular references to homosexuality in the Bible are the only or even the most important resource. Relevant theological insights have to include questions about the forms of human relationship, the nature of sexuality, the role of the family in society, the limits of diversity and, in our present climate of opinion, the limits of tolerance.

A key word under this heading is 'discernment'. People sometimes talk about 'discerning the signs of the times'. If this is taken to mean picking up the latest fashion or climbing on to the most modern bandwagon, then it is not a particularly Christian activity. There is, however, a process of Christian discernment, preferably exercised corporately, which tries to analyse what is going on in the world in its own terms, and then to scrutinize it in the light of a general knowledge of God's purposes as revealed in Scripture and subsequent history. It is not a method of making moral judgements which yields quick or easy answers. The method is difficult and uncertain and is in constant danger of lapsing into the kind of trendiness which is its popular caricature. At its best it can lead to the slow development of a Christian mind on some key moral issues. The highlighting of fidelity as an essential element in personal relationships is a case in point. But there is still much more to be done in spelling out its practical implications.

I have been contrasting four methods of moral decision-making. Let me repeat my warning that these are not to be considered as mutually exclusive or entirely separate from one another. Most actual decision-making employs a variety of methods and rests on a variety of assumptions. Sometimes problems themselves dictate the most fruitful approach, but if Churches are to work more closely together, particularly in the field of public issues, then some understanding of the variety of methods and of their interrelationships is a good starting-point. At least it can encourage us to look beyond disagreements about practicalities to their deeper roots in different traditions, cultures and methods.

One final warning. There is a wide gulf between coming to general moral conclusions and deciding matters of public policy. Public policy decisions have to include many non-theological and non-ethical considerations, not least questions about what is politically possible. Church leaders who venture into this realm therefore must not be surprised if they receive sharp political rejoinders. To enter the political arena is to be judged in terms of it. This may sometimes be necessary but we must know what we are doing.

18
Natural Law and Bioethics

Inaugural lecture at the opening of the Ian Ramsey Centre, Oxford
22 February 1985

In his memoir of Ian Ramsey in *Preliminary Perspective* (Dean and Chapter of Durham 1984), David Edwards describes him as dreaming of just such a centre as this in Oxford, a dream which began to take shape in the mid-1960s, and which crystallized in the concluding words of Ramsey's book, *Models and Mystery* (Oxford University Press 1964):

> Here is a view of a university, not as a mere area for power struggles between professional disciplines, still less as a mere setting in which men go about their segregated jobs; here is a university which holds together and harmonizes the technical and the humane, the specialization and the broad perspective, the mind which is analytically critical and the person who is broadly sensitive and sympathetic, which holds together understanding and insight, models and mystery.

It was during this period that Ian Ramsey was at his most creative in leading a whole series of groups and working parties on major social and ethical issues. It was in these that he pioneered the method of interdisciplinary study in ethics, by stimulating just the kind of cross-fertilization between different styles of approach and types of expertise that he longed to see in his own university. The method thus developed, that of bringing together a variety of experts in different disciplines, has in large measure undergirded the Church's ethical thinking on complex and contentious issues ever since.

I was lucky enough to know Ian Ramsey in those days. In fact from 1964 to 1968 I had the privilege of belonging to a working party set up under his chairmanship to study the significance of natural law in ethics, and it is out of that experience that I intend to speak today. At the centre of our discussion was the question whether such inter-disciplinary work is possible, whether there is a basis for moral judgements on which a wide variety of people, both Christian and non-

Christian, can be expected to agree. What we were trying to do, therefore, could be seen as an essential background to the more immediately practical studies which were then engaging his attention. I suggest that it has some relevance, too, to the tasks this centre will hope to undertake in the future. This at least is my excuse for taking this particular theme, and using some of my time to indulge in reminiscence.

Our brief was set by the then Bishop of Exeter, Robert Mortimer, who in a speech to the Church Assembly on the subject of fornication called for 'a reformulation in modern times of the concept of Natural Law taking into full account the assured conclusions of modern psychology'. This was 1963, the year of *Honest to God*. It was also the year after the publication of *Soundings* in which Harry Williams had ascribed much of traditional morality to cowardice. It was the decade of permissiveness, a decade very conscious of the difficulty in finding any firm ground for doing metaphysics, and when theologically there were still echoes of Karl Barth's attack on the whole natural law tradition.

Ian Ramsey, as I have said, was our chairman, and Gordon Dunstan secretary. Harry Williams, the late George Woods and myself represented the *Soundings* tradition. Eric Mascall, Canon Bentley and Dom Illtyd Trethowan represented the Catholic tradition. There were two others, roughly middle of the road, plus a psychiatrist, the only layman. Interestingly, it was he who was partly responsible for the fact that the group never in the end managed to produce a report. Whereas the rest of us found we could speak with some confidence from our various theological and philosophical standpoints he, the only practising scientist, found himself increasingly overwhelmed by the sheer mass of material on the history, development and psychology of ethics which he felt he needed to master. The result was that his major contribution to the report never materialized. It became increasingly obvious that the extraction of moral insight from even so sympathetic a discipline as psychology is a very hazardous business

There were other reasons why after four years work we failed to produce a report. Two members of the group died, one had to withdraw through ill-health and our Roman Catholic representative was exchanged for another after about a year's work. But the main reason lay in the sheer difficulty of the subject and the impossibility, as it seemed to us then, of compressing our different insights into one reasonably coherent statement. We therefore published a series of working papers in the journal *Theology*, which still, I believe, form a useful quarry for those wanting to pursue the theme today.

We quickly decided that the phrase 'Natural Law' was not the best description of what we were actually trying to explore. It conveys a sense of moral immutability rooted in the way things are, a set of principles somehow discernible either through the exercise of some natural property, reason, conscience or whatever, or through the study of nature itself. At one of our meetings, George Woods put it like this:

> When I speak of nature I do not know what I mean, and in consequence, I have no clear understanding of the adjective 'natural'. I am not at all sure that the word 'law' is the most apt description of that to which Natural Law refers. I am at a loss to know how I ought to determine its content and I find its application by no means easy in particular cases. But I am in favour of the tradition in that it seeks to emphasize the place of reason in ethics, and the essential relation of ethics to metaphysics.

And that, more or less, was where we began. Can there be a reasonable approach to ethics which would commend itself to everyone who is in a broad sense 'human'? And if there is, does it necessarily lead to agreed conclusions on practical issues?

Ian Ramsey had his own characteristic approach to such questions, and we were soon deep into a discussion of disclosure situations, insights and intuitions. The basis of a natural law morality, as he saw it, is not some set of immutable principles from which right behaviour in complex situations can be deduced. Moral reasoning is more like an interplay between certain maxims or key ideas and actual empirical complexities, in such a way that out of their interaction arises a sense of moral claim. Christians are engaged in the same kind of process when they use biblical stories, parables, images as the backcloth against which the moral claims inherent in some dilemma make themselves felt.

Ramsey was highly suspicious of what he called 'external codes'. There is no way of reading off either from nature or from the Bible what has to be done in all circumstances. In a paper written for the working party during this period, subsequently published in his *Christian Ethics and Contemporary Society* (SCM Press 1966), he explored Professor H. L. A. Hart's attempt to ground a fairly traditional view of natural law on the principle of survival. In his paper, Hart had pointed to 'the simple contingent fact that most men for most of the time wish to continue in existence'. On this slender basis he then argued for a series of what he called 'natural necessities'. These included such minimal requirements as living at peace with one another, owning a minimal amount of property, and being able, when essential, to apply coercion. Ramsey was sympathetic, but pointed out that even such general principles as these depended on a kind of disclosure. There is a difference between wishing to survive and being committed to survival, and the difference lies in our recognition of ourselves as persons. It is precisely because we transcend the bare process of keeping alive that we can begin to see a moral claim in survival.

In other words, according to Ramsey, even at this basic level of highly generalized principle, the element of personal disclosure and commitment is inescapable. How much more is this true when actual decisions have to be made. Rigid rules, whether derived from natural reasoning or from Christian revelation, obscure this. But this is not to say there are no principles to guide us. Ramsey preferred to call them mnemonics, rules of thumb. I quote from the unpublished minutes of one of our meetings:

> We need moral principles and there *are* moral principles. But they are not copy-book principles, any more than morality is a slavish following of rules. They each point back to an obligation revealed through and around the empirical facts of countless situations, an obligation matched only by a decision in which we realize ourselves characteristically as persons . . .
>
> Our problem today is not that there are no principles, but that such principles as are enunciated have so often lost their moorings, whether as derived from 'natural necessities' and a basic moral obligation, or as needing to be integrated with Christian discourse and the challenge and commitment which such discourse expresses.

In later papers delivered to the group he went on to explore the use of the Bible, looking for what he called 'a morality of vision'. I quote again:

> The primary significance for Christian behaviour of the Bible, and of the New Testament in particular, is to recreate the challenge of God in Christ, in responding to which there arises Christian commitment which shows itself, in part, in moral behaviour. So the basis of Christian behaviour is to be found in a disclosure situation in which there arises a key idea or basic theme which is one expression of the Christian gospel.

These key ideas are rooted in stories, aphorisms, above all in the best and most widely ranging picture of Jesus which scholarship can recreate for us. It was out of this process of communal reflection on the

Christian tradition in the face of concrete problems that Christian morality developed in the early Church. And still should.

I have quoted Ian Ramsey at some length, not only for piety's sake, and not only because he was the dominant member in our group, but because something of his characteristic approach to all these matters has rubbed off onto the rest of us, and crystallized insights of permanent value.

There can be no easy appeal to simple moral rules in the face of complex new problems. There is a constant need for detailed empirical knowledge. Moral claims arise out of sensitive reflection on actual issues against a background of general moral commitment and insight derived from past experience, whether biblical or secular. At bottom morality has to do with what is characteristically human and personal, and there is thus a kind of objectivity about it; it is more, much more, than conformity to the conventions of a particular society.

These were the bare bones of our agreement. But about the degree to which rules are useful, and the kind of objectivity claimed, there were sharp differences. Is there a givenness about human nature and the conditions for human life, which limit the range of new moral insight? Is it possible to say, even in very general terms, what human beings are and what we are meant to be? These are questions of particular concern in present-day bioethics, and I am sorry to have to admit that twenty years ago we did not get very far with them.

One might, for instance, explore the givenness of human nature in a purely empirical way, by trying to decide what is 'best' for people simply by studying actual behaviour. Our psychiatrist tried to lead us along this path, with the result that we scattered on endless treasure hunts, looking for the hidden value judgements in what purported to be scientific conclusions.

On the other hand, non-empirical claims were equally open to challenge. Hart's claim about survival as representing some kind of moral bedrock, provoked the search for alternatives. The ideas of relatedness and communication were held by some of our members to be even more fundamental. To be is to communicate; to be in relationship is of the essence of being human.

Others favoured a different kind of empiricism, entailing the study of what human beings in many different cultures have actually regarded as being morally fundamental. It is customary to stress the diversity of moral behaviour. But there are also striking convergences, and if there had not been there would have been no point in, or possibility of, finding agreement on declarations of human rights or worldwide professional codes. The moral dilemmas posed by medical and biological advances may be hugely difficult, and may take different forms in different cultures, but we do not start from scratch in the attempt to solve them. Those professionally involved already work within ethical traditions.

My own modest contribution to this part of the group's work was to float the idea that there is a process of moral discovery, in some ways analogous to scientific discovery. It is, I believe, possible to discover new moral truths, truths which once discovered become part of everybody's inheritance. The insights and intuitions Ian Ramsey was so fond of describing may have to be discovered afresh by individuals in the process of wrestling with concrete problems. But they also have a public history, and may depend on all sorts of other insights more deeply embedded in public consciousness. It is their public history, too, which in a weak sense validates them. Just like scientific concepts, moral insights which go on proving their value, gain a kind of permanence which makes it irresponsible to bypass them. The abolition of slavery, for instance, entailed a shift in moral perspective which it would be difficult now to reverse, though it might be deliberately suppressed in a totalitarian state.

All this was twenty years ago, and as I said, we did not get very far. We had no inkling then of the extent to which the whole issue was going to be sharpened in some circles by the publication in 1968 of *Humanae Vitae*, the Encyclical Letter of Pope Paul VI on the regulation of birth. Here was an exercise in the tradition of natural law at its most hamfisted, a classic example of what happens when natural law is identified with natural processes, and physiology made the basis of morals. But if nature as given is *not* an authoritative guide, where and how does one draw the limits? What constraints ought there to be, for example, on making genetic improvements? Physiology may not be our sole guide when we think about contraception, but what is it that makes us hesitate before tinkering with the physiological basis of human personality?

One of the most startling omissions from our exploration in those days was the complete lack of any reference to environmental issues. A natural law based entirely on insights into what fulfils human beings as persons is not well placed to say anything about the environment as such. Yet is there, ought there to be, a sense in which the non-human natural world is treated with respect for its own sake?

And if so, how far do we carry this? How far is it part of our very humanness to go against the grain of nature and subject it to our will?

I am concentrating on asking questions because it seems to me that at the beginning of a new venture it is better to explore difficulties than to attempt to provide answers which are bound, given the present state of the game, to be misleadingly inadequate. I would be failing as a Christian, though, and untrue to the memory of Ian Ramsey, if I did not try to point the way ahead. This is why I want to leap forward to what at first sight may seem an entirely different approach, as represented in Alastair MacIntyre's fascinating book *After Virtue* (Duckworth 1984).

As those of you who know it will remember, a large part of the book is spent in pointing out the failure of the rationalist tradition in ethics, a failure which has led, faute de mieux, to the triumph of emotivism. Whatever so-called rationalists actually claim about the basis of their moral reasoning, says MacIntyre, the fact that they do not agree with one another is the most cogent possible evidence that there are no objective and impersonal moral standards discernible by reason alone. In the end, and this is the essence of emotivism, it is all a matter of opinion, of the way we feel. In the general debacle, the natural law tradition suffers the same fate as secular moralities. In MacIntyre's own words:

> What emotivism asserts is in central part that there are and can be *no* valid rational justification for any claims that objective and impersonal moral standards exist and hence that there are no such standards. Its claim is of the same order as the claim that it is true of all cultures whatsoever that they lack witches. Purported witches there may be, but real witches there cannot be, for there are none. So emotivism holds that purported rational justifications there may be, but real rational justifications there cannot have been, for there are none.
>
> Emotivism thus rests upon the claim that every attempt, whether past or present, to provide a rational justification for an objective morality has in fact failed . . .

How has this come about? Through the fragmentation of a once coherent moral tradition, says MacIntyre, a tradition which held together the different bits and pieces, the insights, the embedded values, the isolated sections of rationality, whose separation now contributes to our present confusion.

There can be no simple return to an unmodified Christian Aristotelianism, which MacIntyre sees as the matrix from which, at least in the Western world, all else has developed. But at least we can recover a teleological approach to ethics, a searching for the good life, a sense that there are indeed goals in being human which are not purely private or idiosyncratic. Just as a variety of human activities, whether science or music or art, generate their own excellences, and require certain sorts of virtue if they are to be pursued successfully, so there are excellences which belong to life itself, and which belong to the communities in which that life must be lived.

Hence the importance of the classic moral tradition. We wholly misunderstand it if we think of it as a set of rules for slavish obedience. The essence of this tradition is that it centres on the search for the good life and the virtues needed to sustain it. It is thus open to the future, and open in the ways it is brought to bear on the actual complexities of life. There is no possibility of spelling out the good life in some formula from which appropriate behaviour can then be read off. The *search* for it is an essential part of living it. But the living of it in turn creates the kind of environment which makes the exercise of virtue possible. And in that kind of environment it is easier to see what ought to be done.

I find MacIntyre's thoughts, if I have interpreted them correctly, resonating with what, twenty years ago, I was trying, very fumblingly, to say about moral discovery. This is my excuse for quoting him alone among modern moral philosophers. I am not aware that he has much sympathy for natural law, but I suspect that among these themes there is room for what one might call natural wisdom, a wisdom rooted in empirical realities, yet not bound by them, a wisdom conscious of its history and made, by an awareness of its own historical conditioning, cautiously responsive to the possibilities of change.

Tradition can be an off-putting word. But in its best sense surely all it means is the sum of our discoveries. A developing ethical tradition centering on the search for the good life, taking seriously questions about human purpose, learning from human mistakes, and constantly open to challenge by those with a transcendent perspective, seems a good basis for the kind of natural wisdom I have in mind.

It will, I hope, be one of the achievements of this centre, to build up a body of such received wisdom. It has been my experience in many years of discussion on intractable problems in medical ethics, that both secular and Christian currents can to a very large extent flow together in contributing to this wisdom. That is why this centre is not just of interest to Christians.

There are times when Christian insight, say into the role of suffering in life, or the significance of death, may differ sharply from the received wisdom of secular society. A Christian centre has a duty to point out those differences. But there is not, I believe, a specifically Christian view of the human status of a fertilized ovum, or of the scientific value of certain kinds of research, or of the relative importance of different types of medical treatment, and I do not see how there could be.

What Christians can most characteristically provide is the motive power to go on searching for the best in the widest human context; the staying power to stick with the quest whatever the difficulties and sufferings and disappointments on the way; and the power of self-knowledge to prick the bubble of pride and to remind ourselves that we are human beings, not God. Ultimately Christians want to make claims about Christ in whom are hidden all the treasures of God's wisdom and knowledge. But pen-ultimately, and that is where we are now, we have patiently to learn wisdom alongside all those who share our desire for it.

19
Constancy and Change

Article published in The Times *under the title 'Dangers of Simplifying Morality'. It was written as a comment on a lecture by the Bishop of London entitled 'The Tyranny of Subjectivism'.*
3 October 1987

THE BISHOP OF London has diagnosed the main ill of Western civilization as what he calls 'the tyranny of subjectivism'. It is an attractive diagnosis, though not without its difficulties. Alastair MacIntyre in his seminal book *After Virtue* (Duckworth 1984) preferred the term 'emotivism', which lacks some of 'subjectivism's' misleading philosophical overtones. Either way the main point seems to be that when a once coherent moral tradition is broken up by attacks from within and without, what remain are fragmentary and unrelated moral insights, resting in the last resort on mere opinion or individual choice. The result – moral uncertainty, chaos, and in the end tyranny.

So far so good. But how to put Humpty-Dumpty together again? How are we to overcome the seductions of emotivism, and restore our civilization's soul? The Bishop in calling for a return to moral absolutes, and for the recognition of 'an authority over and above man', sees such absolutes as 'embodied in the very nature of reality as created by God'. He looks for laws which are 'God-given and reflect the nature of man and society as created by God'. He finds the basis of these affirmations in what he calls 'Scriptural Christianity' and the ancient tradition of natural law. And he identifies the main division in the contemporary Church as between those who accept this kind of moral authority and those who have succumbed to passing intellectual fashions.

Leaving aside the element of hyperbole in this description of his opponents, and ignoring for the moment the question whether these are the only alternatives, one can see that his cure, like his diagnosis, has its attractions. It will ring bells for many who suspect that Christianity in this country has lost its nerve.

But will it do? And in particular is it possible to specify God-given laws which 'reflect the nature of man and society as created by God' anything like as specifically and precisely as the Bishop clearly wants? He is surely right to claim that there are broad moral principles which have their roots in Scripture, and which can also be vindicated by an appeal to rational understanding. Most people would acknowledge the value of persons and the need for human community. The command to love our neighbour carries huge moral weight even among those who see no point in loving God. There *is* an authority over and above man, and Christians have good reason to believe in moral absolutes.

But falling under these general principles there is a bewildering variety of moral practices and value judgements, on which both Scripture and natural law speak with divided voices, and which often span precisely those fields in which the most difficult decisions have to be made. In fact one of the reasons why the appeal to moral absolutes needs to be distinguished carefully from moral absolutism as this is commonly understood, is that between general principles and precise prescriptions there may lie whole areas of disputed interpretation, empirical uncertainty and differing personal experience, which muddy and divert what might otherwise seem to have been a simple deductive path. Belief in moral absolutes does not necessarily lead to clear and unequivocal answers.

There is a further difficulty in what the Bishop says, in the very idea of 'the nature of man and society as created by God'. Are we to assume that this is something given once for all, fixed in a particular period of history, and therefore unchanging and unchangeable, not only in general terms but in detail? To accept that there are certain human constants, central among them the need and the capacity for love, does not preclude the possibility that another constant of human nature may be its capacity for change, growth and development. In fact the major difference between so-called traditionalists and so-called liberals lies just here. It is not that one is faithful to God-given revelation while the other falls victim to mere fashion, but that there are deep differences in belief about what kind of creation it is that God has made and what he is doing in it. For one the notion that human nature is created by God fixes attention on its givenness. For the other creation is a continuous process, an open-ended adventure set within the freedom given by God which allows the created order to discover its potentialities.

Both types of belief can claim to be rooted in Scripture. Static views about the 'essence' of human nature owe more to Greece than to Israel.

And the perception that nature itself is a flux of change and development is not merely some recent intellectual fancy that will pass, but one aspect of an irreversible shift in human consciousness.

The search for moral guidance in such a world is admittedly complex, but absolutism and emotivism are not the only alternatives. Moral insights are neither merely given nor merely invented. In many fields of human life they have to be won painfully, by reflection on Scripture, by attention to tradition, by absorption of the best available knowledge, by a process of trial and error, and by the exercise of creative imagination. Progress may be fitful and erratic, and even at the best of times moral traditions remain incomplete and open to correction. But the answer to moral uncertainty does not have to be unassailable conviction in matters where no certainty is actually possible. The answer must lie in convictions which are reliable enough and realistic enough for the task in hand – no more, no less.

20
A Basis for Medical Ethics

Sermon preached in St Mary's, Scarborough, at the Annual Meeting of the British Medical Association
22 June 1986

IT IS A coincidence that our lessons this evening should have included the Ten Commandments. They were simply the set lessons for today's evensong. But it is a good coincidence because the Commandments remind us of our moral roots. They are a foundation stone of Jewish and Christian civilization. For thousands of years they have been regarded as the very heart of biblical morality. And so for a profession which often finds itself at the sharp end of our society's moral dilemmas, the message that morality has a firm basis in God's Commandments could be both encouraging and important.

The doctors among you don't need me to remind you of the appalling moral choices you sometimes have to make. It is not for nothing that medical ethics has become a growth subject, though I notice that writings on the subject from within the profession often draw only a very thin line between ethics and etiquette. There is a potential difference between things which are professionally appropriate and things which are morally right, and it is a difference which in some circumstances may have to be watched.

But in general it is true, is it not, that the medical profession has become burdened with more and more people's insoluble personal problems, and more and more decisions of principle which may have wide social repercussions. This is partly the consequence of your own successes. New techniques create new moral choices. In part you are trapped in the confusions of a society which is no longer sure of its own moral basis, and so tries to push its decisions off onto convenient scapegoats.

A recent writer tried to imagine the kind of letters which might be published in *The Times* after a leading article deploring the decline in moral standards, with the usual references to violence, drugs, divorce, abortions and so forth. Some letters would dispute the facts – what was the data base for the statistics? Some would question whether the facts, if agreed, represent a moral decline at all. Isn't it healthier that people should make their own choices, at least on matters which affect only themselves, rather than be restrained by fear of punishment or social disapproval? Others might go further and point to the shortcomings of a social system which encourages escape or violent anti-social responses, as the only way in which the relatively deprived can express themselves. A philosopher might criticize all the previous letters by pointing out that the very notion of moral decline is incoherent since moral attitudes are irredeemably subjective and relate only to particular cultures or sub-cultures. *The Times* then rounds off the whole correspondence by saying that there is obviously a need for more research – or if a different leader-writer is in charge, by blaming the Church for 'its deafening silence', and complaining that the Ten Commandments are no longer read frequently enough.

We live in an age of moral confusion in which we disagree not just about our moral choices, but about the basis of our moral diagnosis and the very concepts in which we try to tackle it.

And the Ten Commandments? There is some sharp truth in the cartoon which showed Moses receiving the stone tablets and saying to the Lord, 'You know Lord, I think they'd go down better if we called them voluntary guidelines.'

Where then, in our confused society, can we find our moral roots, and the kind of moral guidance we need so desperately? For those standing in the biblical tradition the answers may at first seem easy. I suspect, though, that many do not realize the sheer difficulty of applying this tradition with integrity to the problems of our very different society. To take only one example, the history of responses to the command, 'Thou shalt not kill', is enough to fill whole libraries. A doctor may have profound respect for human life in all its forms, yet may constantly have to face dilemmas about whose life must be given priority, what quality of life must be safeguarded and so on. The Commandment may provide a background, a sense that there are moral demands on us that are not just the product of our own feelings and circumstances, but it does not provide answers.

For those who do not stand in the biblical tradition, and for whom the Ten Commandments belong only to a distant religious past, there may be no less of a desire to make valid moral choices, but the uncertainties may be even more crippling. What right have we, in the absence of an agreed moral basis, to force our moral insights onto other people?

I have been painting a depressing picture. But it is not all depressing. I believe in fact that there *are* some moral roots in our society, roots from which we can draw nourishment, roots which go back to our religious heritage, but have survived in people who would no longer class themselves as religious. Such roots can therefore be used to sustain moral decisions right across the spectrum of our society. And that is important for a profession which has to serve everybody, irrespective of belief. Given time I believe one could trace them back to that love of God and love of our neighbour which summarize the biblical moral tradition. But rather than try to do that, let me spell out briefly, and in more modern language, what I believe these moral roots are.

I see two basic values, and two attitudes of mind which may help us find our bearings. The two basic values are respect for persons, and respect for the quality of human inter-relatedness. And the two attitudes of mind are wonder, and the readiness to admit ignorance.

Respect for persons seems obvious, and I need not dwell on it. But it is worth pointing out that it is not obvious in all circumstances and in all cultures. Having just returned from a visit to the USSR I am impressed by the extent to which, in that kind of society, ideology is often felt to be more important than actual people. It is a strain which is not entirely foreign to our own society, which is why the basic value has to be asserted again and again. People matter more than things. People matter more than ideas and systems. And this is why systems exist for people, and not people for systems.

But then we also have to respect the quality of relationships between people. And this balances the individualism inherent in what I have just been saying about people mattering. We exist not just for ourselves but for each other. And that means that decisions about ourselves have to include this extra dimension of sensitivity towards our common life.

I have often noticed how in medical ethics one of the most difficult problems is how to get this balance right; the balance between the entirely proper and inevitable concern for the individual need directly confronting us, and the wider implications of whatever we decide to do for all those other people whose needs may be no less real but are not our immediate concern. Decisions always have an individual dimension and a social dimension, and this is why the two values of individual worth and human inter-relatedness always have to be held together. An abortion, for instance, may appear to be an individual decision.

But what is it doing to the family? What are its wider social implications as part of the gradual erosion of feeling in a crucial area of human responsibility?

This is perhaps where our two attitudes of mind may help us – I have called them wonder, and the admission of ignorance.

We have one of those popular posters stuck up at home, with a picture of the Grand Canyon and the words, 'To wonder is to begin to understand'. To wonder is also to begin to worship. And in terms of our respect for people, surely wonder is the beginning of all true care.

A sense of awe and wonder about the world we live in, wonder at the mystery of living things, awe in face of the mystery of human personality from its almost indistinguishable beginnings to its full flowering, this surely ought to be part of any normal human sensitivity. And it is especially crucial in those whose caring role has to be combined with some very sharp analysis of what makes people actually tick. When we have gone through all the explanations, when we think we know, say, what an embryo is in biological terms, there still has to be a sense of awe at something so intimately bound up with the origins of human life.

But with this there has to go an admission of ignorance, an ignorance which undermines all dogmatic assertions that this or that policy is indubitably right. If wonder is the first step towards understanding, humility is the first step in moral maturity. And this is where a reminder of religious perspectives is important. We are not gods. We see only part of the picture. We are inherently fallible. And the very confusions and uncertainty of our day can remind us of that fallibility.

But to know that one is fallible under God is very different from just being a muddled human being. If at times we feel we are groping in the dark and being given responsibilities too great for us, we can also know that the God who sees and knows us in our weakness, forgives and restores us in his love. It thus becomes possible to make the decisions which have to be made, without complacency and without constant anxiety, because the God who gives us his law on Sinai, is also the God of love and forgiveness who has visited and redeemed his people.

21
The Concept of 'Person' in Medical Ethics

The Ludwig Mond Lecture delivered in the University of Manchester
24 February 1988

'TWO MILLION BABIES have been murdered since abortion became legal.'

'Embryo research entails experimenting on human beings who cannot give their consent.'

'His head injuries reduced him to the state of a vegetable.'

'In some severely disabled people the quality of life is negligible.'

'Compulsory castration for sexual offences would be an assault on human personality.'

These are all fairly familiar statements of the kind met in popular writings, and they all presuppose views about the nature and meaning of human life, and what it is to be a person. They are not neutral; ethical judgements are inherent in the kind of language used. Words such as 'babies' and 'vegetable' are heavily value-laden. To describe abortion as 'murdering babies' is already to have judged it as immoral.

It is thus important to look critically at the language used to describe human life, and especially at the term which encapsulates the highest moral claims – the word 'person'. In its present meaning it is a comparatively modern word with deep roots in Christian theology. Nowadays it is a familiar word in ethics, but it is by no means a simple one. I shall try to describe its use in medical ethics, therefore, by spelling out five approaches to the concept, followed by five questions arising out of them. It is not my intention actually to try to resolve any particular ethical dilemmas, but rather to show how important it is to maintain a rich and comprehensive understanding of what persons are.

The first approach is scientific and reductionist. It is characteristic, at least of the so called 'hard' sciences, to try to reduce complex phenomena to simpler more comprehensible components. In science generally this has been an enormously successful strategy and even a phenomenon as inherently difficult to understand as 'thinking' can yield to it. Thus it is possible to break down thinking into such components as the processing of information, the recognition of patterns, the forecasting of consequences, the searching for options, the selection of optimum solutions and so forth. The more closely each of these can be defined, the greater the possibilities of reproducing it in a computer programme. The hope of creating artificial intelligence relies on the success of this process of breaking up the notion of intelligence into reproducible elements.

This approach to persons leads inevitably to the question, Is there anything about them which cannot be analysed in this way? From a reductionist perspective it is possible to acknowledge that the qualities associated with personhood are unique in their range and depth but not different in kind from those possessed by other animals. It is reasonable, for instance, to describe some of the higher animals as thinking, having consciousness, even using language at a very primitive level, and exhibiting the flexibility of response characteristic of human beings. It can be argued from such comparisons that there is no reason to treat persons as anything other than individuals of the species homo sapiens.

The physiological basis of personality, on this view, lies in what a great physiologist called more than eighty years ago 'the integrative action of the nervous system'. Damage the central nervous system through drugs or surgery or accident and the integrated personality can be severely damaged, even destroyed.

I believe it is important to accept the validity of this picture as far as it goes. But as in all scientific accounts, and especially in this one, the question then has to be asked, whose picture is it? who is it who knows these things and who understands what it is to be a person in this reductionist way? Reductionism, indeed most scientific study, entails a process of abstraction from a very complex reality by a deliberate process of leaving out all that is subjective, and hence all that is most inwardly personal.

I am reminded of H. G. Wells's story of the invisible man. Having made himself invisible, he wore clothes and wrapped his face and hands in bandages in such a way that the outward shape of a man could still be seen. On one occasion, though, while passing a mirror without his face bandage in place, he recoiled in horror on seeing an empty void surmounting an otherwise visible body. In much the same way it is possible to recoil in horror from a universe in which all that is most deeply personal seems to have been reduced to nothingness, when the truth is that we are reacting to a picture of the universe created by our own process of abstraction. When the personal is systematically excluded from the process of investigation it is hardly surprising to find it missing from the final synthesis.

Reductionism only gives a partial picture because, inseparable from the objective description of human life, inseparable also from the objective analysis of human consciousness insofar as this is possible, there is the knowing subject, the observer, the I, whose presence is always implicit in any knowledge. This is why in our description of persons two languages are always needed: language about persons and language which expresses our experience of being persons. A professor whom I much revered for his scientific skills used to think that the gulf could be bridged by talking about brains thinking, deciding, experiencing, etc. But this was just confusion. People think; brains only react.

A second approach to the concept of persons is through dualism, the belief that there are two kinds of reality, mind and matter, soul and body, etc. and that these are irreducibly separate and distinct. This has been for many people one of the traditional ways of expressing the specialness of persons, and belief in the soul in particular may seem to be specifically religious. But this is not necessarily so. Dualism encounters many difficulties of which one of the most obvious is how these two quite separate realities are supposed to relate. How for instance do soul and body interact in the human person?

If we accept that humanity has evolved over long periods of time, must we specify a moment at which souls first appeared or were infused by God into what, up till then, had been simply animal bodies? Similar questions arise concerning the development of human individuals, and closer attention to the earliest stages of embryonic development have led to insuperable problems in the attempt to specify a particular moment at which the embryo might become ensouled.

Biblical scholars have, on the whole, not favoured this kind of dualism. Humanity is made from the dust of the earth into which God has breathed life, and the two elements are not to be separated out as two distinct entities. It is preferable to think in terms of a single reality with both inner and outer aspects. We are embodied spirits and the Bible gives no ground for thinking that the real self can exist outside some kind of bodilyness, either here or hereafter. It seems best, therefore, to interpret traditional language about the soul as referring to the self-awareness of persons, a self-awareness which contains within itself further possibilities of expansion through the awareness of God.

The third approach to persons is to see them as a locus of moral attributes and a source of values. To recognize an organism as a person entails valuing it, and this valuation seems to be inseparable from the act of recognition. Those who, for whatever reason, wish systematically to degrade, torture and annihilate other human beings have first to depersonalize them. This is all too familiar as a modern phenomenon in totalitarian states, but it has a long history. Aristotle, we read, 'viewed some men as born to be savages, and others as destined by nature to be slaves, whom he further regards as living machines, and women, apparently in all seriousness, as nature's failures in the attempt to produce men'.

So the practical question is always, who are we going to admit to the club? Growth in moral sensitivity entails widening the circle of those who are perceived to have value in themselves. When Kant discerned that we ought to treat persons as ends rather than as means, he was asserting that intrinsic value belongs to persons as such. But why do we confine this acknowledgement of value to human persons? Current concern about the value of all life, and how far we ought to respect sub-human life because it too is capable of pursuing its own ends, may indicate that we are entering a further stage in the widening of sensibilities.

Our valuation of persons includes not just what they are, but what they may become. Part of what it is possible to perceive in persons is a range of possibilities as yet unfulfilled. Christians have a particular reason for making this claim on the basis of the doctrine of the incarnation. If the humanity of Christ is capable of bearing the image of the divine then in some lesser sense our own humanity must also be capable of some kind of divinization. But there are more ordinary human experiences such as artistic creativity, the exercise of freedom, and the endless process of self-discovery, which likewise point to the open-endedness of our existence as persons. These provide yet further reasons for believing that the concept 'person' cannot ultimately be reduced to scientific categories.

A fourth approach to the concept highlights its social dimension. Persons exist only in relation to one another. 'I need you in order to be myself', wrote John Macmurray. This is certainly true of babies. It is also certainly true of lovers. It is almost certainly true of most people for most of the time. Indeed it is so familiar a truth that I do not intend to elaborate it other than by noting that it may be particularly significant as we think about medical ethics, because so much of medicine has tended to focus on the individual patient. What is done to a person or for a person cannot be separated from that person's entailment with other persons. 'No man is an island. . . .'

The fifth and final approach is theological. Here we meet a curious and little known fact, namely that the word which up till then had been fairly insignificant, was given a new range of meaning through the work of the early Christian theologians on the doctrine of the Trinity. Their aim was to describe both the unity and the distinctness of different apprehensions of God. The Greek Fathers used two terms to express the distinctness, *hypostasis* and *prosopon*. *Hypostasis* literally means 'standing underneath', 'substance', and hence 'basic reality'. *Prosopon* is the word for face or appearance, that through which we relate with one another. Its Latin equivalent is *persona*, the mask through which an actor speaks. The identification of this *prosopon* or *persona* with basic reality, especially reality as encountered in God, was the decisive step in giving the word its supreme significance. It led on naturally to identifying God as personal, and then to understanding human personhood in terms both of our relationship with God and our relationship with each other, just as God is three persons in one.

This is a ridiculously compressed version of a very long story. But it is possible to see in the light of it how Christian theology has an answer to questions about human identity. My identity as a person rests on more than the fact that I have a nervous system which can integrate a wide variety of inputs and responses. Nor is it simply the point of intersection of a large number of social interactions, dependent though I am on other people for being myself. My identity in Christian terms rests ultimately on my relationship with God and the fact that I am chosen, called and enabled to be myself by God. 'I am what I am' in God, and the fact that that description echoes God's self-description to Moses is no coincidence.

Such an affirmation of identity in terms of a transcendent reference point outside the self is given sacramental expression for Christians in baptism, and again it is no coincidence that this is intimately bound up with the giving of a new name. The irreducibility and open-endedness of the human person is undergirded theologically by the concept of relationship with God in which one dimension of personhood is, as it were, open to the infinite depths of God. The other dimension of personhood is rooted in earth, in the physical world, in our status as creatures bound by physical limitations and subject to physical laws. A person so understood also has to be described in relational terms. Just as baptism affirms our identity, so communion affirms our relationships both with God and with each other. 'Human personhood', writes Kallistos Ware, 'like the personhood of God, is exchange, self-giving, reciprocity. As a person I am what I am only in relation to other persons . . .' (*Persons and Personality*, ed. Arthur Peacocke and Grant Gillett, Blackwell 1987, p. 206).

This enormously rich theological concept gathers up and holds together many insights into the nature of persons which may be found isolated from one another or in fragmentary form elsewhere. It forms the basis for the five questions which constitute the second half of this paper, and which I believe have a particular relevance to certain problems in medical ethics. The questions are not equally applicable in every circumstance, nor do answers to them necessarily point to the same practical conclusions. Nor are these the only questions which need to be asked. All I would claim for them is that they are a useful checklist of the sort of questions which need to be asked when considering what it is, or is not, proper to do to those who have a claim to be persons.

1. Given that persons in their relation to each other and to God are a primary locus of value, does an organism whose value is being considered possess an appropriate physical basis for the presence or development of personhood?

The question implies that there has to be a minimum physical basis if an organism is to count as a person. What this physical basis has to be is, of course, a matter of dispute and in practice the lines are drawn in different places in different circumstances. Thus the anencephalic child, born without a brain, lacks the basis for any development of personal life as normally understood, even though such a child outwardly looks like a person and may attract personal feelings in others. At the other end of the scale, the patient who has suffered brain death is now normally counted as dead, even though other parts of the body may continue to function for a considerable time. Choices are particularly difficult when the brain stem survives and the body is thus capable of breathing independently while at the same time, as far as one can tell, all conscious life seems to be extinguished. Here again the way the body is perceived by those with personal attachments has to be set against the physical evidence that the basis for personal life on this earth no longer exists.

Attitudes towards very severe disablement are likely to be changed significantly by the astonishing achievement of Christopher Nolan in writing a prize-winning novel against huge physical odds. I also recall the case, some twenty years ago, of a patient who was totally paralysed except for one big toe and who managed to develop a very warm relationship with nursing staff solely through movements in that one toe. Disablement which involves substantial brain damage poses different problems. We do not really know how much active brain is required for rudimentary developments of personal life to take place, and this is why it is as well to be cautious.

The fact that lines are drawn in different places for different purposes is most obvious in foetal development. Should we ascribe the full value of personhood to a developing human life at the stage when it is capable of independent existence, or when its nervous system begins to develop, or at around fourteen days when individuation begins to occur, or at conception when a unique genetic inheritance is laid down? All choices are to some extent arbitrary and it would help rational discussion if this element of arbitrariness were to be admitted.

2. What actions, treatments or invasive techniques will best allow full personal responsible life to develop?

The main strength of arguments against abortion and embryo research lie in this question. The assumption behind it is that personal life entails a process of development and therefore it is proper to value the personal possibilities present even in the earliest stages of life. The fertilized ovum is clearly not a person in the sense of possessing personal attributes. It is, however, a bundle of possibilities whose history is continuous with the history of the person who, given the right conditions, will one day develop from it. There are grounds, therefore, for ascribing value even to the newly fertilized ovum.

It is possible to turn this argument on its head, however, and argue that the slow growth of personality poses the question whether it is ever possible to specify a sharp dividing line between organisms with or without full personal value. A truer way of specifying value might be in terms of a sliding scale, on which it might then make sense to specify particular points for particular purposes, e.g. the fourteen days from conception recommended in the Warnock report. The ascription of a certain degree of value might then have to be weighed against the seriousness of whatever interference was proposed.

The idea of development implied by this question also has relevance to the way in which medical treatment is understood and accepted by those undergoing it. Illness may provide opportunities for personal growth, but a patient left in ignorance or treated as merely passive lacks this opportunity. This is one reason why the obtaining of consent is such an important part of good medical practice. It is not just that doctors need to be protected by enlisting patients on their side, but that the patients themselves cannot use their experience constructively unless in some measure they know and approve of what is being done to them.

With some illnesses and some invasive techniques, of course, this is impossible. Drastic surgery, say through the removal of a brain tumour, may have a clear moral justification in liberating a person once more to be themselves. The frequently expressed moral doubts about leucotomy relate to the fact that it may change personality in unpredictable ways. Similar problems could arise in the use of chemical agents for the fine tuning of behaviour. Treatments of this kind raise the question whether there is a core of personality which ought not to be violated.

Perhaps a better way of approaching such a question is by asking how far what is done to a person can be integrated meaningfully into his or her personal history. A general distinction which might prove useful is that what is known, and accepted, and lived through, can build up a personality, whereas what is merely done to a person who remains passive, so far from aiding the development of personal life, may threaten it.

3. What effects are medical actions, treatments etc. likely to have on the relationships between persons?

There is a strong tendency in medicine to treat patients as isolated individuals. This has not always been so, nor is it entirely true today. Family medicine lost ground in the great era of scientific advance, but the wisdom of seeing patients as standing within a network of relationships is now being recovered.

It is important to ask, for instance, what effect illness and death have on the relatives of those affected. Nor is it just family relationships which are important. There are complex interactions between patients in the same ward, and between patients and nurses. This awareness that each person must be considered within a social context is going to be particularly important in coping with AIDS, where diagnosis has immediate social implications. Suicide is another well known example of an action which involves many more people than the person actually committing it. The legacy of guilt left by suicide is one of the reasons for regarding it as morally wrong.

The same is true, though in a different way, of euthanasia. This is frequently justified on the grounds that everybody has a right to do what they want with their own life. The argument ignores the fact that the concept of 'one's own life' is an abstraction. There is no way of avoiding one life touching another, one person's actions putting pressure on another, whether by inducing guilt or by prompting the question, 'Would I really be doing my family a service by having myself put away?'

4. What are the likely effects of our actions on general perceptions of the value of persons?

This is an extension of the previous question to society at large. Our actions not only affect those in our immediate circle but contribute to assumptions about what is generally accepted in our society. New medical techniques may induce slow changes in attitudes as they become more familiar. Transplant surgery is an obvious example. One of its side effects has been to change many people's attitudes towards their own bodies. Not many years ago it was hard for most people to think of different parts of their own bodies as having in some measure a separate life of their own. Transplant surgery has also created new possibilities of coming to terms with the tragedy of early death, particularly accidental death, and there are many people who have found comfort in the idea that such a death has not been entirely useless.

On the other hand it could be said that widespread abortion may well have changed public attitudes towards the sacredness of life in a less desirable direction, and that euthanasia could do so even more. Individuals may have good personal reasons either for wanting an abortion or for wanting euthanasia, but in weighing the ethical pros and cons one of the factors to be considered ought to be the long-term effect on society's perceptions of a whole series of such actions. There is a mutual interaction between what we do, the kind of society we help to create, and its reflection back to us of what is possible, desirable and permissible. This can develop into a vicious circle of gradually coarsening sensibilities unless we stake out some limits.

The proposal to use foetal brain tissue in the treatment of Parkinson's Disease is a particularly difficult example in which natural revulsion and the possible gains for many tragically disabled people both make strong appeal. It seems to be the kind of case in which a firm limit would have to be set to ensure that no abortion could be performed simply to secure foetal tissue.

5. What are the implications of the limitations of our knowledge of persons?

Here we begin to trespass on religious ground. Persons are ultimately mysterious, not just because our knowledge of them is limited as a matter of fact, but because it is essentially limited by that open-endedness which is the essence of personhood. 'We do not know what we shall be.' A recollection of religious perspectives can remind us of the need to be cautious. Doctors maybe do not need many reminders of human ignorance; their daily work makes them all too conscious of it. It is the planners of possible human futures who need it most.

A distinguished moral theologian has recently described what he calls the SLOOP factor. The term comes from architects who frequently find what they label as 'space left over on plan'. They do it by accident. The moralist should do it on purpose. With persons there is always a SLOOP factor because personality has its ultimate roots in the mystery of God.

PART IV

MORAL ISSUES

22
Innocence

Sermon preached in York Minster
Christmas Day 1987

'This will be a sign for you; you will find a babe wrapped in swaddling clothes and lying in a manger' (Luke 2.12).

THE 'SIGN' IS the sign of a new beginning; a new hope; a new light shining in the darkness; the dawning of a new day in the long story of God's dealing with mankind; a new outpouring of love; and all this weight of expectation and longing carried in a new life – 'a babe wrapped in swaddling clothes and lying in a manger'.

The story of Bethlehem has endless power because it signifies all these things – and more. But this morning I want to concentrate on just one theme, a theme we especially associate with a new-born baby – innocence.

It is a particularly poignant theme at Christmas time because so much of the traditional imagery of Christmas seems to express a kind of nostalgia for lost innocence. The virgin snow, and the Virgin mother. Wonderfully jolly coachmen from some never-never land of merrie England. Animals straight out of Walt Disney. Dear old Santa Claus with nothing more menacing to say than Ho! Ho! Ho! Shepherds and wise men who are really children dressed up in rugs and cardboard crowns. Memories of Christmas past when children's eyes were shining with excitement, when it always snowed on Christmas Day, and before turkeys looked like frozen footballs wrapped in plastic.

Unforgivable nostalgia; but buried within it, I suspect, a search for lost innocence, for the world as it might have been before it all became so complicated, and murky, so full of tragedy, so torn apart by division, so unfair, so threatening, so worldly-wise.

Innocence is not a virtue which is highly regarded these days, except in children. We rightly feel anger and disgust at the abuse of children, at the exploitation and destruction of innocence in the ways which have been so vividly retailed to us in the press in recent months. I hope we also feel dismay at the pertness and knowingness of some children who are pushed into adult ways of thinking and behaving all too soon. There *is* an innocence of childhood which needs to be safeguarded and cherished. And Christmas is a good time to reaffirm it.

But is there also an innocence of adulthood? We sing in our carols about the spotless Virgin and the sinless child. It is harder to know what to make of the innocence of Jesus the man.

It certainly was not the same as ignorance. Nor was it naivety. Nor was it the kind of innocence which has to be sheltered, kept out of conflict, untouched by pain and sorrow, unconscious of the huge weight of the world's evil. On the contrary it was the very weight of the world's evil which somehow, mysteriously, he bore.

We see, rather, a kind of fierce integrity, an innocent straightforward relationship with God, an uncluttered moral insight, what the Bible calls 'purity of heart'. And that was how he could go straight to the hearts of those who needed him. The innocent eye saw through them, saw beyond the silliness of lost sheep, beyond the anxious doubts of a father with an epileptic son, beyond the impetuousness of poor well-meaning Peter, to the child within.

'Innocent vision' is not the whole truth about Jesus. It ignores the depths of wisdom and subtlety, the breadth of his humanity, the heights of his relationship with God. But it is part of the truth about him. And it is a truth I am emphasizing this morning, not only because it is Christmas, but because our age seems especially in need of it.

Think of the quite extraordinary deviousness of much of what goes on. We have welcomed this month the Reagan-Gorbachev summit and the INF agreement: a wonderful Christmas present. But the inner reality of it is a horrendous mixture of bluff and double bluff, suspicion, cautiousness, compromise, checks and counter-checks, brinkmanship, and hopes and fears for the future. Please God it will work, and lead to greater trust and a more stable peace. But at the moment the agreement, and the huge effort needed to reach it, stand as monuments to the appalling complexity of international politics. There is very little room for innocence round the negotiating table.

Or think of the deviousness of some personal relationships. Just what did the manager mean in asking after my health when all he ever says is 'Good Morning'? Do I look ill? Have I been making a mess of things? Is this the first move in a plan to get rid of me? Or promote me? Or make advances? The complications flowing from a single remark can be endless.

Or think of the picture of human deviousness and casual sin fed to us through the media. We constantly have to be titillated by scandals. In the world of sit.coms. and chat shows it seems to be assumed that the morals of Hampstead set the pace for all the rest of us. We are bombarded by images of a cynical society where innocence is a faintly ludicrous handicap.

And yet, and yet . . . that can't be all. We are haunted by the image of a child for whom the angels sang. We cannot escape the challenge of a life which was transparent to God. We cannot turn our backs on the truth that in all the mess and confusion and frightening complexity of life, the love which came down at Christmas still points us to the central purpose and meaning of it.

The innocent eye cannot be recovered simply by wishing for it. But we can go in heart and mind to see the babe lying in a manger. We can look to him whose innocence of vision can begin to take hold of ours, who can restore to life a new sanity, direction and strength.

When the shepherds came to Bethlehem they wondered and worshipped. So, please God, shall we.

23
Loyalty

Hulsean sermon preached to the University of Cambridge
24 January 1988

'And Ruth said to Naomi, Intreat me not to leave thee, or to return from
  following after thee: for whither thou goest I will go; and where thou
lodgest I will lodge: thy people shall be my people, and thy God my God:
where thou diest I will die, and there will I be buried: the Lord do so to
me and more also, if ought but death part thee and me' (Ruth 1.16-17).

THIS IS MORE than great poetry. It sets out a moral conviction to which
most of us, I imagine, instinctively respond. Loyalty of this order is
impressive, admirable, remarkable especially when offered to a
mother-in-law, but above all noble. It has a touch of quality about it.
No matter that the words are words of a penniless foreigner. They
presuppose an exalted view of human relationships. This is the stuff of
which great civilizations are made.

I remembered them last week when visiting the Age of Chivalry
exhibition in London. Here was an elaborate system of loyalties
embracing all the orders of society, and reaching up to the Crown, and
beyond the Crown to God. The very word 'Chivalry' to describe a
period of history brings out something of its moral quality, and it is
hard not to be captured by the romance of it. Yet hovering in the wings
were the divided loyalties which led to civil war; and beyond them the
figure of Don Quixote, warning us how quickly noble visions and
exalted purposes can turn into empty rhetoric.

At the turn of this century the philosopher Josiah Royce tried to
rehabilitate loyalty as the centrepiece of a total system of values. He
saw it as the link between public and private morality, as providing the
essential structure of defined relationships within which individuals
can explore their range of freedom without trespassing on the freedom
of others. Society, in his view, is a web of loyalties which both restrain
and nourish us, loyalties given and received.

Josiah Royce is not much remembered these days. Nor is loyalty the
most obvious of virtues to spring to mind when thinking about the

roots of morality. Ruth's declaration to Naomi still has power to stir our imaginations. But for many people loyalty as a virtue by itself, let alone the key virtue, has become problematic. This is why I believe it is worth taking a closer look at it, particularly at a time when we are conscious of difficulties about the meaning and scope of loyalty in our own society. I am not just thinking of the Official Secrets Act, but of much of our institutional life, universities and Church of England included. And I believe loyalty is a proper subject for a Hulsean Sermon, because it raises just those questions about the rootedness of morality in belief which John Hulse would have approved.

What has happened to make loyalty seem problematic? In part, of course, it is the sheer multiplicity of loyalties which claim our attention in a complex society. We are conscious of inhabiting too many competing worlds. Loyalties can become stretched, weakened, torn, trivialized.

But this cannot be the whole story. Divided loyalties are not a new phenomenon. Sophocles explored them in unsurpassed depth in *Antigone*, at the very time perhaps when some unknown author was writing the story of Ruth.

A civilization with *Antigone* in its bloodstream has constant reminders of the conflicts of loyalty between the individual and the state, between youth and age, men and women, the claims of today and the claims of the past, between human laws and the laws of God.

All these conflicts presuppose, however, that the language of loyalty is common currency. And it is doubts on this level which seem to be peculiar to our age.

There has been a moral shift. Public affairs are largely governed by utilitarianism, and loyalty does not stand high as a utilitarian value. But allied with the change in moral perception there have been far-reaching social changes. Loyalty is a useful quality in a highly structured society with fixed roles and relationships and permanent institutional constraints. In such a society human identity tends to be defined in terms of these fixed structures. It was said of St Augustine's sacramental theology that it created a principle of stability and security which 'gave the Christian a firm hold on immediate immutables and tangible fixities while Roman civilization crumbled . . . A man's faith, a man's baptism, a man's priest, a man's wife and family, were his for ever, and nothing could take them away. These were a bond of unity, for unity demands stability, between man and man, between generation and generation, and were an essential part of the framework on which Christian civilization was built' (Bernard Leeming, *Principles of Sacramental Theology*, Longmans 1963, p. 233).

But this points to the kind of society which in the modern period has been fast disappearing. It is not so much that we are forgetting the importance of roles and structures and institutions and the tangible fixities which sacramental life was intended to represent. Our age has relegated them to second place. Instead of defining personal life such rigidities seem, in modern perceptions, more likely to constrict it. The search has been going on for something behind the roles, something no longer half-crushed by structures and institutions, something more authentic, more basic, more personally real. The moral focus has shifted from loyalty to autonomous freedom.

One way in which this is reflected is in the language of human rights. Rights, says the UN Declaration, pertain to individuals 'irrespective of race, colour or creed'. The implication is that all other differentiations, sex, social status, age, nationality, are equally irrelevant. And who would want to quarrel with that? But it is an interesting reflection of the extent to which the autonomous individual as a moral subject can now be abstracted from all those differentiations and relationships which in former times would have made him or her significant. Rights belong to the isolated self. Very often they are perceived, and show their usefulness, as rights *against* structures and institutions.

I am not for one moment denying the value of all this. We have gained hugely in our respect and care for individuals. Structures and institutions, even obligations of loyalty, can sometimes be suffocating.

In a small way the evidence in the latest edition of *Social Trends* about the number of couples who seem to want to live together and have their children without actually getting married, points to this same ideal of autonomy. I don't believe it is just tax advantages and fear of commitment. Bound up with it is a muddled feeling that not being married is somehow more authentic.

But the ideal of autonomous freedom also has its negative side. There have been losses as well as gains in changing attitudes towards social structures, and these are most obvious in the agonizings about personal identity which fill the literature of the twentieth century. Who am I if I don't belong anywhere? What does my life mean if I have no ultimate obligations? How can any choice be significant if I am simply choosing to please myself?

All the desperate insecurities which were once kept at bay by firm social structures come crowding back in. And we need no reminding how deep the reaction against them has been. A century of agonizing has led us paradoxically to a new moral censoriousness, new rigidities, loyalty elevated into fanaticism.

Four years ago the Christmas editorial of the *Economist* looked ahead in the light of other world movements to the recovery of Christian identity: 'It will not be an identity of ifs and buts and mutual understanding. It will be confident, born again, bloody-minded. Our descendants will look back with curiosity on our bizarre age, a brief by-way of western history, in which people did not believe much and, what little it was, were quite ready to allow that other people might think differently. God's house will still have many mansions and they will be full of some saints, countless sinners, and a good many soldiers drawn from both.' My postbag is depressingly full of letters from little Christian fascists who exactly fit this description.

I have tried to analyse very sketchily why I believe loyalty is a problematic virtue in our age, wistfully prized yet distrusted, easy both to undervalue and to overvalue. Let me now try to be constructive, to see what place loyalty might have in a society which has taken seriously the discovery of individual freedom. And I begin with an essay written by G. K. Chesterton, 'In Defence of Rash Vows'. He began by detailing the lengths to which some medieval Christians would go in order to demonstrate their devotion; remarkable and unnecessary feats like chaining two mountains together or walking to Jerusalem blindfolded. Why did they do it? Because in committing themselves to some absurd task they were making an appointment with themselves in the future. They were being loyal to what they believed they had it in themselves to do. Unlike our modern couples who believe that anything as binding as marriage might make their relationship inauthentic, they knew that the high moments of vision and commitment were what made them into full human beings. Chesterton went on: 'To be everlastingly passing through dangers which we know cannot scathe us, to be taking oaths which we know cannot bind us, to be defying enemies who we know cannot conquer us – this is the grinning tyranny of decadence which is called freedom.'

Loyalty and a true sense of identity, in other words, may prove to be inseparable. Psychologists make the same point when stressing the importance of promise-making and promise-keeping in the development of personality. They are part of what gives unity and coherence to a personality through time. Whatever our criticism of the forms which loyalty may have taken in ages now remote from us, we cannot dispense with it altogether.

But loyalty to what? The classic answer is loyalty to God as the fundamental element in all loyalty. 'You shall worship the Lord your God, and him only shall you serve.' Only God is great enough to receive the offering of a whole life. Lesser loyalties must exist as part of this greater loyalty. If they try to usurp its place, or to put themselves beyond criticism or the possibility of defection, they become corrupt and idolatrous. So, for example, loyalty to a nation is always subject to loyalty to God. Even loyalty within marriage is subject to loyalty to God.

But what about loyalty to an idea? or to some moral imperative? or to a belief about God himself? This is where in our modern world the roads diverge into fanaticism or autonomy. To identify our beliefs about God with God himself is the essence of fanaticism. The opposite error – to believe that it is in some way possible to stand over against God and criticize him from some independent standpoint, is the essence of the autonomous freedom which modern human beings think they have grasped for themselves.

It seems to me that to resolve this dilemma we have to start from the other end, not with our loyalty to God but with God's loyalty to us. This is where the Christian gospel starts, not with the needs of society, not with structures and hierarchies, not with individual aspirations however noble, but with an initiative of love. And every human initiative is, or ought to be, a response to that.

So human love is possible because God's love is actual, and we are loved before we learn to love. Human loyalty is possible because God's faithfulness never fails. We are trusted despite our betrayals. Judas is one of the twelve. Human commitment is possible because mercy and forgiveness embrace us on every side.

The struggle for autonomy, therefore, does not have to be against God but in God. And the deepest Christian wisdom about freedom is that we find it when we find ourselves as we were meant to be.

Is this just rhetoric? I do not think so. Our stability, our security, our identity are given to us. They rest in God's love for us. They transcend all the particular forms, structures, institutions, mediating influences, which convey them to us. And so we are free to be critical, free to stand over against these intermediaries as well as within them, because the fundamental relationship can *take* criticism, has taken criticism, mocking, scourging, death, without being broken.

Loyalty in such circumstances is not blind or fearful loyalty, but the loyalty of those who know that they are wanted, forgiven, accepted and loved. It is a free loyalty, freely given and freely received.

If this is what lies at the heart of the virtue I have been trying to describe, then what does it mean in terms of the lesser loyalties of every day life? One obvious implication, surely, is that loyalty has to be evoked before it can be expected, and that those who expect it can evoke it only by first displaying it themselves. From here it is but a short step back to questions about the sources of trust and generosity in ourselves, and in our society; and to thoughts about what our own lives, and the life of our society might become if those resources were strengthened.

Perhaps after all loyalty merely leads us on to something more basic still. It seems to be the kind of virtue which can only flourish where other deeper virtues have laid a stable foundation.

When Ruth set out to follow Naomi she knew nothing of the tremendous consequences of her act of loyalty. Nor did it seem a particularly exalted thing to do. She only knew she loved Naomi because she had first been loved by her. And from that everything else sprang. Ruth in the fulness of time begat David. And David in the fulness of time begat the Christ.

24
War and Peace

Sermon preached to the University of Essex
10 November 1985

'When Jesus drew near and saw the city he wept over it, saying, "Would that even today you knew the things that make for peace! But now they are hid from your eyes"' (Luke 19.41–2).

AND SO THE lament has gone on, for century after century. We know the message of peace. We share the longing for peace. But to know the things which make for peace seems beyond our human powers. Wars continue – nationalist wars, civil wars, guerrilla warfare – with escalating violence and brutality. It is easy to feel that nothing has improved in 2000 years. But this would be a mistake. What our century has seen, I believe, is a profound change in attitudes to war. Instead of regarding it as something really rather noble and glorious, huge numbers of people now regard it as, at best a tragedy, and at its worst an obscenity.

And the change is marked in the very title of this day – Remembrance Day. Not Victory Day. Not like Trafalgar Day or Guy Fawkes Day or even VE Day. A day to pause and remember the cost of war, its senseless waste, its ruined lives. This is an important thing to do, even for those who cannot remember the Second World War, let alone the First. The mood in which war is emotionally rejected must not be allowed to evaporate.

But this does not by itself bring us any closer to knowing 'the things that make for peace'. The problems were brought home to me very sharply by three successive visitors one day last week.

The first was a Ugandan bishop who described the vicious circle in which his country is caught. The civilian government is dependent on the army for its support. The army itself is out of control and a major source of murder, robbery and terrorism. The devastation of the economy means that there are no jobs for members of the army to go to, even if it could be reduced in strength. And as long as the army remains the effective power, the economy is not likely to recover.

There seems to be no point in the vicious circle where those who long for peace can take effective action. And this is true not only of Uganda, but of many other countries where militaristic regimes create the same insoluble problems.

My second visitor was a group of Ba'hais who came with a plan for world peace. Like all such plans produced by religiously well-meaning people it boiled down to saying that if only everybody would agree to work together, and maintain world standards of justice and devise world instruments of government, we could all live at peace with one another. Maybe. But the trouble about visions of world harmony is that they never include workable instructions about how to get there.

My third visitor was a very keen Christian working in a parish with another very keen Christian, both full of love and zeal and with gifts of the Spirit, and both incapable of staying in the same room with each other for more than five minutes, each accusing the other of being insecure, domineering and out to destroy them.

It was a depressing day. If the actual problems of our militarized world seem insoluble, if grandiose peace plans are unworkable, and if even Christians cannot live with one another in peace, what are we to do? Do we simply weep over Jerusalem and wait for its destruction?

When Jesus wept it was not in pessimism or despair. There was nothing fatalistic in it. He wept at people's failure to grasp the actual hope and life and peace held out to them by God. And this, it seems to me, is where Christian thinking about peace has to begin, with the determination never to give up praying and working and sacrificing for peace, in the belief that beyond all the appalling practical problems, all the mistakes and misunderstandings, and more enduring than all the evil that we are conscious of even in our own hearts, there is 'the peace of God which passes all understanding'. There is the promise that 'all shall be well. And all manner of thing shall be well' – to quote Lady Julian of Norwich. There is the gospel of the reconciliation of all things in Christ.

But this still leaves the question, what apart from praying do we actually do?

The so-called Peace Movements have one kind of answer. They channel longings for peace, the feelings of frustration at the slowness and uncertainty of many political processes, into active protest and practical proposals. The various nostrums, 'no first use', nuclear freeze, nuclear-free zones, general disarmament, outright pacifism, all have their attraction; and especially for Christians who feel that if the gospel is to mean anything in a dangerous world with a ridiculous number of arms, then there ought to be some simple policy on which all Christians could agree.

I do not wish to criticize such movements, which have an important part to play in our society. But I refer to them as 'so-called' Peace Movements because there is an unfortunate sense in which they have hijacked the word 'peace' as if it applied only to their particular policies. The implication is that those who do not agree with these policies are not really peacemakers but war-mongers in disguise.

This is not helpful. It creates unnecessary polarization. It feeds the roots of extremist politics. And it fosters the illusion that there are simple, right and unequivocally Christian answers to complex international problems. 'Every human problem has a solution', somebody once said, 'which is simple, neat – and wrong.'

The truth is that there are different beliefs about the best ways of creating and maintaining peace, and sincere Christians are found on both sides of the fence. This is why I believe a special task for Christians in the complex business of peacemaking may be to ensure that different kinds of peace-makers learn to understand and respect one another!

Rather than start a 'more peaceful than thou' competition, it may be more useful to ask what actually causes wars.

The root problem is the possession of arms, say some. Get rid of weapons and you get rid of war. But is that true? Weapons may cause fear, but there is no evidence from history that the possession of weapons by itself has ever been the main cause of war. Was Jerusalem destroyed as the result of an arms race? Surely not; the causes lie much deeper in the feelings, fears and fantasies of the time.

But if it is an illusion to suppose that weapons by themselves cause wars, then it is an illusion to suppose that reducing or removing them will create peace.

This is not to say that disarmament is a futile aim. The world needs it, if only for economic reasons. The world-wide wastage of resources on arms is a scandal and a disgrace. But to make disarmament a major goal without at the same time tackling the deeper causes of war, is to concentrate on the symptoms rather than the disease. The hard truth is that if next week's summit were to produce deep cuts in weaponry on both sides, the world might seem a saner place, but it would not necessarily be one ha'porth safer.

Wars in the past have been caused by fear, by misunderstanding, and by the mistaken belief that it is possible to win. Most of them have begun as adventures, daring strikes which have then gone terribly wrong.

This is why peacemaking has to concentrate on removing fear, removing misunderstanding, and removing temptation from those who might otherwise think that victory could be bought at too cheap a price. Remove these, and disarmament can follow.

But how? To a large extent the causes I have referred to lie in people's minds, not just in the minds of leaders, but in your mind and my mind. Once we see this we can begin to do something about it.

We can begin with ordinary friendship – simply discovering other people, making contact, removing misunderstandings, learning to distinguish between legitimate and illegitimate fears, building up a sense that we belong to one world.

I happened to be in Jordan just after it was announced that Bishop Khoury would be visiting this country as a representative of the PLO. The effect among the Christians in Jordan was electric. Here at last was a positive cause they could identify with in the search for peace amid the appalling confusions of the Middle East. Here was a tiny hope of creating a bit more international understanding of what Palestinians actually feel. And we all know what happened. Fear, suspicion, internal rivalries, intense lobbying, muddle and incompetence, took their toll – and the extremists won another round. But the hope was there, the possibility was there. It only needed a bit more magnanimity, a bit more imagination and courage, and it could have been a small step towards peace.

And what is true of the minds of individuals is true of the atmosphere of a nation. Nations like individuals can project their problems outside themselves on 'the enemy'. Nations can suffer paranoia. They can be divided and weak and temptingly vulnerable or aggressively self-protective. Or they can be genuinely sensitive to world problems; they can be generous; they can develop the inner strength to face uncomfortable facts. And whether they do it or not depends on the attitudes and assumptions of countless ordinary citizens.

Peacemaking, in other words, begins at home: in the kind of people we are, and in what we believe about those who are different from us. It begins here in the university, in the contacts we make with others, and especially in the unique opportunity of living in an international community.

If that sounds rather undramatic, in much lower key than Christian

visions of defeating evil and violence by some kind of invitation to be
crucified, then remember that for most of us the real cross we have to
bear is the cross we face every day in the challenges to our pride, and
self-interest, and over-hasty judgements and rejection of others.

Jesus wept over Jerusalem because its people could not see the
obvious things which were happening in their own streets. The things
which belonged to its peace were the ordinary things which belonged
to its righteousness, its faithfulness, its inner integrity. The things
which belong to *our* peace begin in our own hearts, begin where we are
now. May God's peace be in us, and among us, and flow through us to
the world.

25
Pacifism

*Sermon preached in York Minster to the Anglican Pacifist Fellowship
3 October 1987*

'I am for peace, but when I speak of it they make themselves ready for war'
(Ps. 120.6).

THE DISAPPOINTMENTS EXPERIENCED in peacemaking are as old as the
longing for peace itself. The vision which seems so luminously clear to
one person, evokes no response in another. Actions designed to
conciliate may simply arouse suspicion and increase mistrust.
Sacrifices lovingly offered can fall into the dust.

I begin by striking a somewhat gloomy note because in celebrating
fifty years of the Anglican Pacifist Fellowship it is as well to be honest
about what has and has not been achieved. And it is wise to set this fifty
years within the much longer Christian pacifist witness, and within the
larger context of history.

The bad news is that we live in a world as divided and dangerous
as ever. We hear of wars and rumours of wars, assassinations,
oppression, struggles for liberation, militant fanaticisms and deep-
rooted antagonisms. And we have to face the tragic irony that many of
these are inspired by religious motives, and appeal explicitly to religion
for their justification. People kill each other in the name of God – as
they always have. In fact there is a case for saying that all wars are at
bottom religious wars, because only religious emotions are powerful
enough to sustain commitment to all the horrors and sacrifices
involved.

The bad news of human perversity, including the perversity of
religion, is the baseline from which a witness to peace has to be given.

What is the good news? The good news is that despite the
disappointments and the brutalities, and despite human perversity,
some things have changed. I am talking now about recent history, not
about the ultimate good news of the gospel. We shall come to that later.
But simply on the plane of history I believe it is possible to see some

hopeful signs – not everywhere, not universally recognized and accepted, at times no more than flickering lights in the surrounding darkness, but lights nonetheless.

I want to mention three such signs of hope. First a growing acknowledgement that there *is* such a thing as the international community, that despite deep differences between the peoples of the world, we belong to one another and depend on one another and therefore that all of us have an interest in preventing war everywhere. This is not a new idea. It has always been a dream of those who seek peace. A sense of universal belonging ought to be a normal and natural part of Christian faith. But it is an idea which has at last begun to gain greater credibility, not only among Christians but among people of all faiths and none. And that is hopeful.

The second sign of hope has been the development during this century of codes of behaviour and aspirations to which most nations at least pay lip-service, however much they fall short in practice. It has been widely recognized that there are fundamental human rights and obligations which transcend purely political considerations. Again, this is not a new idea. It is still very inadequately expressed and realized. But it is happening.

The third sign of hope is a growing disillusionment with warlike attitudes. People talk about war in different terms from a century ago – in terms of waste and horror rather than in terms of excitement and glory. It hasn't happened everywhere – certainly not where nationalist struggles are still in progress. But where it *has* happened the attitude of mind, the belligerence, which in the past has often tipped seemingly irresolvable conflicts of interest over into actual war, is now missing. Belligerence can come back if we are not careful, but it is not what it was. And thank God for that.

My three signs of hope may seem very secular and unspiritual. But when we ask *why* these things have changed in our world today, then part of the answer has to be that through all these years there has been a persistent witness to the more excellent way of love, a persistent reminder that the way of violence is self-defeating.

'I am for peace, but when I speak of it . . .' they may not seem to hear. Yet something goes home.

It would be absurd to claim that this is the only reason why attitudes have slowly and fitfully been changing. But it is *one* reason. And as a non-pacifist myself I want to state clearly and unequivocally how important the pacifist witness has been as part of the conscience of mankind, as a constant nagging reminder to those engaged in practical affairs that love is what it is all about.

But, of course, you want more than that. We all do. We want the good news of the gospel to become the good news of an actual historical revolution – a changed world. It is in the way we go about this that we come up against the fundamental difference between pacifists and non-pacifists. It is not a difference about the meaning or power of the gospel. It is not a difference about the significance of the cross. It is not basically a difference in commitment, though I admit that pacifists often put other Christians to shame. It is a difference in how we see the relationship between what I shall call 'prophecy' and what I shall call 'policy'.

Our Christian faith entails a prophetic vision of the world as it is in all its horrors, and the world as it should be in all the glory of its transformation in Christ. Like all prophetic vision it goes to the roots of human attitudes. It faces human beings with the ultimate demands of God. It poses sharp contrasts, paints in vivid colours, appeals to our deepest emotions. This is the stuff of real religion.

Policy statements, by contrast, can seem thin and bloodless. Policy is a matter of ifs and buts, of weighing evidence, assessing possibilities, searching for practical ways forward. Policy has to take into account the actualities of power and the ability to effect change. It has to balance interests. It can seem a long way from the simplicities of the gospel. Yet even in church affairs there have to be policies as well as prophecies. And the greater the responsibility people bear the more likely they are to worry about policy, and let prophecy look after itself.

In fact we need both. Indeed we need more than both. Without prophetic vision there is no fire, no drive, no sense of ultimate goals. Without careful policy-making there is no effectiveness. Words of peace simply fall to the ground and are lost. But without some bridge between them, policy goes cynically in its own direction, prophecy becomes mere rhetoric. What is this bridge? What is this third element in the picture?

I suggest it is the process whereby God actually teaches us through history – a pretty basic Christian concept. What it means in practice is that we have to reflect on and learn from human experience – on history as the arena of the Spirit's action. This is one reason why I took time at the beginning of this sermon to identify three signs of hope as a basis on which one can begin to see what kind of difference prophetic witness actually makes. It is on the plane of historical events that

176 *Confessions of a Conservative Liberal*

Christ meets us. We must continually hope and pray for things beyond our imagining. But we must also ask in what way the prayers of those who have gone before us may have been answered. We must explore the roads which others have trodden between prophecy and policy.

Between the vision and the action, lie reflection and experience. Between the seed and the fruit, lies the slow process of growth. Between the words of peace spoken in the name of God, and that peaceful world for which we pray so hard, lie the countless tasks undertaken by millions of people, in very different ages, in very different styles, with very different understandings, who in Christ's name have helped to turn back the tide of evil by the power of love.

26

Theological Reflections on AIDS

Article published by The Times *under the title 'By Wayward Values to New Vulnerabilities'*
13 February 1987

WHAT CAN THEOLOGICAL reflection hope to add to the millions of words already written about AIDS? The short, but ambitious, answer is 'a framework of meaning'.

Those who leap to condemn AIDS victims for moral enormities presuppose one kind of framework of meaning, one where retribution is writ large. Others who sit down silently beside the victims to bear part of their suffering with them presuppose another framework, one in which meaning is generated by compassion. The pragmatic 'technological' approach ('use a condom') sidesteps the question of meaning, but only at the cost of making the experience of the disease strictly meaningless, a matter of hanging on, hoping to be lucky, until the researchers come up with the answer.

As I see it, reflection on meaning is an essential feature of our humanness, whatever the context. I offer these thoughts therefore as a preliminary attempt to make emotional and religious sense of a problem which threatens to engulf us for the remainder of this century.

The character of the virus itself may provide a first clue. It has been described as fragile, 'a pathogenic weakling'. This is why it needs intimate contact, blood to blood, for its transmission. The link between infection and sexual intercourse is thus no accident. The most intimate physical relationship between human beings provides the most secure environment in which this pathogenic weakling can gain a new foothold. The other known means of transmission equally presuppose a special degree of intimacy, the brotherhood of the needle, open flesh to open flesh, mother to child. Fragility and intimacy form part of the same pattern.

A second, and perhaps less obvious, clue lies in what the virus does. The invasion of the immune system is a medical disaster, but in an indirect way it too relates to the theme of intimacy. The immune system, like the human skin, protects the boundary between the self and the not-self. How it works is still in large measure mysterious. The fact that it works is part of the physiological basis for individuality. An individual organism retains its genetic distinctness and identity by refusing to allow replacement of its own genetic material from another source. Only in reproduction does the fusion of distinct genetic material take place. In almost every other circumstance the barrier between the self and the not-self remains inviolate – unless and until the AIDS virus begins to erode it.

I do not know whether there is any scientific connection between the fragility of the virus and its ability to attack one of the physical citadels of self-hood. In symbolic terms, though, a connection seems clear enough. A virus, which depends upon intimacy for its transmission, also happens to be one which exposes those who receive it to extreme dangers of invasion from without.

It seems only a short step from this conjunction of properties to a general reflection on the link between intimacy and vulnerability. It is not for nothing that intimate relationships have usually been hedged around with conventions, ceremonies and taboos. They involve dangerous moments of exposure, both physically and psychologically. The most intense emotions of shame, rage and hatred can be aroused when intimacy is abused. Most murders take place within the family. The fragile personality is most at risk when engaged in the self-exposure which intimacy demands. The frontier between the self and the not-self is the battleground on which individuals struggle to define their personal identity. The familiar sequence, dependence, independence, interdependence signals the movements backwards and forwards across the defences.

The role of religion in containing these dangerous experiences only works on the level of convention, ceremony and taboo if religious symbolism touches the actual springs of behaviour. In theory there is every reason why it should. One of the main tasks of Christian theology, for instance, is to explore the ramifications of love, both human and divine. It has powerful things to say about the intimacy of love and the vulnerability of lovers. The symbolism of Christ on the cross brings together in shocking juxtaposition the nearness of God to our human condition in its fallenness and his vulnerability to its consequences.

But much of the symbolism which once carried religious meaning has become degraded and trivialized. The conventions about intimacy have been repudiated as outworn, arbitrary, too ridden with fear and guilt about sex to be reliable guides in a supposedly enlightened age. The accumulated wisdom which set restraints on intimate human relationships has in large measure been squandered. It is small wonder that in a society which has grown so uncertain in its handling of intimacy, new forms of vulnerability should make their presence felt. AIDS is only one of them.

The relegation of modesty as a virtue is one of the small tell-tale signs of what has been happening. Many people, if asked, would spontaneously think of it as a rather old fashioned virtue, a first cousin to prudishness, a hangover from the petticoats on Victorian piano legs. Yet some of the things which go with modesty – privacy, space to be oneself, the right not to be forced into intimacy when one is not ready for it – can be important, not least for the growing child. Modesty, understood in these terms, is part of the self-restraint which lets other people be themselves. A convention of modesty can enrich human relationships by increasing the range and variety of responses between people before overtly sexual factors begin to make their presence felt. It is the exact opposite of what used to happen in the San Francisco bath-houses, now closed by AIDS, where sexual champions used to count their partners in tens and hundreds.

A theology which seeks to discover some meaning in AIDS has to look beyond the overtly sexual to some of the deeper failures of our society in not safeguarding the quality of our relationships. The sexual revolution of the 60s has had irreversible consequences, and that is why no mere reimposition of moral strictures is likely to be acceptable or lasting. But the fear, guilt and hypocrisy which used to surround most matters sexual are not the only alternative to licence. Perhaps AIDS can teach us a more positive lesson, the need to show more respect for personal integrity, the need to strengthen the link between sexual intimacy and other forms of intimacy, the need to rescue love from trivialization and re-emphasize its power to wound.

The defendant who recently said in court that for her sexual intercourse was no more significant than having a cup of tea, may well think of herself as modern and liberated. For me her remark symbolizes the emptiness of a culture which has thrown away restraint, and now finds itself with an empty house invaded by seven devils more dangerous than the first.

27

A School for Sinners or a Society for Saints?

Diocesan Letter, December 1987, written before the General Synod debate on sexual morality in November 1987

I WRITE THIS as the General Synod prepares for an orgy of discussion on sex at its November meeting, with two major debates on consecutive days. The first of these, on AIDS, will centre on an admirable report by the Board for Social Responsibility. I hope the report will be widely read. It contains good factual information, it faces some of the difficult practical issues, it stresses the urgent pastoral needs of AIDS victims, and it underlines the importance of changing much current sexual behaviour. AIDS has provided an additional and compelling motive for everyone to take seriously what Christians have always said anyway, namely that sex when separated from its proper context of love, commitment and fidelity, can become debasing and destructive. Promiscuity is not just dangerous, it is wrong.

The second debate, on a private member's motion, would seek to underline the same point, but in a subtly different style. It is a partisan attempt to bind the Church of England to an unequivocal condemnation of adultery, fornication and what it calls 'homosexual acts' in all circumstances, and to exclude from office any clergy guilty of such actions. I hope that by the time this letter is read the Synod will have shown its good sense by radically amending or dismissing this motion. The drawing of such rigid lines, and the hounding from office of those who offend, are deeply alien to the character of our Church. Sometimes it has to happen. In some matters there is already a harsh discipline designed to safeguard the expectations which people properly have of their priests. But for the Church to commit itself inflexibly to such rules would be to take a big step along the road to becoming a persecuting sect.

This second motion and the assumptions underlying it are dangerous because they are so superficially attractive. Of course the Church needs to have clear standards. Of course it is concerned about the sexual laxity and confusion of our times. Of course homosexuality raises great problems for those who find many of its expressions deeply repellent. And of course clergy ought to be exemplary in their behaviour. But how are high ideals and hopes to be turned into practical policies in the day to day lives of Christian people living in a world which has undergone a sexual revolution? It has been the genius of our Church that it has constantly tried to uphold high ideals while not losing contact with facts. And in the field of sexual behaviour the facts have changed, not only the facts about how large numbers of people actually behave, but facts about sex itself, from the control of its consequences to the deeper understanding of its psychology and meaning, and of its potential as a gift of God for the enrichment of life.

It is also a fact that many Christian people, for reasons which seem good to them, do not find traditional Christian teaching about sex fully answers their questions, and are not impressed when the only word which comes across to them with any conviction is the word 'Don't'. This is especially true of homosexuals. Many are not prepared to accept that St Paul settled the matter once and for all by condemning homosexuality as understood in his own day. It was then assumed that this was simply a matter of irresponsible and licentious choice. It is known now that many homosexuals have no choice at all about their sexual orientation. The question facing them is not whether they will be homosexual and/or heterosexual but whether, given their sexuality as it is, any form of sexual expression is permissible. So far most Churches have not found it possible to give a clear answer to that question. At least we owe it to Christian homosexuals to listen sympathetically to what they say about their own condition. The Synod motion would have closed the doors and shut them out.

It would have closed the door also on many puzzled heterosexual adolescents who have no wish to be promiscuous, who may have high ideals about love, but who cannot see that it is necessarily wise or helpful to postpone all sexual activity until marriage. Young people are growing up in a world in which it is common knowledge that sex, both now and in previous generations, has frequently been the basis of much hypocrisy. Furthermore it is a world which offers them endless new temptations and opportunities. Clear standards can be a help. But inflexible policies with repeated exhortations to 'do better' often fail to answer their very real dilemmas. What seems to be needed is a combination of firmness about the real heart of sexual morality, the giving of the whole of oneself in fidelity, and gentleness in dealing with the actual perplexities which surround it, chaotic sexual experiences, fumbling personal relationships, and insidious social pressures. A Synod motion which is all firmness and no gentleness does a disservice to those who are trying to be honest about themselves and their world.

A further worry about this attempt to impose new sexual rigidities on the Church is that it tends to get the whole business of sexual sin out of proportion. Sex is always good for a headline. It is also misleadingly simple to lay down the law about particular sexual actions and hold them up for public condemnation, in contrast to less definable sins like jiggery-pokery in the City, greed at one's table, unkindness to one's children, and blindness to the world's sufferings. But what a strange Church we would have become if a night's foolish passion were always and in all circumstances enough to lose a clergyman his job, whereas another man could neglect his parish for twenty years and remain immovable. Last summer's sexual scandals among American tele-vangelists were seized on with glee by the media because it is always fun to watch hypocrisy being unmasked. But the serious side of the story is that the ministries themselves were odious, and the sexual misdemeanours were only symptoms of a self-righteous megalomania much more deeply worrying.

A sexually disordered society is one in which human relationships have gone wrong, not only sexually but in many other ways as well. To reinforce the popular image of the Church as more concerned with sexual sin than with any other human failing, may be satisfying for those to whom sex is a particular problem. It may also be damaging to the Church's wider mission by focusing attention on symptoms rather than causes.

It is worth pondering that Jesus actually said very little about sex.

28
Animal Welfare

Diocesan Letter, August 1985

LIVING AS WE do on the edge of a river my wife and I have had ample opportunity to observe the ducks. Some of them we have come to know as individuals. Some we have reared by hand and allowed to return to the wild. A little further down the river, where the bank is accessible to the general public, there are those who lure the ducks with food and then shoot them at point blank range.

Anger and shame at the way human beings behave towards animals are curiously mixed emotions. As gardeners and householders we are only too anxious to get rid of slugs and rabbits and rats. Our pesticides are indiscriminate. We make friends with cows and pigs, and then eat them. We agonize over a lost cat or an injured dog, and acquiesce in thousands of their kind being used in medical research. Few of us who cheerfully eat meat would really like to know what goes on inside abattoirs, and shoppers looking for cheap food have a vested interest in not asking too many questions about factory farming.

In short, we are in a muddle about our relationship to other creatures. When I say 'we' I mean our civilization, a whole way of life which has achieved its present level of comfort and security by ruthless exploitation of the natural world. Few would want to return to the stage of civilization, still shared by millions of our fellow human beings, in which a crop failure, a plague of locusts, or an epidemic can spell utter disaster. We have had too many terrible reminders in recent months of how precarious human societies can be. But alongside this exploitation has grown a feeling for nature, which expresses itself in conservation programmes, in a delight in animals for their own sakes, in a sense of kinship with 'all creatures great and small', and in a nagging sense of guilt about what we do to them.

The muddle arises, I suspect, partly out of the very security which our exploitation has won for us. Those who struggle on the margins of survival cannot afford to be sentimental. Those who pioneered modern medicine through what may seem to us now to have been horrifying experiments, were battling against ignorance, pain and disease on a scale which in their eyes entirely justified what they were doing. The new sensibility about animals is not a wholly modern thing. It has been growing for centuries, but we are now in a position to reflect about it more urgently and more dispassionately than those in previous generations who felt they had no choice.

Our understanding of ourselves as part of an evolutionary process has also sharpened the issues. On the one hand we have been made aware that the gulf between human life and other forms of life is not as great as was once supposed. It is true that we are 'made in the image of God'. But the whole creation also reflects his glory. Human beings have unique possibilities of relationship with God. We can justifiably claim that evolution reaches its climax in this God-given awareness of the divine source and ground of the whole process. There is no reason to suppose, however, that this relationship with God is totally exclusive. Does God not delight in the other things he has made? And if he does, and if he has enabled us to see more clearly the links between them and us, how should we treat them? Paradoxically, though, the exploration of this relationship in an evolving world, has also revealed the extent to which all living creatures exploit each other. Big fish eat little fish . . . and so on ad infinitum.

I do not pretend to be able to find a way through this muddle. I simply draw attention to it as one which our civilization is going to have to tackle, and in which Christians ought to play a more constructive role than has often been the case in the past. There is a danger in becoming so obsessed with issues of direct personal importance, that we neglect to be good stewards of the wonderful world in which God has put us, a world we have to learn to share with his other creatures.

The alternative is the kind of vicious polarization of attitudes which takes its most extreme and unattractive form in the violent tactics of some of the animal 'liberation' movements. Animal welfare groups in general often do their cause a disservice by the stridency of their literature with its 'shock-horror' approach, by their one-sidedness, and by their failure to respond sensitively to the muddle in which most people actually find themselves.

I can appreciate and share the feelings of anger at unnecessary cruelty. I am saddened by the insensitivity which some people, including Christians, still display towards animal suffering. But I am convinced that we cannot develop more humane attitudes towards animals by hating our fellow human beings. The way lies through a deeper understanding of the rich and complex lives of animals themselves, through a greater respect for their different forms of sentience, and through a readiness to see them as having their own value in the eyes of God.

29
Powerlessness

Diocesan Letter, January 1988

AMONG THE MANY social issues which the bishops coming to Lambeth this year have said they want to discuss, powerlessness heads the list. It is easy to see why. Many Africans have good reason to feel powerless. The political impotence of black South Africa, the economic constraints in parts of that continent which carry crippling debts, the sense of hopelessness in the face of agricultural disasters, the huge and unmanageable threat posed by AIDS, these and other African problems clamour for attention.

A different kind of powerlessness is the daily experience of many Asian Christians, who have to struggle to maintain their identity in cultures dominated by another religion. The dreadful poverty of much peasant life in South America reveals yet another face of powerlessness. Even in our own country the symptoms are apparent in the emergence of a so-called 'underclass', a sizeable group of people with few prospects of escaping from their present position at the margins of society, badly educated, financially stretched, poorly housed, and generally excluded from decision-making about the things which most affect their lives.

Powerlessness is everywhere. And not only in places where bishops with social consciences might expect to find it. I receive many letters from seemingly prosperous and successful people who dislike this or that aspect of social change, but feel powerless to do anything about it. Powerlessness can infect industry, with shop-floor workers, trades unionists and managers all in their different ways feeling trapped by the system. Politicians may seem to have power, but many of them are more conscious of its limitations than its opportunities. Some people do, of course, exercise real power, and most people have small amounts of power in limited areas of life, even if only the power to tyrannize one other person. Great wealth brings power beyond the dreams of ordinary folk, but it also brings its own form of powerlessness; witness the barricades round the homes of the very rich as they seek to guard their possessions.

The sense of powerlessness reaches even into the Church, and some of the upsurge of feeling in the events surrounding the now notorious Crockford Preface, must surely be explained by the touching of this particular nerve. 'They', whoever they are, must be held responsible for all the things 'we' don't like. The other group, whichever it is, is perceived as a threat to ours and is trying to exclude us. And there is nothing to be done. 'The system' moves ahead with its own inexorable logic. In fact the feeling of banging one's head against a brick wall seems to be almost universal.

My reason for this lightning survey of a few of the different experiences of powerlessness is not to claim that they are all alike. The frustrations of a suburban housewife are not in the same league as the sufferings of a South American peasant. But there is a common thread. Both, in very different degrees, may feel that they are not in control of their own destinies; and they are not sure who is. And what is true for them is true for most people. Powerlessness, as I have said, is everywhere.

So who is in charge? The answer in most modern societies is – nobody. Things happen, not because any one person has said they will happen, but through an elaborate process of consultation, committee work, adjustment, compromise, manoeuvring, inadvertence, and 'going by the book'. Bureaucracy spreads its tentacles into almost every area of modern life because it is the easiest way of making complex decisions with apparent fairness, and without any individual having to bear too great a burden of responsibility. Its disadvantage is its facelessness. And the other side of that coin is the feeling among the powerless that there is no way of grappling with a faceless monster.

Even on the international scale this remains true. Try to trace the levers of effective power in the world of international debt, and they keep on disappearing. Everybody blames everybody else, and waits for somebody else's decision. The powerlessness of the oppressed may seem to have a more simple remedy, but the irony of most revolutionary social changes is that they simply create new forms of oppression.

It is useful to recognize this characteristic of modern societies. Much fruitless energy can be expended in trying to tackle frustrations by looking for villains, and the need to be angry with somebody can cause a lot of unnecessary pain. I am not saying that there are no villains and no causes for anger. Sometimes there are, and even if there are not and responsibility is widely spread, those who accept their share in it may grow in moral stature by doing so. But the frequent use of the word 'witch hunt' in contemporary polemics is surely significant. It prompts the question, why in the days when people really believed in witches was hunting them such a popular sport?

The answers are to be found in Keith Thomas' great book *Religion and the Decline of Magic* (Penguin 1973). In a nutshell the main reason, he says, is that witchcraft 'served the useful function of providing the victim of misfortune with an explanation when no other was forthcoming'. Sometimes, where there was negligence and incompetence, it offered an attractive excuse for failure. And in contrast with the other major explanation of misfortune then available, namely divine displeasure, it 'held out precisely that prospect of redress which the theologians denied. By personalizing their misfortunes, the victims were able to remedy their situation' – by attacking the supposed witch.

It is not hard to hear the echoes in our own day. Look for the villain, and many awkward questions are shelved. But theology, thank God, has moved on. We are more likely today than in the seventeenth century to think of God as sharing the experience of human powerlessness, meeting us in the midst of misfortune, enabling the weak to discover their true strength. The realization that God is with us in our weakness, far from discouraging effort, opens up the prospect of doing what *can* be done to remedy evil without indulging in fantasies about changing 'everything'. God is in the small steps, the tiny movements of love and reconciliation, the glimpses of hope, the acts of self-sacrifice, the seemingly endless search for practical solutions for the world's ills. And that enables us to see a loving face even in the most faceless of systems, and a loving presence at work even in the depths of powerlessness.

PART V

CHURCH AND MINISTRY

30

Protestantism and Protest

Article published in The Times Higher Educational Supplement *on the occasion of the Martin Luther Quincentenary*
9 December 1983

I RECENTLY HAD the somewhat unnerving experience of being the object of a violent demonstration. A protester threw herself in front of my car as it left York Minster, and others tried to lie in the road. Had it not been for the skilful driving of my chauffeur, there could have been serious injuries. As it was, the demonstrators were swiftly dragged away by the police. One of them explained afterwards, 'We just wanted to show our displeasure about Margaret Thatcher coming to York for the enthronement when this month [a local company] is closing down as a direct result of her policies. But we were also protesting at cutbacks in the National Health Service, the problems of the jobless and Cruise missiles coming to this country. No way was it an anti-religious demonstration against the Archbishop. There were a lot of Christians in the group.'

Such all-purpose protest against the wrong person sheds a curious light on our times. It may seem a far cry from the solemn rejoicings surrounding the quincentenary of Martin Luther. Yet Luther's 'Here I stand. I can do no other' still represents the authentic voice of the protester, and it is not for nothing that the word 'Protestant' was first used in a Lutheran context, even though Luther himself did not invent it. I hope, therefore, that some reflections on the relationship between Protestantism and protest may be an appropriate marginal comment on this year's celebrations.

The actual word 'Protestant' was born at the Diet of Speyer in 1529 where the evangelicals, as they then called themselves, protested against unfair discrimination. The Diet had agreed that Catholic minorities should enjoy religious liberty in Lutheran regions, whereas Lutheran minorities should only enjoy such liberty in Catholic regions where there was a serious danger of civil disorder. The name stuck when the opposition asserted that 'they must protest and testify publicly before God that they could do nothing contrary to his word'. By linking protest with testimony they gave the word a positive connotation which many Protestants would still claim to be of its essence. By the mid-sixteenth century, however, the negative sense predominated, and it had become widely used as a neutral term applicable to all forms of anti-papalism.

It is perhaps this negative side of it which has made most Churches reluctant to use it in their titles. Out of 318 member churches of the WCC only 16 explicitly call themselves Protestant, and most of those are in and around Indonesia. The Episcopal Church of America quietly dropped its Protestant prefix when nobody was looking. Within the Church of England the word never found its way into any of the official formularies, much to the annoyance of those who wish to emphasize the English Protestant heritage. The only liturgical context in which it appears is the Coronation service, where its anti-papalist implications have an obvious secular, as well as a religious, reference. Extreme Protestant groups within the Church of England attach high value to this isolated instance of its use, but for many Anglicans the word is an uncomfortable one which is avoided whenever possible.

Why this caution? It is more than a rejection of negativity. Other reformed Churches may not use it in their titles, but they have no objection to it as a general designation. The notion that Western Christendom can be divided into Catholics and Protestants may owe more to the convenience of statisticians than to peoples' own feelings about where they themselves stand, but at least the labels are not rejected. Church of England hesitations rest partly on the belief that in England the Reformation took a unique turn. But I suspect that there is also an underlying sense that the word Protestant signifies something altogether too narrow. It is not just the Paisleys of this world who induce the feeling. Protesting is an activity which belongs properly to a minority, and a Church which regards itself as secure and socially accepted is thereby likely to lose the cutting edge of its protestation.

A Free Church friend, when asked what he was still protesting about, thought first about Rome, and instanced one or two points of continuing disagreement. But his second thoughts went back to the more positive notion of testifying, and he began to expatiate on the sovereignty of God and the constant need for radical criticism. In doing so he had shifted from the defence of a particular denominational stance to the more general enunciation of a principle. In modern times

this shift of emphasis owes much to the work of Paul Tillich.
It was Tillich who drew a clear distinction between Protestantism as
an historical phenomenon, one among a number of denominational
forms of Christianity, and what he called 'the Protestant principle', a
principle of universal significance of which historical Protestantism is
only one particular embodiment. This principle, for Tillich, was an
essential thread running through all genuine forms of Christianity,
whatever their label.

> The most important contribution of Protestantism to the world past,
> present and future, is the principle of prophetic protest against every power
> which claims divine character for itself – whether it be church or state,
> party or leader. Obviously, it is impossible to build a church on the basis of
> pure protest, and that has been the mistake of Protestantism in every
> epoch. But the prophetic protest is necessary for every church and for every
> secular movement if it is to avoid disintegration. It has to be expressed in
> every situation as a contradiction to man's attempts to give absolute
> validity to his own thinking and acting . . .
>   (*The Protestant Era*. University of Chicago Press 1957, p. 231)

Churches which call themselves Protestant may lose hold of the
protestant principle, as defined by Tillich, just as devastatingly as
those which have never claimed to adhere to it. Creeping respectability
takes hold of all. In fact, the idea that being a Protestant might have
anything to do with modern forms of protest against a rag-bag of social
ills would be a strange and offensive one to many of those to whom the
word has come to signify solid, stable, undemonstrative virtue.
Furthermore, protest within the churches, where it is found at all, is
more likely nowadays to be directed towards objects outside the
explicitly religious sphere, than against fellow Christians. The fact that
the exact opposite of this is true in Ireland is a cause of offence and
incomprehension.
Yet surely Tillich was right to see Protestantism and protest as part
of an authentic religious stream which flowed from the Old Testament
prophets, through the New Testament and surfaced in full flood at the
Reformation. The stream has often flowed in trivial and unworthy
channels. Squabbles about churchmanship, fixation on externals, the
use of shibboleths to identify genuine Catholicism or genuine
Protestantism, have all tended to obscure the deep sense in which the
Catholic spirit and the Protestant spirit both need each other.
Present-day divisions of the Christian world into conservative and
radical may eventually come to be seen as equally unproductive and

unnecessary. The conservative spirit and the radical spirit need not be regarded as alternatives. In a recent book I have tried to make the point that both are essential for any true understanding of God. Thus it is only possible to know God as a reality transcending one's own feelings and intuitions by attending to what is actually given us in the traditions about him. But we can only know him *as God* insofar as we recognize the utter inadequacy of those traditions to convey more than 'the outskirts of his ways' (*Church and Nation in a Secular Age*, Darton, Longman and Todd 1983, pp. 153ff.). Continuous dialectic between the conservative spirit and the radical spirit does not make for an easy life, but then why should it? Religion, as von Hügel was fond of saying, is not meant to make us comfortable.

The spirit of protest, whether ecclesiastical or intellectual or moral, cannot be removed from Christianity without the danger of faith lapsing into idolatry. In this very general sense, those who shouted outside York Minster while the bastions of society enthroned a new archbishop within, were all part of the same game. Whether a purely political protest was appropriate at that particular moment is another question altogether, and my own belief is that Christians who took part in the protest misjudged the occasion. Nevertheless, the general conjunction of ceremony and raw feeling, tradition and immediacy was, and is, a potentially fruitful one. The incident itself was trivial. But by setting this kind of thing within the much broader framework of the general outworking of the Protestant principle, it may be possible to pinpoint some of the opportunities and constraints which contemporary protesters should bear in mind.

First, and most obviously, Protestant history demonstrates how the right protest at the right moment can unleash huge and uncontrollable forces. However much Luther had a shrewd idea of what he was doing, he can hardly have guessed all its consequences, or approved them if he had. The protester has to make his protest, conscious of the danger, not knowing whether his hand might be the one which lights the powder train which blows up a nation, or church, or culture. Such moments in history may be rare, but they are a reminder of risks as well as opportunities, an inducement to a sense of responsibility as well as hopefulness.

Their rarity prompts the thought that contemporary protest might be more effective as a weapon if there was greater economy in its use. When innumerable feet are trampling all over potential powder trains, and when the protesting attitude has become so familiar as to be disregarded, actual change becomes less likely than when protest is more restrained. It was surely the fact that the Church of England is not normally regarded as a protesting body which led to the unusual nervousness in government circles about its attitude to nuclear weapons.

A second lesson from Protestant history follows closely from what has just been said about the scarcity value of protest. The protesting spirit can easily become institutionalized. Protest itself becomes a way of life from which it is difficult to withdraw, at least outwardly, even though the real initiative in self-criticism has passed elsewhere. This is one of the dangers faced by the Greenham Common women. In becoming a quasi-institutionalized symbol of protest they are reduced to making and arousing stock responses. It is possible to admire them for their self-sacrifice and the strength of their conviction, but wherever the real nuclear debate is actually taking place, it is clear that it is no longer on Greenham Common. And the same is true of other ritualized forms of protest. Crowds shouting 'Out, out' are ministering more to their own feelings of helplessness than to any real process of political change.

A third lesson might concentrate on the inherent limitations of negative Protestantism. It is fairly easy to criticize protesters for not being constructive, and there is justice in the reply that they cannot be expected to do everything. When the majority ignore what seem to them to be manifest evils, it is enough to declare that evil is evil without specifying precisely what should take its place. But the danger of negatively based protest, especially in an age when the roots of evil and the responsibility for it may be hard to identify with certainty, is that it can slide into carping criticism of everything-in-general, an attack on 'the system' as such, whatever that might be held to mean.

The challenge to testify to some alternative vision, and to work out its implications, need not be construed as a move in the game to show up protest as futile. There is a deep sense in which the integrity of protest itself depends on the possession and articulation of some positive beliefs. The original Protestants may have been reacting to unfairness without having a clear idea of exactly what they wanted to achieve. But they were in no doubt that their motive was obedience rather than resentment. So a pertinent question to today's protestors might be – 'What imperative do you believe yourself to be obeying?'

A final lesson, and perhaps the most pointed one, follows directly from what has just been said. Negative Protestantism relies on its ability to identify, and rally support against, some external enemy, whether Pope or Prime Minister or 'system'. The Protestant spirit, on the other hand, directs its first criticisms internally. It is the limitations of its own apprehensions, the inadequacy of its own responses, the shortcomings of its own obedience which are the first objects of attack. The protest has to be made because God stands in ultimate judgement on all human endeavours. And this is why specifically Christian protest, even when, as in Luther, it is at its most provocative, always starts in the uncomfortable knowledge that judgement begins at the household of God.

31
One God

Sermon preached in York Minster during the meeting of the General Synod in York
12 July 1987
'God spake these words and said, Thou shalt have none other gods but me' (Exod. 20.1).

I TAKE THIS first commandment as my text for this morning because it is the uncompromising foundation of our faith. 'None other gods but God.' It is not specifically about idolatry. That comes in the second commandment. Here in the first we have what almost amounts to a definition of God – 'he beyond whom there is no other'.

Of course, it didn't begin like that. It is obvious from the Old Testament that this uncompromising monotheism developed slowly. The God of the Israelites was seen in the first instance simply as more concerned about them than other gods, more significant, more powerful, and in the final analysis all-powerful. The first commandment can be read in these early stages as a call for allegiance. 'There might be other gods, but in fact you are to remain faithful to the God of Abraham, Isaac and Jacob.' By the time we reach Isaiah the emphasis has changed. Other gods simply don't exist. 'The Lord, the Almighty, is the God of all the earth.'

It is a short transition from saying this to saying that this is in fact what the word 'God' means. Gods are not a class of objects of which there might possibly be many, though in practice there only happens to be one. Not that at all. The very notion of God includes the notion of oneness. What we mean by God is the one who creates all things, sustains all things, empowers all things and ultimately draws all things to himself. Any other concept of God reduces him to one among a set of objects; and that is to destroy the concept altogether.

Forgive this rather abstract introduction, but the point is an important one. What begins as a command becomes in the end a definition. This 'God of all the earth' becomes the fundamental presupposition of the whole biblical tradition.

There is an interesting parallel in physics. When the early physicists began developing the concept of energy they stumbled on the idea that it can take different forms. There can be heat energy, chemical energy, the energy of moving bodies, and so on, and one kind of energy can be transformed into another without the energy itself being lost. Burn coal, and chemical energy is transformed into heat energy; use the heat to drive a steam engine and it is transformed into mechanical energy. But what remains unchanged in all these transformations is the amount of energy itself – the so-called law of the conservation of energy. It was a law worked out through hard practical experience.

But as time went on, and as new forms of energy were discovered, the law ceased to be thought of as a discovery and became a basic assumption. The whole thing was turned on its head. Physicists no longer looked anxiously to see if energy was conserved. They defined energy as what was conserved in the various transformations. And the basic assumption came to be regarded as so reliable that when the equations didn't work out they invented new forms of energy to balance the books – and subsequently discovered them! It is an amazing story of the way in which a concept developed to become the key to a whole new way of thinking and acting.

'Thou shalt have none other gods but me.' The parallel is not exact for obvious reasons. God is not a concept – he is the ultimate reality. God is not discovered – he reveals himself as human beings are able to respond to him. But belief in the oneness of God is not an optional extra in the Jewish–Christian tradition. It is the assumption from which all else starts. The supposition that there could be 'other gods' in any meaningful sense destroys the notion of God itself.

I have been labouring what may seem a rather obvious point. But it has some profound practical implications. If there is only one God, the God of all the earth, then some of the possessive exclusive claims made about him begin to look rather silly. If he is by definition concerned with everything and everybody, then the variety of transformations in which he may be known has to be taken seriously. Again I don't want to press the analogy with energy too far, but it is at least possible that different claims to have received the revelation of God have some unifying thread running through them.

This is dangerous ground. Christians have not been very successful yet in working out how we relate our faith to other religions. We get into difficulties as we try to set our belief in the finality of Christ within the context of undoubted knowledge of God which lacks this Christian reference. We are not even very good at understanding and sympathizing with each other in our different Christian traditions. So perhaps this is where we need to make a start, here at home, before we scale the greater heights of inter-faith dialogue.

In struggling to emphasize the oneness and universality of God I am not advocating some great theological mish-mash in which all truths are equal and all the things which each of us holds dear are reduced to insignificance.

Here again the analogy with energy may help us. There are definable forms in which energy manifests itself, just as there are viable and definable forms of faith and theological understanding. Unless we want to claim exclusive privileges for only one of these, as if heat were the only form of energy, then we need to be sensitive to the links and transformations between them. Indeed, unless we are, we are in danger of disastrously misunderstanding the nature of energy itself.

Do we make the same mistake about God? Sometimes when I hear Christians talking about each other I have fears that we do. God seems so tightly wrapped in so small a package.

So let me end with a practical suggestion. And since members of the General Synod are worshipping with us this morning, let me make it especially to them.

Let each of us resolve to live out our Christian discipleship in terms, not just of one of the different traditions which go to make up our Anglican inheritance, but in terms of at least two of them: some combination of Catholic, evangelical, liberal and middle of the road. This would give our claim to comprehensiveness some real content. It would take us away from a stultifying kind of co-existence into a real mutual enrichment. Forgive another scientific analogy, but it is the difference between a mixture and a compound. Both may contain a number of different ingredients. But in a mixture they just lie side by side. In a compound they have reacted together to become something new.

To take each other, and each other's traditions, seriously in these terms, is to take God seriously. For there is one God and no other. And we cannot discern him rightly unless we discern him through all that he has revealed of himself, and in the face of all that he has made.

32
Martyrdom

Sermon preached in York Minster at an ecumenical service jointly led with Cardinal Hume to mark the four hundredth anniversary of the death of Margaret Clitherow.
31 March 1986

'Do not fear those who kill the body but cannot kill the soul.
Fear him rather who is able to destroy both soul and body in hell'
(Matt. 10.28).

HERE IS THE classic justification for martyrdom. Fear God rather than man. Fear the betrayal of allegiance more than the bearing of pain. Fear the denial of inner integrity, the loss of what is most inwardly precious, more than the worst that human brutality can do to human flesh. Faith is made perfect in death, for those who die with Christ rise with him. So look beyond the sufferings of this present time to the glory that shall be.

Margaret Clitherow stands in this honoured tradition. Today we give thanks for a saint whose martyrdom was the fruit of deep and bitter religious division. And by the grace of God we can give thanks *together*. We can look back on a dark and terrible period of English history when good convinced Christians did unspeakable things to each other in the name of Christ. And we can thank God that he has led us out of the nightmare to rediscover each other.

The fact that this particular martyrdom was suffered by an ordinary citizen of York, a mother and housewife whose last action was to dispose of her stockings and shoes to her twelve year old daughter, brings it all closer, and makes it all the more poignant. And the fact that we have been able to walk from her house to this place of worship, and do it side by side, powerfully reminds us of how far God has led us on our pilgrimage to unity.

Thank God for the martyrs. And we may be tempted to add, thank God they belong to the sixteenth century and not to ours. Though tragically in many parts of the world Christians still suffer and die for their faith, though torture is still the stock in trade of many countries which claim to be civilized, though people are still imprisoned for purely religious reasons, the obscenity of Christians martyring Christians belongs to the unhappy past.

Or does it?

There are frightening paradoxes in religion. Our sixteenth-century forebears who made martyrs of each other may have been brutal, but they were not brutes. They felt they were acting for the highest and holiest of reasons. They may have been blind but they were not hypocrites. Indeed through suffering and inflicting suffering they experienced a strange kind of purification. And the impulses which led them to do it run just as deep in twentieth-century hearts.

Religion is about what matters most to us, the deepest springs of emotion, the highest ideals, the greatest fears, the bitterest disappointments. And so when it goes wrong it can go devilishly wrong. All the emotions stored up for the greatest potential outpourings of love can be unleashed in hatred and violence and scorn. All those supports of faithfulness which in better times can undergird religious stability and perseverance and the readiness to go on hoping against hope, can solidify into bigotry and blindness and intransigence.

I had a letter some time ago which ended with the charming words 'May your soul rot for ever in hell', signed – six ecumenical Christians from Watford.

It is not only those rather pathetic people who write rude letters to archbishops, who reveal the face of the persecutor under twentieth-century masks. Wherever these things are felt deeply, whether in the polarized religious communities of Ireland, whether in the small group of committed enthusiasts who are convinced they alone have got it right, whether in the suppressed fears and suspicions of each other nurtured by one-sided versions of history, there may lie the same emotions which led the good citizens of York to crush a housewife to death.

Religion is dangerous stuff. Explosive. Easily corruptible. And if not all the corruptions are as nasty as those I have been describing, but merely petty and quarrelsome and stand-offish, they may be no less dangerous to the individuals concerned. Fear not the little things which can corrupt the body, but the little things which can corrupt the soul.

Historically speaking one of the reasons for today's indifference to religion in countries where religious persecution once reigned, is precisely this frightening vision of what religious enthusiasm can do.

We are still paying for the fires and the hangings and the crushings of four centuries ago. And on a lesser scale we go on paying for our divisions, and for the aura of petty religious squabbling which still wafts around us in the public imagination. It is not for nothing that 'couldn't care less' is perhaps the most deadly disease in our modern society.

But it provides no real answer. To possess no deep springs of emotion, no idealism, nothing we really care about, nothing to live and die for, is to lose half of our humanity. It is to create a dangerous vacuum into which all kinds of secular fanaticisms can pour. The modern world makes its martyrs – secular ones – with no less brutality than the world of Margaret Clitherow.

Religion won't in the end go away. And the question is how to live with this dangerous reality, how cope with this paradox of religious impulses which can rise to such heights and fall to such terrible depths?

I came across a phrase some thirty years ago which has stuck with me ever since – 'the redemption of religion'. Those feelings which can be so strong, the visions, the idealism, the inner energy, this raw material of religion, need to be redeemed. It is part of what the Bible calls 'the natural man'. It has a potential for good or evil. It can unite us or divide us. It can take us to heaven or dash us to hell.

We are not redeemed just by being religious, not by the intensity of our feelings or the depth of our commitment. We are redeemed only by Christ. Our religious impulses have to be brought again and again to the place of forgiveness. The things which can so easily distort religious commitment, pride and fear and self-seeking and humbug, have to be offered up and given back to us by God as faith and hope and love. The lust for certainty, the need to be right, the wish to dominate and control, have to be brought to the cross of Christ and endure the searching gaze of one who died helpless and forsaken. The religious fortress mentality which keeps us separated from one another, and ultimately tempts us to make martyrs of one another, has to be broken down, the stone rolled away from the door of the tomb. And through the open channels, set free by the love of God, the vision, the idealism, the emotion can flow uncontaminated – Holy Spirit, the spirit of our true selves, holy because flowing from the hearts of those whom Christ has made his own.

That was a compressed piece of theology. My essential point is quite simple. Religion by itself isn't enough; it tempts us to make martyrs of each other. Irreligion isn't enough either; it exposes us to other forces and tempts us to go our separate ways. The religious impulses inside us have to be brought to the place of redemption, there to be offered, consecrated, broken and shared.

There is a well-known story about St John the Evangelist on his deathbed with disciples crowding around, friends listening for one last message from the great visionary and theologian who had given them so much. 'A final word', they begged, 'what now do you see as you stand on the threshold of heaven?' There was a long silence, and the old man slowly raised himself.

'Little children, love one another.' 'But you have said that before', his disciples protested. The old man sank back. 'There is no more to say.'

Indeed, there isn't. And if we begin there, even martyrdom can become a strange paradoxical witness to the triumph of love.

33
St Cuthbert

*Sermon preached in Durham Cathedral at a service to celebrate the 1300th anniversary of the death of St Cuthbert
20 March 1987*

A BISHOP OF Durham cannot escape having to come to terms with history. To be the heir to Cuthbert's patrimony is no light burden. Other saints in other places may come and go, and we pay them due respect. But Cuthbert in a curious way persists. His legacy is part of the air we breathe, part of the feel of North East England, part of a tradition which still has life in it. For me some of the moments in this cathedral which stand out most vividly in my memory are moments spent in silent prayer before that grey stone slab with its single word 'Cuthbertus'. So this is no ordinary 1300th anniversary. We are celebrating our roots as Northern Christians.

Why should this be so? What is it about this particular man which arouses such feelings? Someone has described him as 'fashioning within himself a brilliant spiritual synthesis'. It sounds a bit self-conscious, but one can see what is meant. In Cuthbert we find a combination of extreme asceticism in the Celtic tradition, with something of the new Roman image of episcopacy – the Roman sense of dignity and order – the living fusion of two streams of Christian culture. The man who wore Cuthbert's cross was no ragged hermit. Again, we find a man with his eyes totally fixed on heaven, looking upwards through the hole in the roof of his cell on Farne Island, yet a man who loved nature, who was close to animals and felt at one with the earth. We find a man of huge spiritual power, and enormous humility; a tirelessly courageous man who loved Christ and loved his people, even the most unlovable of them. A saint who in the manner of his death and the strange events which followed it, unleashed spiritual forces which influence us to this day. 'A brilliant spiritual synthesis.'

But he would have disliked hagiography. And he would not have wanted to hide the fact that there were tensions even in the monastery at Lindisfarne, tensions which burst out in quarrels after his death.

Saints do not belong to some never-never land. They belong in this world where people are sinners. Cuthbert's intense concern with holiness was all the more necessary because his mission was to a world which was coarse and brutal and divided. And I believe he would want us to celebrate him, not just by extolling his qualities, but by bringing him into conversation with *our* world, no less sinful, no less divided, no less hungry for some genuine glimpse of holiness.

So let us look at him, the monk, the lover of nature, the man in whom spirituality and earthiness were integrated, the man whose conscious- ness had not been divided, as ours has, between the objective scientific understanding of nature, and the passionate intensity of belonging within a world shot through with the glory of God.

Cuthbert would have known what Dostoevsky meant when he wrote, 'My brother asked the birds to forgive him; that sounds senseless, but it is right; for all is like an ocean, all is flowing and blending; a touch in one place sets up movement at the other end of the earth . . . so kiss the earth and love it with an unceasing, consuming love. Love all men, love everything . . . water the earth with the tears of your joy, and love those tears.'

Dostoevsky put those words in the mouth of a holy monk Father Zossima in *The Brothers Karamazov*, and those who know the novel will appreciate the irony. Father Zossima died. And the young novice, Alyosha, the hero of the story, who has built all his faith on this man's sanctity, has been expecting a miracle. Surely the corpse of so holy a man must remain uncorrupt. But on the very day of his death the visitors to his coffin notice a disturbing smell, which grows stronger and stronger until it is unmistakable. It was the smell of corruption, starting, as some of Zossima's more malicious fellow-monks put it, 'in excess of nature'.

Alyosha goes through a spiritual crisis which is finally resolved when he learns to love the world in its corruptibility, and he goes out and waters the earth with tears of joy. There in that little cameo, it seems to me, we have a nineteenth-century version of the miracle of St Cuthbert. Our world is all too conscious of corruption and decay; no longer the springtime of a budding civilization. But in our world too, for all its cynicism, for all the malicious delight in scandal, for all its dissolution, God can still be known, earth can still be loved.

Think of another picture. Our worship has already reminded us of Cuthbert praying in the sea. The Celtic saints felt at home in the sea – quite an unusual thing in those days. Somehow the roar and splash of the waves seemed to provide a kind of bass accompaniment to the melodies of Celtic prayer.

But now move forward 1200 years to another deeply serious man, Matthew Arnold on Dover beach in 1867. For him the waves had a different message. He saw the ebbing tide as a symbol of the long slow retreat of Christian faith, a sad accompaniment to the agonized wrestlings of the earnest Christians of his day who felt their world crumbling about them in the face of new knowledge.

> I only hear
> Its melancholy, long, withdrawing roar
> Retreating to the breath
> Of the night wind, down the vast edges drear
> And naked shingles of the world.

The world has changed. The simple naturalness of Cuthbert's faith is no longer easily accessible to us. We are burdened by complexity, perplexity. For us 'the sea has many voices' saying different things.

But just as we can know and love God in a world which is corruptible, so we can know and love him in a world which is perplexed. Matthew Arnold got it wrong. God is not away there in the retreating sea, an ever more distant vision leaving us stranded on the shingle. God is in the turbulence which rages inside us. God is in the questioning, in the agonizing. His waves and storms beat over us, as they beat over Cuthbert. But it is precisely in this turmoil that we can grasp the still centre of the turning world, where the pure in heart see God.

One final brief picture. There is a remarkable little story about some monks from South Shields being blown out to sea on five rafts. The inhabitants of South Shields, who didn't particularly like them, were rather enjoying the spectacle. Whereupon Cuthbert rebuked them, and prayed for the monks; the wind changed and they all came safely back to land.

We in our sophisticated, safety-conscious world cannot rid our imaginations of a red-bottomed hulk lying in the shallow waters off Zeebrugge. And remember also yet another nineteenth-century writer, Gerard Manley Hopkins, agonizing over the wreck of the *Deutschland* in 1875. Here too was a God whose power was felt in the sea through terror and death: five nuns drowned at midnight . . . Yet the same God who answered Cuthbert's prayer. In Hopkins's own words:

> . . . past all
> Grasp God, throned behind
> Death with a sovereignty that heeds
> But hides, bodes but abides.

Cuthbert's world has vanished. But not his faith. Nor his God. In our own less innocent environment we need his clarity of vision and singleness of purpose. Bede said of him that he 'watched, prayed, worked and read harder than anyone else'. We thank God for him.

That single word 'Cuthbertus' means 'famous' and 'bright'. In his case, famous because bright; shining both in his age and in ours with the brightness of the love of God.

34
Ministry, Ordained and Lay

Diocesan Letter, February 1985

WHAT ARE PRIESTS for?

I ask it partly because this year our Church is going to be trying harder than ever to encourage suitable candidates to hear the call of God and offer themselves for ordination. So it is as well to be clear why we need them.

But I also ask it because last October's Lay Conference in Scarborough highlighted the strong desire among many lay people to have their skills and talents used more effectively in the service of the Church, and their frustration when sometimes this fails to happen. In today's Church it is impossible to think about ordained ministry without at the same time thinking about lay ministry, because clergy and laity are partners. Our tasks and responsibilities intertwine. But they are also different, and it is my purpose in this letter to spell out the difference.

This is all the more urgent because many excellent lay people who offer themselves for ordination, cannot understand what has gone wrong if their offer is not accepted and they are advised to continue to exercise a lay ministry. There may also be others who ought to be ordained, but who have never been challenged to see that there is a special and worthwhile job to be done.

So what are priests for? And what qualities are needed? I start with some of the qualities and functions which clergy and laity ought to share.

We ought all to be pastors, because pastoral work is about caring for people and being sensitive to their needs. There may well be special skills needed to deal with difficult situations, and clergy are expected to have training in some of these skills, but being a pastor is not an exclusively priestly function. Many laity do it extremely well without calling it by that name.

The same is true of evangelism. All Christians, ordained and lay, ought to be witnesses to the gospel. Opportunities and circumstances differ, and clergy have the advantage of being visible examples of Christian commitment simply by virtue of their office. But there is nothing to prevent a lay person being just as effective in spreading the faith, if not more so.

Both clergy and laity need to think and to study and to pray, to use their knowledge and experience and try to relate them to what is actually going on around them. In this general sense all are teachers and prophets, just as all need to be disciples.

Where then do the differences lie? Not so much in functions of the kind I have been describing, as in the idea of the priest as a representative, representing the Church, and Christ in the Church, and Christ to the Church. The essence of ordination lies in setting the seal of Christ on an individual life so that it comes to represent, officially and explicitly, God's will to order his Church in a particular way. This is the meaning of 'Holy Orders'.

Ordination is thus a sign of the 'givenness' of the gospel. The ordained ministry acts as a kind of reference point in the continual process of responding to the Spirit while remaining faithful to Christian tradition. It represents the unity and continuity of the Church in Christ, and this is why much of the symbolism of ordination relates to the idea of 'handing on'.

All this means that the most characteristic priestly tasks, the ones which distinguish clergy from laity, have to do primarily with the business of linking what is happening here and now in the local congregation to its roots in the gospel, to its wider context in the whole Church, and to the resources of the whole Christian tradition.

By the same token, the most characteristic lay task is to claim for Christ, and to fill with Christ's presence, whatever bit of God's world or whatever form of human activity the lay Christian is responsible for.

Thus a Christian mother, for example, may see her primary responsibility as creating a Christian family. A priest's task, in relation to her, will be to help her to locate that family in the context of the whole purposes and family of God.

In the same way a Christian business man may spend most of his energies trying to do his job with integrity. The presence of a priest is a standing reminder that there are other realities and other values which also have a claim on him and provide a resource for him.

These different roles are expressed most fully in the Eucharist. Some Christians nowadays, who want to take the idea of lay participation to its logical conclusion, see it as no more than a set of prayers which anybody can say provided a priest 'does the magic bits'. But this is totally to mistake the character of the service. It is to lose the careful balance between what is going on in a local congregation with its own concerns and its own interrelationships, and the universal worship of the Church into which the congregation is lifted, and which the presence of an ordained celebrant represents. This is, incidentally, why it is important that he alone should say the parts of the ASB services reserved for the President, so that his wider representative role is not obscured.

It would be easy to go on multiplying examples, but I hope I have said enough to indicate some of the personal qualities a priest should have if he is to fulfil this particular role, qualities which become even more important as lay people take more seriously their own Christian ministries. It is not enough just to be a good pastor, evangelist or teacher, not enough just to be faithful in prayer, though all these things matter hugely. There also needs to be an imaginative and humble grasp of what it is to act as a representative, a flexibility of mind, a width of vision, a broad sympathy with many different kinds of experience. Then what he is as a person, as well as what he represents through his office, can be a visible reminder of the need to look beyond ourselves and our own local concerns to the whole action of God in Christ through the Church.

A tough job? Not for those who live by the promise, 'My grace is sufficient for thee; my strength is made perfect in weakness.'

35
Lay Theology

Article published in the Church Times *under the title*
'A Doctrinal Role for the Laity'
2 January 1987

THE HOUSE OF Laity flexed its muscles at the November General Synod. The Synod responded by making sure that the role of the laity in decision-making remains at the top of ARCIC's agenda. This is surely right and proper. In a Church which describes itself as 'The People of God', all the people of God must play their part in all aspects of church life, including the definition of doctrine. Our Church is irrevocably committed to this understanding of itself by our acceptance of synodical government.

So far so good. But now the hard questions begin. To affirm a role for the laity in doctrinal matters is not the same as saying precisely how that role should be exercised.

Some may think of it mainly in terms of Synodical power politics. One excited member of the House of Laity talked to me about forcing his point of view on the bishops. Others are more modest, but believe that they have a role in countering the clerical dominance in theology, not least by rescuing it from jargon-laden abstractions. There are also increasing numbers of straightforward Bible-reading Christians who feel that they have direct access to theological and moral truths and seem puzzled that there should be any real argument about them. At the other extreme are highly competent lay theologians, who demonstrate that their status as lay people has nothing to do with lack of theological expertise.

All of which suggests the need to think beyond a theology *of* the laity towards a very different range of questions about what might be expected from theology *by* the laity. And that entails asking first about the kind of basis on which theology rests, and whether there are any elements in this to which lay people might have special access. Only then does it make sense to ask about the distinctive role of the laity in doctrinal decision-making.

I start with a very broad generalization. Theology stands on two legs. One of these consists of all that is given in Christian tradition – the Bible, church history, scholarship, the thoughts, writings, artistic creations and moral insights of countless faithful people – a tradition which is in principle accessible to all who take the trouble to study it and learn from it. It is not simply an academic tradition, though it has an academic component; mastery of it, whether intellectually or spiritually or in terms of broad Christian wisdom, is a demanding business. There is, in other words, a basic theological expertise which consists of knowing, in various ways, and at different depths, what the Christian tradition is.

The other leg on which theology stands is experience. 'If any man will to do his will, he shall know of the doctrine, whether it be of God . . .' (John 7.17). There is a knowledge which comes through obedience, through doing, through commitment and belonging. There is practical wisdom as well as scholarly wisdom. There are gut feelings of rightness, which may be difficult to explain or articulate, but which are enormously important in determining what people actually believe and how they actually behave. To a greater or lesser extent religion always contains direct and unanalysable elements, and without them the other leg, the tradition, would be mere words.

Sensus fidelium, the gut feeling of the faithful, reception by the Church at large, form a necessary counterpart to the work of the experts. But just as the tradition needs the *sensus fidelium*, so this kind of direct experience and gut feeling needs the work of critics and scholars to save it from lapsing into mere uninformed prejudice. Many who are horrified by any thought of the infallibility of the pope, cheerfully accept the infallibility of their own convictions.

Theology needs both its legs, expertise and experience. Much Christian experience comes simply through being part of the living tradition of the Church, through worshipping, hearing the Scriptures read, meeting others, attempting to live a Christian life. This is not the prerogative of the laity any more than theological expertise is the prerogative of the clergy. But while there is a presumption that clergy – though not only clergy – will be students of the tradition and take seriously their commitment to pass it on in ways appropriate to our day, there is an equal presumption that lay people will have a deeper knowledge of some aspects of the secular world than clergy, and will find their Christian experience uniquely shaped by it. Thus, though some lay people may be excellent theologians and some clergy may be poor ones, the likelihood is that the majority of lay people will make their special and necessary contribution to the Church's thinking by reflecting on their secular experience in the light of Christian faith.

I want a House of Laity in which scientists are valued as scientists, teachers as teachers, mothers as mothers, the unemployed as those who have experienced the underside of our society, and where all value each other's experience of living Christianly in a largely unreceptive world. But I am not particularly interested in a House of Laity filled with amateur Bible students who are not willing to acknowledge that there is an expertise in these matters, which is every bit as demanding as any other professional expertise.

The Basic Christian Communities of Latin America show what can be done. In them the discussion of Christian faith is very close to the dreadful actualities of life among the very poor. Their theologians legitimize and build on their insights, relating them back to the tradition, and drawing out new and unexpected understandings of tradition as a result. I am not commending this as a model for the General Synod, only as a contemporary example of a distinctive lay role in the task of doctrinal development.

The so-called Frontier Groups which flourished in the immediate post-war period, were probably the nearest equivalent in Britain, though they tended to operate at the opposite end of the social spectrum. Such groups brought together lay people with similar skills and interests to work out together the implications of Christian faith in their particular secular contexts. A body like the Institute of Religion and Medicine is an obvious heir to this kind of thinking. So is the new Institute of Business Ethics. And many others. These are the seed beds of a genuinely lay theology.

All honour, then, to the House of Laity for wanting to assert a doctrinal role for lay people. But first we need to be clearer about what it is.

36
Baptism Policy

Diocesan Letter,
February 1986

I HAVE BEEN asked to write about our policy as a Church concerning infant baptism. It is a matter which troubles and divides people, and has recently come to the surface again through the publication of the report of a Working Party from the General Synod Board of Education, *Communion before Confirmation?* (Church House Publishing, 1986).

The report, which received a lukewarm welcome at last November's General Synod, bases its proposals on the claim that baptism alone is the full rite of Christian initiation. If this is so, it follows that children who have been baptized, and who are old enough to be able to receive Communion with some minimal understanding of what it is about, should be allowed to do so. Confirmation, if it happened at all, would then be reserved for a later age when young adults may wish to make a further commitment.

The proposals are highly controversial. There are strong arguments on both sides. But one thing is immediately obvious. Any acceptance of baptism as the sole requirement for full communicant status, would raise urgent questions about the conditions on which it is administered. And that is the topic on which the present disagreements are felt most sharply.

Let me first dispose of two extreme views. There are those who accuse some clergy of the Church of England of practising 'indiscriminate' baptism. The impression given is that any child brought along is baptized with no questions asked, no instruction given and no attempt to make parents face the seriousness of what is being done. If this kind of thing happens in some parishes, then it is to be deplored, but I think it is highly unlikely that many baptize indiscriminately in this literal sense of the word.

At the other extreme are those who refuse to baptize infants at all, other than in the most exceptional circumstances when parents and godparents can give copper-bottomed guarantees about the child's Christian upbringing. The refusal of infant baptism in all circumstances is not really compatible with ministry in the Church of England, but as with the other extreme I doubt whether there are many parishes where the fences around infant baptism are so high that it scarcely ever takes place.

The main area of debate is in the middle ground between the advocates of generous and rigorous baptism policies, and it is here that we need to develop mutual understanding and to take a long view of the effects of different policies on the Church. It may also be useful to link this debate with the Lent 1986 programmes on 'What on earth is the Church for?'. Baptism policies not only affect the Church; they also reflect different understandings of it, so there is everything to be said for keeping the two topics in close relation to one another.

Infant baptism, for example, represents an ideal of family and community solidarity, whereas adult baptism represents an ideal of individual choice. Different ideals tend to be associated with different churchmanships, the extreme communal end of the scale being represented by Eastern Orthodoxy which also practises infant Communion. At the extreme Protestant end of the scale individualism becomes so interiorized, as in the Society of Friends, that adult baptism gives place to no baptism at all.

Parallel with, but not identical to, this churchmanship scale is what one might call a missiological scale, a scale depicting how a church sees its mission in relation to the society around it. Some churches see themselves as very much part of the local community, distinct from it but responsible to it, and with plenty of interchange across the boundaries. This is the basic concept of a parish church, and one of its key features is its accessibility and its openness to all. Such an understanding of the church inevitably implies a generous policy towards baptisms, and there can be very hard feelings among parishioners if their own understanding of what the church is and what belonging to a parish entails, are not borne out by the actual parish policy.

Other churches see themselves primarily as fellowships of believers, with a missionary task towards their local community, but one which needs to be marked by clear distinctions between the 'committed' and the rest. Such a church can have an internal strength, which is often very impressive, and which is usually reinforced by a rigorist baptism policy. But to those outside, it can seem to exist primarily for the sake of its own fellowship. Its internal dynamic will tend to raise the barriers higher and higher.

It is easy to see why, in difficult times, this latter understanding of the church is gaining ground. But it does so at the cost of unchurching large numbers of people whose faith does not take the required form, and alienating those who, given some encouragement, might have retained at least a tenuous sense that the church is for them too.

I have been drawing some crude distinctions. Most parishes, as I say, fall somewhere between these extremes. My own belief is that we must not be mean about the sacraments, not treat them as prizes for good behaviour. But we can require parents who bring their children for baptism to prepare for it by a careful study of the service. If the baptism itself is public, then this degree of public commitment is probably enough of a deterrrent to those whose request is merely frivolous. Beyond that, surely, we have to rely on God's grace to illuminate and transform the often fumbling sense that this little child has an eternal significance.

37

Ecumenism: What Problems? What Hope?

*The Morningside Annual Lecture delivered in Morningside
United Church, Edinburgh
20 November 1987*

IT IS A particular pleasure to be able to come and talk about ecumenism in Scotland, because it was in Scotland that I had my first real experience of what working together as Christians may entail. You have already been told that I was for five years Rector in Jedburgh and I was recalling how during that time a remarkable degree of co-operation developed between the four churches in that little town. There were two Church of Scotland parishes, there was my own Episcopal and there was a Roman Catholic, and, during my time there, we managed to have a monthly Bible Study for all the clergy in the town; for much of the time we had shared evening worship every Sunday and, during the period of preparation before Easter, we had an ecumenical youth club for the whole town. We developed a system of shared visiting whereby we all visited in particular areas and then passed on our results to the minister whose church anybody claimed to belong to. We had a regular meeting with the clergy of the area and the doctors to discuss particular troublesome people and I even had the privilege of being a member of the Kelso Presbytery, in an honorary capacity.

All this took place after the failure of the Anglican-Presbyterian proposals for unity and before the Second Vatican Council, and I ask myself, 'How much further have we actually got in twenty-five years?'

Obviously there have been some notable advances, and the very existence of this church is a sign of the willingness of some people to take that decisive step into unity, as is the existence of the United Reformed Church in England. But have we got much further, really?

I begin by referring to my own personal experience, because it seems to me that if ecumenism is to be worth anything it has to be rooted in what people are actually doing face to face. Very often when people talk about ecumenism it seems to be something that somebody else is doing in some conference or some other body, or it seems to entail the discussion of complex proposals year after year, which never seem to get anywhere. So what I want to start by saying is that unless ecumenism is rooted in encounter between people and co-operation between people, it is boring, it is time-consuming, it is complex, it is frustrating and it is ultimately irrelevant to the real business of being Christian.

But if it is rooted in face to face encounter, in real experience, then one comes to see that it is essential and that none of us can be fully Christian without the others. I often quote a little story of a very zealous Christian who died and went to heaven and stood at St Peter's gate and knocked. St Peter came, and this chap knew he had been zealous, and thought that he would get entry straightaway, so he said to St Peter, 'Here I am'. St Peter looked at him and said, 'That's fine, but where are the others?'

When I left Jedburgh, I had the privilege of being Principal of a college in Birmingham which was then an Anglican college, and during my time there we turned it into an ecumenical college. This was through union with a Methodist college in Birmingham, and we also had some participation from the United Reformed Church, and we developed very close relationships with the local Roman Catholic college. This union between colleges took place extraordinarily rapidly. In fact I arrived as Principal in September 1967, and by February 1968 we had a scheme in print. We had to do that for the Methodists, because the Methodists gear everything to the Annual Conference and their agenda has to be in print by February at the latest. I have always claimed this for the Guinness Book of Records as the quickest piece of ecumenical negotiation which has ever taken place. We managed it because we left out most of the small print.

Sometimes, in ecumenical schemes, those who are concerned about union tend to scrutinize the small print very, very carefully, to make sure that their particular interest is safeguarded and nobody is going to take away from them their precious way of doing things or their precious piece of theological property. It seemed to me that if we were actually going to enter into union, and if we tried to work it out before we started, there was no point in doing it at all, because we would have learnt all the lessons before we were united. But the whole point of coming together is that we have to learn from one another. And we can only learn from one another if we come together in a minimum structure, open to what the Spirit is actually going to tell us.

So we had a very sketchy scheme with many of the major questions unanswered before we actually went into union. And then we listened, and we learnt, and we discussed, and out of our being together we created something which was certainly very exciting to live with. Now, as fifteen years have passed, it has become a bit more respectable and quiet, but I am convinced that the only way to learn about ecumenism is actually to do it, and not just to talk about it.

This is why it seems to me that in our ecumenical efforts today one of the things that we have to do is to try to create significant experiences for people, so that they may actually encounter one another in a setting where they feel secure and where they feel their own tradition, their own insights, are valued. One of the things that has come out of the 'Not Strangers But Pilgrims' process has been that opportunity for Christians to meet together and to discuss fundamental matters about their own Churches. It is only as we actually meet one another and open ourselves to each other that we can remove our blinkered view of our own Church. Given that, then there is scope for serious and detailed discussion, much of which is already taking place.

Let me spell out briefly therefore, something about the actual complexity of the ecumenical scene. I am going to do this, I am afraid, from an English perspective because this is the only one which I can speak about with any first-hand knowledge nowadays, but I am sure one could translate it into a Scottish context very easily.

As some of you may know, next year is the year when bishops from the Anglican Communion come together to Canterbury for a three-week-long Conference, to discuss the whole Anglican Communion. One of the major topics we shall be discussing is 'international ecumenism'. That has meant bringing together in a single, extraordinarily complex report, the fruits of all the conversations which have been going on on a world scale. If I just list them you will see what is entailed.

There have been the conversations with the Roman Catholics, the so-called ARCIC talks, still continuing. We have had conversations with the Lutherans, particularly in the United States, where Lutheranism is very strong. We have also had conversations with the Orthodox, which suffered a hiccup when they got worried about the ordination of women, but they are still going on. We are at the beginning of conversations with the Oriental Orthodox, that is the Orthodox in the

Middle-Eastern area. We had conversations with the Reformed Churches which resulted in an excellent report, and, of course, also on the international level there has been the work done by the World Council of Churches on the 'Baptism, Eucharist and Ministry' document: a very significant advance in understanding on those topics.

Those are the major things which have been happening in my own Church on an international scale. One of the difficulties is that in conducting so many conversations we can find ourselves saying different things in different conversations, and that is why it is essential in 1988 to bring all these together and look at them as a whole and see whether we are presenting a coherent ecumenical approach.

Out of all this we are struggling to find a common terminology about what we are trying to do. If we look beyond the things with which the Church of England is involved to the world ecumenical scene then the position is extremely complicated. As a member of the Central Committee of the World Council of Churches, I have seen at first hand some of the massive documentation arising out of discussion of the 'Baptism, Eucharist and Ministry' documents. How all this material is going to be handled and collated I don't know, but the activity is enormous.

There is also, as some of you will know, a great deal happening on a much more local level, and one little discussion in which I am involved is between the Church of England and the Church of Scotland, where we consider our different roles as established Churches. This is really quite an interesting basis on which to discuss because we are not going straight for the main controversial topics; we are asking, 'How do we see our respective responsibilities towards our two nations?' It provides an alternative way of creating mutual understanding.

There is also, in addition to the discussions on the more familiar topics of ministry and Eucharist, a new study being mounted by the World Council of Churches on the apostolic faith. This is an attempt to go through the main Christian Creeds and to discover how in the twentieth century we can express our common faith in the light of a hugely complex past.

Within all this activity I think it is possible to see some real marks of progress and I want now to list one or two of these. Then we shall look at some of the problems, and then I want to say a word or two about what I see as the way ahead.

So, first of all, the marks of progress. The first of these I see as the widening of the constituency. I have mentioned a whole series of bilateral studies in which Churches pair up. This is quite a good way to come to understanding because in a pair it is possible to reach a considerable depth in the discussion and to concentrate on the particular issues which affect the relationship between those two Churches.

But there are also the multilateral efforts, in which the attempt is made to talk with many partners. What this means in practice is that participants are not allowed to develop an easy, cosy relationship with one partner with whom they might have a lot in common, and thus move away from other possible partners in the ecumenical scene. In England, for example, we began with bilateral conversations more than fifteen years ago with the Methodist Church. These got a long way, and then failed because some people in the Church of England felt that we were losing a very important part of our Catholic heritage. We then had the Covenant Proposals, which involved not only Methodists, but United Reformed and Moravians; the Roman Catholics and Baptists were in with us for a time, and that gave a more realistic edge to the discussions but, as you will know, the Covenant proposals failed too.

One of the things which I think is most significant about the recent efforts at ecumenism in the whole of Britain through the 'Not Strangers But Pilgrims' process is that we now include virtually every Church in the British Isles. The bringing into an ecumenical discussion of the Roman Catholics, the Orthodox, the Pentecostals, particularly the black-led Pentecostals – some thirty different Churches in the British Isles – certainly complicates the scene enormously. But I believe it means that we are going to be rooted in the real complexities of church life in Britain, and we are going to have to be listening all the time to the voices from many different partners. I believe that this widening of the constituency is one of the more exciting features of the ecumenical scene in these last years. It is a recognition that ecumenism is about the whole Church, not just about those who happen to feel that they have some things in common.

One of the major factors in ecumenism in the last twenty years has been the aftermath of the Second Vatican Council, and gradually, over those twenty years, Roman Catholics have entered seriously into ecumenical discussion. They are now, I believe, learning much faster than the Orthodox Churches, which have been at it longer, and learning much faster about the shifts in self-understanding which are needed if one is to take ecumenism seriously.

I think I am not being unkind if I say that still, within the Orthodox Churches, their vision of a united Church is an enlarged Orthodox Church. Up till fairly recently the Roman Catholic vision of a united Church has, I believe, been an enlarged Roman Catholic Church. But one of the very significant things which happened at Vatican II was the beginning of a recognition that other Churches had their own valid life within the total Body of Christ. There were some small signals to this effect in the Vatican II documents which are now being exploited and used; and there is a much clearer recognition that we can speak as equal partners in the ecumenical dialogue.

This is a highly significant change, because, as the Roman Catholic Church enters seriously into this field, we can for the first time begin to talk realistically about the whole of Christendom, the whole of the Christian community. It is a Church which is large enough and powerful enough and distinctive enough to shake up the ecumenical pattern and to inject something really new into it. This is, I know, for many people highly threatening, but I think we have to recognize it as the new fact of our time.

Furthermore, as some of you will know, this new presence is being used as a lever to change the British Council of Churches. All bodies, Churches, councils, whatever, tend to settle down into a comfortable pattern and can only begin to rethink radically when something large enough hits them.

The 'Not Strangers But Pilgrims' process arose out of two strands of thinking. One of these was the recognition within the British Council of Churches that it needed to change, and also that it needed the Roman Catholic Church and other Churches if it was to be truly representative of Christians in Britain. The other strand arose out of the Pope's visit to Britain, which made the Roman Catholic bishops in England, Wales and Scotland think much more seriously about their ecumenical role, and themselves suggest a new initiative. These two strands converged in a widely representative meeting of church leaders, which I had the privilege of chairing, and out of it the Inter-Church Process was born, the 'Not Strangers But Pilgrims' process and the recent Swanwick Conference.

I was privileged to play a leading role because, having moved in ecumenical circles for a long time, I could credibly issue an invitation to a new start. I make the point simply to show how new starts may sometimes be needed; but they require a sufficiently big force coming in, in this instance the Roman Catholic Church, to create the momentum. And this is what has happened.

A similar change is, I believe, desperately needed by the World Council of Churches, and what Roman Catholicism would be likely to do for it would be to bring much greater rigour into its thinking. One of the dangers in the ecumenical world is that theology can become sloppy. This has been a particular danger in the World Council of Churches.

One of the sadnesses in these recent advances has been the self-exclusion of some of the more extreme evangelical and Pentecostal groups. The British Evangelical Council, for example, in writing about the 'Not Strangers But Pilgrims' process, said 'Ecumenicity that is not based on vital Christian truth is actually a danger to Christian people, as it obscures the distinctiveness of the gospel'. That is a theme found constantly running through ecumenical discussion: 'Here we have a distinctive truth and the danger is that this will be lost if we enter into serious dialogue with other people.' Some people, I am afraid, exclude themselves, fearing that danger more than they fear the danger of not uniting with their Christian brethren.

There are real problems, because in talking about ecumenism involving all Christian people where does one draw the line at ecumenical inclusiveness? Interestingly, one of the churches which made a submission for inclusion in the 'Not Strangers But Pilgrims' process was the Unification Church – the Moonies – claiming that they are a Christian Church! Well, where *do* you draw the line? We did not include them.

A second mark of progress is, I think, real theological convergence. This is the achievement of the World Council of Churches 'Baptism, Eucharist and Ministry' Report, a report which, I may say, took sixty years in the making. Convergence does not come quickly! One of the major fruits of the Anglican-Roman Catholic International Commission is the discovery that if one goes back to the roots of Christianity in the Scriptures, and in living Christian experience, one finds that Christians do in fact share much more than they ever imagined. They may express this in different language; they may feel very strongly that they belong to different traditions, but around experience and around the interpretation of the Scriptures an enormous amount of convergence can take place.

Also we recognize that most of what is said in the historic Christian

Creeds is shared by all of us. The ARCIC discussions, as again you will know, recently claimed to have made a breakthrough on the question of salvation and justification – one of the main theological reasons for the Reformation. And they claim that there was a failure of communication, that at that time people were talking across one another and were, indeed, endeavouring to preserve basically the same truths, but doing it in different languages.

One of the things which has taken place in the 'Not Strangers But Pilgrims' process is a sharing of our thoughts about the nature of the Church, and, superficially, these may be very different indeed; but we find as we put the different stories together that we are all concerned with the same themes, though we express these with different emphases and in different styles. Every Church is, in one way or another, concerned both to express its nature as a local church, a living fellowship of Christian people engaged in face to face meeting, but also to express in some way or another its part within the universal Church, the total body of Christ. Now the way we do that differs, but the fact that we do it is the same for all of us.

Again, every Church is in some way concerned about its continuity, because Churches are not things which are just created because people feel like it. We all have our historical roots, we all try to preserve our relationships with our tradition, our roots back in the Scriptures. Again we do that in different ways, but it is the same thing that we are doing.

If any of you have seen the little book called *Reflections* (BCC/CTS 1987) which came out of the 'Not Strangers But Pilgrims' process you will find in it confessions by many different Churches about where they stand on matters of ecclesiology, confessing what it means to belong to that particular Church, and the different styles in which this has been done are quite fascinating. It is worth reading just for that alone. For example, the Roman Catholics, in confessing where they stand, do so in a highly theological way: it is all set out very logically in terms of articles in the Creeds and so on. The Church of Scotland, in confessing where it stands, does so in a 'confessional' style, going back to historic documents in its own history, and then trying to interpret these. The Church of England in doing so, does so in a historical style, telling a story of how the Church of England came to be. And these three approaches are very, very characteristic of the three denominations.

I believe that unity begins to become effective as we begin to discern a common faith within these different styles. One of the things that I learnt most of all from my time in Queen's College, Birmingham, was to identify the way in which Christians would express the same basic values in different ways in their Churches. So there is a huge amount of learning still to be done but also some very encouraging signs of progress.

A third sign of progress is the participation at all levels, and I have already referred to this. Ecumenism cannot just be something for the experts: it has got to take place at local level, and the pressure for it has got to come from people in the local churches who are saying, 'Why cannot we work more closely together, why can't we be one?'

One of the exciting things in the 'Not Strangers But Pilgrims' process was the pressure which came from those who met around the local radio courses in Lent 1986. The clear message was, 'We have made discoveries in meeting together: we want to be closer together as one; we value also our differences, we are not just thinking in terms of mergers; but for heaven's sake, you at the top, get on with it!'

Alongside these local experiences we need big ecumenical occasions. I think we have now reached the time at which coming together for the Week of Prayer for Christian Unity and for Christian Aid Week, important though those are, are not enough. They can deaden us in helping us to feel, 'We've done our ecumenism for this year and now let's get on with being ourselves for the rest of the year'.

One of the ideas flying round the Swanwick Conference which brought all this thinking together was the idea of having an occasional *Kirchentag* – there is no English word for it – great church days, great occasions on which thousands of people come together, to sit together under the Scriptures, to meet with one another, to get a sense of the largeness and vitality of the whole Christian body. World Council of Churches Assemblies perform that function. Bring together some three or four thousand people, live together for a fortnight or so, and there is a sense of the range of Christian experience on a world scale, and people go home with a vision which lasts them for the rest of their lives.

So, we need to study together, we need the big ecumenical occasions which can involve lots and lots of people, who would not normally be involved in ecumenical conversations. We need also the face to face contact which comes through doing tasks together, and my hope is that the pattern of ecumenical co-operation for the future will not be in the setting-up of elaborate, permanent committees which look round for things to do, but through the pinpointing of specific tasks which need to be done in specific places and then mobilizing Christians to do these tasks together. They may be quite short-term tasks or quite long-term ones, but I think in this kind of way one will see some point and purpose in what is being done together, and a much larger group of people can be given the experience that they need of actually working together with fellow-Christians. This can also be done on a local church basis; and also on the basis of professional or personal expertise or spheres of interest, whatever these may be. It is absurd for members of the medical profession, or lawyers, or industrialists, or trades-unionists, or housewives, or whatever, to come together simply on a denominational basis to talk about what it means to be a Christian doctor, or a Christian housewife, etc. Why can't we do this together? We are not threatening our church boundaries when we do so. There is enormous scope, I believe, for ecumenical learning through this task-orientated work together either on a Church base or on the basis of particular interest and vocation.

I was reflecting the other day that in 1948 when I was very much involved as a student in Christian work, I had not the remotest notion that the World Council of Churches was being inaugurated, in Amsterdam, in 1948. It did not impinge one iota. That is a terrible indictment of me. But it is, I think, typical of the way in which things can be happening, things of perhaps world importance, and yet not impinging on the ordinary Christian.

Fourthly, we look for advance where advance is possible, and do not get too worried about areas in which it is not possible. In recent years ecumenism has been obsessed with the problem of ministry. I do not think there are going to be any quick breakthroughs there. If we shift our concern from ministry to mission I think we can get very much further.

And that is why in the 'Not Strangers But Pilgrims' process those who were at the Swanwick Conference, and at earlier conferences, had to face the pain of not being able to share together eucharistically. With participation from the Roman Catholics, and to a lesser extent with the awkward Anglicans, eucharistic sharing is not going to come quickly.

But this need not stop us doing many other things. One of the most moving moments in the Swanwick conference was when those who were unable to share eucharistically came forward in different Communion services to receive a blessing from those from whom they could not receive Communion. We can take steps of this kind together, recognizing each other's worship, recognizing each other's ministry, and yet realizing that there are still barriers which may take a long time to overcome. Meanwhile let us do the things that we *can* do together.

This is not a new idea; in 1926 the slogan was, 'Theology divides but service unites', and I have a feeling we have now come full circle. In the end, of course, your theology cannot be separated from service, because if we are going to work together on major moral and social issues, we have got to theologize about them. If we are going to do mission together, we have got to have a theology of mission. But we do not have to start by tackling all those questions which have proved so intractable in the past.

I believe, therefore, that there has been progress; there is a great deal of hope. But there are continuing problems, and not just the major theological ones I have been talking about.

First, there is a tension between the ecclesiastical and the secular aims of ecumenism. Some people think of ecumenism primarily in terms of the renewal of the Church – perfectly right. Others talk much more about the renewal of the whole of humanity. I believe it is desperately important not to separate these. Our concern for unity must not be just to produce bigger and better Churches, but to be a sign of the unity of the whole of mankind. But there are differences of emphasis and we need to recognize this.

Some of these come to the surface when people get very worried about what they perceive as the highly politicized efforts of the World Council of Churches. Another way in which the tension manifests itself is in the question, 'How far must our ecumenical dialogue extend into interfaith dialogue?' That again is a topic on which the World Council has been working very hard. My own belief is that we must not lose this vision of 'the whole of humanity' somehow being involved in God's purposes and to be brought into God's Kingdom.

There is a second tension between national and international ecumenism. Are we really looking for ways of going ahead simply in our own national setting, with its peculiar problems and peculiar opportunities, or must we try to advance on a broad international front? The criticism of national schemes of unity is that they seem to emphasize nationalism at a time when one of our great needs in the world is to transcend nationalism. But on the other hand, can unity be real if it is not local?

This particular point is arising for us acutely in the Church of England at the moment because, as with yourselves, some Anglican Churches have already entered into union in India and Pakistan. One of the disadvantages of doing that on a national basis is that united Churches then become isolated. If, for example, we invite bishops of the Church of South India or North India to our conference of Anglican bishops, other partners in the South and North of India schemes can easily say, 'This is a takeover bid by the Anglican Communion'. On the other hand, if we don't invite them they are then isolated and feel that in becoming united they have lost their membership of a worldwide communion. There are real tensions here which need to be dealt with very sensitively.

Thirdly, there are huge problems about authority. In the years ahead the questions of authority in our respective Churches are going to be a main focus of discussion. This has come to the fore already in the 'Not Strangers But Pilgrims' process, where, as soon as anyone mentions the words 'church leader' in that very broad context, people immediately have very different ideas and all sorts of hackles go up. Some will say, 'You have easily identifiable church leaders, your bishops and archbishops and whatever, so you know what you're talking about'. But in another Church they will say, 'We have no church leaders at all; we are entirely democratic; it is the whole Church which has the authority.' But ask who actually makes the decisions and it turns out to be the permanent secretary.

We need to ask ourselves as Churches: where does power reside? Who actually makes the decisions? Who can speak for the Churches ecumenically? How do we balance against one another these different concepts of authority? Within Roman Catholic thinking the *magisterium* makes the final judgements. In other contexts there are leaders who are basically spokesmen; in others nothing at all can be done without agreement among all the faithful.

We tried to resolve this issue at Swanwick by saying that authority, ecumenically, must continue to reside in the Churches themselves. We cannot delegate authority to another body to act on our behalf. But we must find ways in which those who can command the resources in the Churches and who can get things moving, can actually meet together and use those resources in common tasks.

I hope the pattern which will emerge eventually out of these Swanwick discussions will in some ways be a much more decentralized pattern than we have been used to in the British Council of Churches. It will entail the identification in every Church of some people who can speak on behalf of it and actually get things done, and enable these resources to be shared. Such people are going to have to be very carefully monitored and stimulated by much larger bodies, because all power corrupts, as we know, even in the Church. Perhaps especially in the Church.

We are also very conscious of the inadequacies of our existing ecumenical instruments. What has tended to happen with local Councils of Churches, the British Council of Churches, and the World Council of Churches is that these have tended to become bodies which are seen to stand over against the Churches. We have set them up; we have told them to get on with various things; and then we criticize them for doing it. We have starved them of funds. They see a role as being gadflies for the Churches, but they do not have the authority to do and say things on behalf of the Churches, so their prophetic role is stunted. This is a road-block which we are trying very hard to get through.

Finally, two words on where ecumenism is taking us. The first is a phrase which came out of the Swanwick Conference, the phrase 'enlarged identity'. We are all worried about a possible loss of identity through ecumenical commitment. The idea put forward by Swanwick was that, by contrast, ecumenism enlarges our identity by allowing us to feel also part of one another's traditions. It is not a question of 'giving up precious things', as we are sometimes invited to do, but of receiving one another's precious things. Let me leave you with a key thought in this connection: people are usually right in what they affirm and wrong in what they deny.

The second word is 'interdependence'. This lies at the heart of the Swanwick proposals. We look not for uniformity, not for elaborate new structures, but for reconciled diversity, for a sense of dependence on one another made real by the sharing of resources. This is the point of making sure that the Churches remain accountable for work done in their name. We cannot delegate ecumenism to some other body and then ask it to do tasks which we are not prepared to do ourselves. The message for the future is that we are all in this together.